Words of Praise for *Mind Programming*

*"In reading Eldon Taylor's book **Mind Programming: From Persuasion and Brainwashing to Self-Help and Practical Metaphysics**, I embarked upon a journey beginning at Psych 101 and ending deep into postgraduate Metaphysics; a reading experience that delivers a near-visceral adventure that begins with imagination and ends in near-manifestation. Eldon reveals the extraordinary reality of a virtually unrecognized dimension where each of us live every day but are completely unaware—the subliminal realm. I recently produced a motion picture featuring 23 <u>Living Luminaries,</u>* each of whom shares pearls of wisdom and enlightened insights as to how we can all achieve true happiness and our purpose in life. Although it was an extraordinary cast, in retrospect I wish there had been 24. Eldon Taylor brings an invaluable teaching to seekers of wisdom and understanding. The world of higher learning has a new 'high bar' with his work."*

— **Michael J Lasky,** producer and founder, Gotham Metro Studios, Inc.

*From the new film *Living Luminaries (on the Serious Business of Happiness)* featuring 23 "luminaries" such as Eckhart Tolle, Marianne Williamson, Don Miguel Ruiz, Michael Bernard Beckwith, Geronimo JiJaga (Pratt), Dr. Obadiah Harris, and many extraordinary masters of conscious disciplines

"Dr. Eldon Taylor's new book is a <u>must read!</u> If you've ever questioned your purpose in life or felt bound by a culture that's driven by mass media, you now have at your fingertips the knowledge and tools to break the chains of this cycle. Eldon goes in-depth to illustrate and expose how we've been programmed from birth by social constraints; and he methodically reveals the psychological techniques that advertisers, politicians, corporations, and the media use to control us. He then provides strategies and solutions to free your mind from these tactics and rise to a new level of consciousness. As you read this book, you'll feel the blinders being removed and will truly see the world in an entirely new light."

— **Jeff Warrick,** documentary filmmaker, *Programming the Nation?*

*"I've known Eldon Taylor for 20 years and have been fascinated with his research regarding subliminal communication. Mind programming can be used to control your mind for good or bad. **Mind Programming** presents tools to give you the power to program your own mind to empower you to realize your goals and desires. Book One deals with the dark side of persuasion methods, while Book Two gives you tools to train your own mind in the ways you want it to be trained. I especially appreciate his emphasis on forgiveness in healing and his serenity affirmations."*

— **Paul G. Durbin, Ph.D.,** retired Brigadier General, U.S. Army chaplain

■ ■ ■ ━■■

MIND
PROGRAMMING

Also by Eldon Taylor

Choices and Illusions: How Did I Get Where I Am, and How Do I Get Where I Want to Be?*

Subliminal Learning: An Eclectic Approach

Subliminal Communication: Emperor's Clothes or Panacea?

Thinking Without Thinking: Who's in Control of Your Mind?

Subliminal Technology: Unlocking the Power of Your Own Mind

Exclusively Fabricated Illusions

Just Be: A Little Cowboy Philosophy

Simple Things and Simple Thoughts

The Little Black Book

Wellness: Just a State of Mind?

Plus hundreds of audio and video programs
in multiple languages.

■ ■

*Available from Hay House

Please visit Hay House USA: **www.hayhouse.com**®
Hay House Australia: **www.hayhouse.com.au**
Hay House UK: **www.hayhouse.co.uk**
Hay House South Africa: **www.hayhouse.co.za**
Hay House India: **www.hayhouse.co.in**

MIND PROGRAMMING

From Persuasion and Brainwashing to Self-Help and Practical Metaphysics

ELDON TAYLOR

HAY HOUSE, INC.
Carlsbad, California • New York City
London • Sydney • Johannesburg
Vancouver • Hong Kong • New Delhi

Published and distributed in the United States by: Hay House, Inc.: www.hayhouse. com • *Published and distributed in Australia by:* Hay House Australia Pty. Ltd.: www. hayhouse.com.au • *Published and distributed in the United Kingdom by:* Hay House UK, Ltd.: www.hayhouse.co.uk • *Published and distributed in the Republic of South Africa by:* Hay House SA (Pty), Ltd.: www.hayhouse.co.za • *Distributed in Canada by:* Raincoast: www.raincoast.com • *Published in India by:* Hay House Publishers India: www.hayhouse.co.in

Design: Tricia Breidenthal • *Edited by:* Suzanne Brady

Library of Congress Cataloging-in-Publication Data

Taylor, Eldon.
  Mind programming : from persuasion and brainwashing to self-help and practical metaphysics / Eldon Taylor. -- 1st ed.
    p. cm.
  ISBN 978-1-4019-2331-0 (hardcover : alk. paper) 1. Brainwashing. 2. Deprogramming. 3. Control (Psychology) 4. Thought and thinking. I. Title.
  BF633.T38 2009
  153.8'5--dc22   2008038954

ISBN: 978-1-4019-2331-0

12   11   10   09   4   3   2   1
1st edition, April 2009

Printed in the United States of America

To my sons:

Roy Kenneth, whose intellect keeps me honest;
and William James, whose heart keeps me grateful.

I love you both!

■ ■

CONTENTS

If acts of goodness be not accumulated,
they are not sufficient to give their finish to one's name;
if acts of evil be not accumulated,
they are not sufficient to destroy one's life.
The inferior man thinks that small acts of goodness
are of no benefit and does not do them,
and that small deeds of evil do no harm
and does not abstain from them.
Hence his wickedness becomes great
till it cannot be covered and
his guilt becomes great
till it cannot be pardoned.

— *The Ethics of Confucius,* edited by Miles Menander Dawson

■ ■

PREFACE

"If you want a quality, act as if you already had it. Try the <u>as if</u> technique."

— William James

It may surprise you to know that a hotly debated issue among many academics today is essentially an argument for the absence of free will. There are many reasons for this. In recent years, numerous studies have demonstrated that the conscious mind only thinks it's in charge. In fact, it appears that the subconscious is making decisions and the conscious mind is making up stories to explain those decisions. Albert Einstein paraphrased the German philosopher Arthur Schopenhauer this way: "A human can very well do what he wants, but cannot will what he wants."[1]

Within the halls of academia today is strong support for the idea that humans are no more than "meat machines"—biological mechanisms programmed to behave in certain ways. Daniel Dennett of Tufts University is quoted as stating, "When we consider whether free will is an illusion or reality, we are looking into an abyss. What *seems* to confront us is a plunge into nihilism and despair."[2]

Is free will an illusion? If the subconscious makes the decisions, what or who programs the subconscious? I hope to show you several major contributors, some rather obvious and some you may seriously doubt.

As we navigate through the seemingly endless possibilities that pull our strings and push our buttons, that program our appetites and set the tone for our moods—as we look behind the closed doors to who, what, when, and where our minds and behavior are manipulated—

we also visit parks full of terrific opportunities for expanding our awareness, enhancing our mental abilities, improving our lives, and gaining many other benefits, including health and longevity. It's for this reason that I chose the title *Mind Programming* for this book. (The only other option I could think of was already taken: *Mind As Healer, Mind As Slayer*. That says it all.)

It's my wish that you find this work engaging and empowering. I do have a bias, and I'll share that with you right now. I believe in the human potential and its evolution toward love and peace. I believe in *you*. I think that within every one of us resides a vast reservoir of ability that typically goes untouched. When we each awaken to our individual potential, we lead the way to a conscious awakening of the planet as a whole, for as Lao-tzu might have said, "The world awakens one person at a time." I trust that with knowledge comes power, that you'll enjoy the best in all that you create for yourself, and that in some small way this book may assist you in doing so.

My own path, when I look back at it, seems to include many lives in one lifetime. I've been a successful salesman and sales manager; an entrepreneur; a racehorse trainer and paddock judge; a lie-detection examiner and investigator with my own intelligence and counter-intelligence agency; a spiritual counselor and minister; a motivational coach to elite athletes, businessmen, and performers; a best-selling author; an expert on hypnosis and subliminal communication; and more. It has been a wonderfully full and vital journey that I could never have planned in advance.

So what's the point? Through my various training and experiences, a common denominator has been repeated: mental control. Whether someone is an athlete or an interrogator, that person gains a mental edge from understanding how the mind mixes with emotion, how that affects the body, and the circularity of it all.

Human beings are wired so that they give away "tells," or clues, in everything they do or say . . . or don't do or don't say. In addition, predictable psychological mechanics make it relatively easy to manipulate people—who include you and me.

What you do, what you own, what you plan, what you believe, who you think you are, what you want, and so much more are all the result of beliefs and values you've been trained to have, to be, and to want. Some of this is simply enculturation, but when it takes on the intent of deliberate manipulation, then *enculturation* per se is an inadequate term.

I believe that you deserve to know what's possible, what's being done by others, and what *you* can do to take back the power of your mind. I want my sons, Roy and William, to be as free from these influences as possible—or at the very least fully informed. This book is dedicated to this principle and, therefore, to Roy, William, and you.

INTRODUCTION

*"You will become as small as your controlling desire;
as great as your dominant aspiration."*
— James Allen

I've spent 30 years studying the mind, yet I really entered the field through the back door. My initial interest had nothing to do with personal growth or spirituality but with the practicalities of my work as a lie-detection examiner and investigator. The more I learned about the workings of the mind, however, the more I began to appreciate the incredible potential we all hold within.

In my earlier book *Choices and Illusions,* I examined how our choices aren't our own because of enculturation and peer pressure. In this book, I'll look at how far others have gone to understand the workings of our minds just so that they can manipulate our thoughts, desires, and beliefs. We're familiar with this to some degree—for example, we're all very aware that salespeople use such tactics all the time. However, many of us have no idea quite how far and deep this research has gone.

Some may find the information to be too much and claim that they have no interest in conspiracy theories. Others continue to believe that subliminal communication doesn't work. Only by showing you the full extent of the attempts made to control your thoughts—to brainwash you, if you will—can I convince you of the reality behind thought control.

This work is really two books in one. Although some may only be interested in one or the other, I've included both for the sake of completeness. Book One sets the stage. It explains how the mind functions and shows in great detail how much work has been done by certain individuals in learning this information for the express purpose of taking advantage of you. There isn't much that's inspirational in Book One, but the information does finally lay to rest the notions that "Subliminal doesn't work," "You can't be made to do something that you don't wish to do," and "No one uses it." The details are quite instructive, and the interest of the researchers can no longer be denied.

Book One covers most of what I've learned about subliminal communication. Much of my work has been about proving to myself what's effective, when, and how—if at all. I'm now convinced that the mind has immense abilities both to create the life of our dreams (health, wealth, love, and so on) and also the ability to bring us everything we say that we don't want (sickness, poverty, loneliness, and the like). I'll present a plethora of information about persuasion technology, particularly subliminal methods, and how it's used against you. The evidence is simply overwhelming and irrefutable. I'll also introduce you to the positive side of subliminal communication and the research that has been done to show how this technology can be of great benefit.

Once you've read Book One, you'll fully appreciate the need for Book Two. It holds the keys for dealing with day-to-day life in the 21st century. It contains many tools, techniques, and exercises that will assist you in becoming the person you're supposed to be.

A metaphor best explains the purpose of these two books: Imagine that your mind is like the fresh, sparkling water flowing from a high mountain spring. As the water travels down the mountain and through small villages, it picks up some contaminants but is still considered clean and drinkable. In our analogy, these small villages correlate with our early childhood—or at least a desirable early childhood.

As the water continues its descent and heads through larger towns and small cities, it picks up more contaminants. It no longer looks clear and sparkling but is still considered acceptable for drinking, especially if it's boiled first. These larger settlements equate with much of the manipulation in our lives that's almost unavoidable, ranging from the tactics of the salesperson who persuades you to buy a larger TV to the codependent manipulations of those who have already lost their own minds.

Next, the water passes through a large industrial city. Waste is dumped wholesale into the stream, and it becomes brown and sluggish. No fish could possibly live in it. This water must go through a sewage-treatment plant to make it potable once more. The large city equates to the gross misuses of persuasion technologies in advertising, music, and movies. Those who employ these methods care only about what they gain from it. They want you to buy stuff you don't need and that may even be bad for you. They want you to feel emotions such as hate, anger, and fear.

In this city, violent incidents become everyday events. School shootings, mall shootings, hate crimes, small-mindedness, road rage, and more are commonplace. Crimes occur on the streets in broad daylight, and no one comes to help the victim. The world is dark, gray, and ugly. It's full of sayings such as "Don't get even—get evener," "Life sucks and then you die," "The good die young," and on and on.

It might seem as though this is as bad as things can get for the water that began its journey as a cool, mountain spring—but it isn't. Downstream live those who wish to pour toxic nuclear waste into the water. Fortunately, they're at the outskirts of the city right now, and if we all work together, we may be able to prevent this kind of abuse from entering the current of our lives.

The toxic dumping equates to the brainwashing attempts that many say have never taken place. Here, you'll find people who aren't just after your purchasing power or your vote, but who seek to control the very fibers of your being: power for the sake of power alone.

Book Two can be looked upon as the purification plant. It contains tools, philosophies, and beliefs that will take the heavily contaminated water and slowly but surely return it to its clear, sparkling, pure state. Once this stream begins to be restored, it can choose a different path, perhaps through meadows, fields, rocky canyons, and happy villages. There can be a different ending—perhaps in the sea. Book Two isn't a destination, but the beginning of a most fabulous journey. It gives you techniques and exercises designed to put you firmly back on the path you're supposed to take—one of learning, loving, enjoyment, and living the wonderful thing called life.

As you read through Book One, you may decide that it's too technical or too dark for you. If so, read only the summaries at the end of each chapter and then proceed quickly to Book Two. As you continue your own journey, you may wish to share what you've learned with someone else. Perhaps that person will need to be convinced that training the mind is necessary. In that case, the material in Book One will be very helpful.

Also in this book is an InnerTalk® subliminal CD for your own experimentation. Some say, "The proof is in the pudding," and for that reason I want you to have the opportunity to *test* the "pudding." The CD is great for when you feel stressed or hurried and prefer a little serenity. Try it—you'll like it! (Please see Appendix 4 for a complete list of the affirmations recorded on this program.)

To use this CD, simply play it quietly in the background as you go about your day, or even all night long while you sleep. While you may hear some talking going on the background, the idea is not to focus on this. Also, don't be concerned if you can't hear it—the amount perceived will vary from person to person and with how relaxed you are. You don't need to turn the volume to a higher level—as long as you can hear the music, however quietly it's playing, the InnerTalk messages will be priming your self-talk. The more you play this program, the more you'll experience the benefits.

Enjoy your journey.

BOOK ONE

THE TWO FACES OF PERSUASION

"If you can control the meaning of words, suspend critical judg-ment, and appeal to a mechanistic drive, you can control the masses. These are the basic tools of the manipulator."

— Eldon Taylor

PART I

THE MIND AS SLAYER: THE DARKER SIDE OF PERSUASION

CHAPTER 1

The Genie

*"To get up each morning with the resolve to be happy
. . . is to set our own conditions to the events of
each day. To do this is to condition circumstances
instead of being conditioned by them."*

— Ralph Waldo Emerson

Imagine that within you was a genie, a veritable creation machine capable of bringing you anything you desired—good and bad. Let's imagine that you were unaware of this genie within or had heard about it but disbelieved. Perhaps you'd tried to believe and discovered that it was bogus—the whole thing about the genie within was just so much superstitious mumbo jumbo.

We're all familiar with such phrases as "the power of the mind," "mind over matter," and "the mind-body connection." We've heard of spontaneous healings and achieving or creating the life of our dreams. Most of us have even experienced some of this, even if it appears to be in very limited ways.

Almost everyone today has at least heard of the book and movie *The Secret.* They were marketed in an absolutely magnificent manner, and although they contain no real secrets, they nevertheless retold in new ways the inner mystical teachings of all ages. *The Secret* informed readers and viewers that one's mind was a genie of sorts, for whatever it held in sufficient detail it would *attract* or *create,* and these two words were actually interchangeable in this context.

Maybe you watched *The Oprah Winfrey Show, Larry King Live,* or some other program and heard of the magnificent wealth and abundance that people had attracted using *The Secret.* Perhaps you grabbed a book, CD, or DVD all about the Law of Attraction and pored through it to glean the exact hows, whys, and wherefores.

Now armed with the secret knowledge and the testimony of so many, you created a vision board and printed out affirmations that you pasted everywhere so you'd constantly see them. You began visualizing all the things you wanted to attract and even started down the road of daily meditation. You got on the Internet and looked up such terms as *New Age* and *metaphysical.* You subscribed to numerous mailing lists, tuned in to New Age Internet radio shows, and began to buy self-help books. Alas, nothing wonderful happened.

Unfortunately, that's the experience of most people who tuned in to the idea of the genie within. Some, however, found a different result. They manifested their home, a special relationship, or the like. Not many achieved this, mind you, but some. Why?

The mind is that genie, and it's the doorway to the manifestation process, although its role is often misunderstood. It's an entry point, a doorway, not the manifestation tool per se. The mind provides the pictures, not the feeling. It organizes our activity to build a vision board, post the affirmations, and so forth. It invests some learned belief (expectation) in the process. Actually, the mind's highest role is inhibition. Let me say that again: *The mind's highest role is inhibition!*

The Human Mind

Like it or not, we're all the product of millions of years of survival evolution. Wired in every one of us, no matter what our calling—including the highest evolved of spiritual beings now walking the earth—are primitive mechanisms that respond to primitive and sometimes rather gross stimuli. Often, stimuli that we consciously claim as reprehensible are nevertheless processed subconsciously in ways that drive us toward seeking more of the same. Those mechanisms respond to fight and flight, taboo images, socially fearful rejections, and similar stimuli in a mechanical way—thus, the term *mechanism.*

The human brain is a marvel of evolution, and one of its most splendid developments as far as human consciousness is concerned is the cerebral cortex. One of my early teachers, Professor Carl LaPrecht, used to say, "Whenever you find something in nature in great abundance, pay attention. It is critical to the system." The cortex or gray matter is by far the largest part of the brain. And it's within the cortex that inhibitory power resides.

The cortex is the brake. Cortical power inhibits impulses that aren't in our best interest or the result of our best intentions. The cortex shuts off the television when the content is violent, suggestive of disease and illness, or otherwise contains matter that's purely garbage. Our minds are like large trash containers: we can put anything into them. And like Dumpsters, they're difficult to clean out. Dumpsters don't tip over easily, and to clean one requires climbing inside, perhaps with a garden hose, a bucket of hot water, cleaning products, brushes, and so forth. What a tedious and nasty job.

All of us have minds, of course, and evidence suggests that when we come into the world our minds aren't blank slates, despite the tabula-rasa argument by the German philosopher Immanuel Kant.[1] No, it appears that certain predispositions and even some types of knowledge (cell memory and more) are already written in our minds when we make our first inhalation. Still, the content of our mind that's acquired following birth is the beginning of what we shall eventually hold as both our identity and our knowledge/beliefs.

The Law of Attraction

You may have heard of the three components of the Law of Attraction—*ask, believe,* and *receive.* This sounds really easy until you question the degree of your belief, and that's where most people fail.

I actually divide belief into three components that must be activated in the proper sequence to manifest using the inner genie. These components are:

1. The emotional input that's passionate and convinced

2. The confidence/mental element that can simply and truly visualize something and then let it go, knowing it will happen

3. The spiritual sincerity that realizes at the deepest level of our beings that we're a gift from the Creator. Knowing that, we release our vision, for we believe *this or something better, according to the highest good of all concerned.*

Anything that would distract from thinking, feeling, and knowing these three components will, in direct proportion, sabotage our efforts at manifesting our desires.

Given this understanding, it becomes easier to see why some people first manifest their desires, only to lose their treasures and find themselves worse off than they were before, some fail to manifest at all, and others seem to manifest the opposite of what they're seeking.

With this under your belt, you might ask, as I did: *Why do most people seem handicapped by the inability to use the genie within and create the reality they deserve?*

The Dumpster analogy is the first clue to answering this question. The garbage some hold in their minds would be frightening if it were visible to the public eye. As Strongheart, the German shepherd hero of the movies, put it in his letters to Boone, "What a dreadful sight to see people's faces as incomplete as their minds."[2] I would paraphrase: "What a horrible sight to see people's faces as grotesque as the worst in their minds."

I'd like to imagine a world full of joy, peace, balance, and harmony. That's truly difficult to do when nature seems so callous and carnivorous. As I think about this, I realize that I'm anthropomorphizing nature, so I turn my thoughts to humans, where I find such horrible acts that a lion killing a lamb is innocent in comparison. How do we truly find peace, balance, and harmony? How do we gain spiritual sincerity and merge this with the right balance of mental and emotional stuff to manifest a *world* full of peace, balance, and harmony?

For some, manifestation is about things such as cars, swimming pools, houses, riches, sexy this and that, and the gratification of other sensual desires. For the spiritually sincere, manifestation is first about peace, balance, and harmony and then about health and individual happiness. These are complex issues that labels alone don't cover, so we can let the subject rest with this: each individual has a purpose for being here; and when individuals seek to manifest according to their purpose, they're enlightening themselves and the world around them.

Back to the main point: the mind is both ignition and brake. First thing in the morning, I open my eyes and begin talking to myself. My thoughts may recognize a dream or immediately turn to the new day's itinerary.

The mind goes immediately to delivering the inner world of thoughts, beliefs, ambitions, goals, and so forth. That constant stream of consciousness—self-talk—informs us of our mood, attitudes, likes, dislikes, and so much more. It's this stream of consciousness that reflects the contents of our "Dumpster."

A Warning

We started this chapter by imagining a genie within. I believe that this inner genie actually exists, but if you don't, that's okay. What I intend to show you is that the genie has been creating all along, even if you think that it's only some concocted get-rich scheme. In fact, the worse your life might seem, the higher the probability that the genie is working hard at fulfilling your every fear (emotion), thought (expectation), and spiritual insight ("Life sucks, and then you die"). It's in precisely this way that your hopes and ambitions are slain. Thus, your mind has been turned into the slayer.

To adequately illustrate my point, I must make a case that will at times lead us into some dark areas. For years, I practiced criminalistics.

During that time, I ran lie-detection tests, conducted investigations, did forensic hypnosis, and more. I remember well a case in which a young man was accused of murdering his mother after sexually abusing her. This was about as dark and sinister a crime as it was possible to work on. Thoughtfully reconstructing all I knew about this case had (forgive the expression) its "upchuck moments." The accused son had been convicted of the crime when I became involved. The moral I wish to share with you is this: the boy didn't commit the crime, and we proved it. He's free today as a result. If I'd refused to explore that so-called dark side, things might well have been much different, because it was largely my findings and testimony that freed him.

Again, in order to make the case, we must journey through some nasty things just as detectives do. I wish there was another way, but there isn't. Indeed, there's so much misinformation that our arguments, either pro or con, must rise above the fray in all respects. Sometimes that means going to the proverbial horse's mouth.

There was a time in my life when I worked to have good street contacts (informants). Developing these contacts could mean going down to their hangouts and fitting in. If you stay with me, I promise that we'll come out of those places with a deeper understanding of ourselves and the world around us. I warn you, though, if you're totally innocent and wish to stay that way, don't come! Close the book now. If, however, you're like most people and truly wish to understand how your choices have been programmed, how your thinking is often controlled, and how the art of persuasion is used against you and by you every day, then stay with me. This and much more will be found in the pages that follow.

One more warning: Parts of this book are not for children. Please keep it out of their reach. It isn't the *Kama Sutra,* and you're not going to find erotic adventures inside, but there are some brutal psychological facts and misuses that are visually portrayed. I'm certain that some of what follows will offend, and I apologize in advance. But I also know that you truly *do* have a genie within; and once you get the garbage out of the Dumpster, once you call upon the cortical power to stop the input processes that insert the junk, and once you see the easy antidotes to cleaning out the garbage, the journey will have been more than worthwhile.

The Genie

*The genie within is your birthright and
manifesting the glory of the Creator
by carrying out your purpose
is the highest and best gift
you can give the Giver.*

Part of my purpose in life has been revealing and resisting improper uses of persuasion techniques while cultivating and developing their proper uses. I hope that when you've finished reading this book, you'll find that I've lived up to my understanding, at least in part.

Summary

Our minds are the source of our imagination and ambition. I've suggested a genie within as a metaphor for the ability our minds have to create the life of our choosing. Yet accessing this genie isn't quite that simple. Although we like to think of ourselves as being the most evolved of the animal kingdom, wired into our being are primitive mechanisms. Life, peer pressure, enculturation, and planned manipulations of these mechanisms all influence our inner genie. As a result, our lives can appear to be out of our control. How did the manipulation even begin?

■   ■ ■ ▬■

CHAPTER 2

Are We Being
Manipulated?

*"To be a star you must shine your own light, follow
your own path and be not afraid of the darkness,
for that is when stars shine brightest."*

— Author unknown

I'm not a conspiracy person; in fact, I generally dismiss so-called conspiracy theories. Still, in a world where the ability to manipulate exists, is it out of bounds to ask, "Are we being manipulated?"

The answer is "Of course." We're manipulated every day by someone and probably have been all our lives. Our choice in clothing, the automobiles we drive, the foods we eat, the things we do for recreation, the opinions we hold, and even the lenses through which we see ourselves have been framed in such a way that it's impossible to separate our identity from the process that has brought us all to where we are today. Words such as *enculturation, ethnocentrism, egocentric,* and the like all address the assumption that our environment shapes our impressions and personalities and, as a result, our judgments and beliefs. Most of this manipulation is commonly considered just a fact of life, and indeed it is.

Propaganda is a word defined by Merriam-Webster as "the spreading of ideas, information, or rumor for the purpose of helping or injuring an institution, a cause, or a person; ideas, facts, or allegations spread deliberately to further one's cause or to damage an opposing cause." Propaganda has been overtly employed in the past to convince entire societies of the rightness of their wrongful actions. Most of us know that much of the story, but do you know where propaganda originated and the extent to which it's used? How is it possible to persuade entire populations to go against their moral or ethical codes, such as what was witnessed by the world during the Holocaust?

How are reasonable people convinced that unreasonable actions are warranted and just? What lurks in the psychology of the masses that mobilizes group vigilante actions inconsistent with the beliefs of individuals? Are there people, groups, agencies, and governments that seek to learn and exploit these human vulnerabilities? Is it foolish or simply naïve to think otherwise?

Where do we begin? Do we go all the way back to the very cradle of civilization, or could we start with something much more contemporary? For our purposes here, let me begin with the story of Edward Bernays and what we know today as propaganda.

The Birth of Propaganda

As the 20th century opened, Bernays's uncle, the famous psychotherapist Sigmund Freud, was advancing his theories of the dynamic, active, decision-making unconscious mind. Notable American philosopher-psychologist William James rejected this model. In *The Principles of Psychology,* James asserted that the mind is limited to conscious processes alone, and so-called unconscious events are "only physical." James stated that the two distinctions of consciousness were simply different metaphysical substances: consciousness was the crown of human reason; unconsciousness was merely a bodily function.[1]

Although the work of James has survived as a true classic in the behavioral sciences and, indeed, was well ahead of its time, his rejection of an intelligent unconscious was an error. Over time and through much controversy, it has emerged that the mind consists largely of an unconscious that arguably provides the conscious with what it will think.[2] This research was originally carried out by Benjamin Libet in 1967 and has been repeatedly verified, most recently by John-Dylan Haynes at the Bernstein Center for Computational Neuroscience in Berlin: "Studying the brain behavior leading up to the moment of conscious decision, the researchers identified signals that let them know when the students had decided to move 10 seconds or so before the students knew it themselves. About 70% of the time, the researchers could also predict which button the students would push."[3]

It was the subconscious mind that Bernays sought to exploit. He called his approach the "engineering of consent" and based it upon the work of his uncle Freud, thereby lending the term *scientific* to his techniques. In his most influential book, *Propaganda,* Bernays argued that the manipulation of the masses is absolutely necessary for a democracy and its economy to work:

> The conscious and intelligent manipulation of the organized habits and opinions of the masses is an important element in democratic society. Those who manipulate this unseen mechanism of society constitute an invisible government which is the true ruling power of our country. We are governed, our minds are molded, our tastes formed, our ideas suggested, largely by men we have never heard of. . . . In almost every act of our daily lives, whether in the sphere of politics or business, in our social conduct or our ethical thinking, we are dominated by the relatively small number of persons . . . who understand the mental processes and social patterns of the masses. It is they who pull the wires that control the public mind.[4]

For our purposes here, it's important to understand that Freud's influence was more than just that of an intelligent unconscious. More important was the central role played by sexuality in developing personality and shaping unconscious strategies and defense mechanisms. Understanding this orientation shaped the world of advertising in almost all venues over time.

Freudian Psychology

A brief overview of Freudian psychology may be helpful here. Freud associated psychological development with sexual energy (psycho-sexual). According to him, as our sexual energy changed, so did our psychological development. Three of Freud's stages of development are oral, anal, and phallic.

Underlying this is the theme of polymorphous perversity, the ability to find erotic pleasure from any part of the body. During these stages, the child finds pleasure in ways that would be considered perverse in an adult. The first stage is oral. During the first two years of his life, the infant is focused on oral gratification. The second stage is thought of as the anal period, which is associated with toilet training and which a child experiences during years two and three. The third stage is the phallic, when a child experiences pleasure in phallic feelings and which is generally experienced between ages three and six.

If development is arrested early, then the child could remain stuck at one of the levels into adulthood. For Freud, stage-one problems in adults are a need to smoke or overeat. These could represent an incomplete oral stage, such as early weaning, punishment that accompanied nursing (perhaps a slap when a teething child bites), or prolonged nursing that lasts in some cases into the third level. Stage-two problems usually arise as a result of punishment during potty training. This is where the idea of being anal-retentive originates. In stage-three development, Freud believed that the child saw the parent of his or her own sex as a rival for attention from the parent of the opposite sex, and that's where the notions of the Oedipus and the Electra complexes come from.

Further, according to Freudian theory, the personality is structured into three components: the *id, superego,* and *ego.* The id is instinctive and primal, seeking to maximize pleasure and minimize pain. It's thought to comprise both the life force and the death instinct. It also drives sexual desire because propagation is a part of the life force. Freud's notion of the libido arises here; and because this includes both life and its opposite, libidinal impulses can contain death urges. This is important to understanding the subliminal embeds from the print media, and the death and dying scenes often portrayed subliminally in advertising.

The superego is the authoritarian inner voice of our enculturation. It's the home of our socialized "ought to" notions. The superego seeks to impose morality and speaks to us through our conscience.

The ego mediates between the id's hungry drives, which often conflict with social mores, and the superego's urge to repress them. The ego gives rise to what most think of as finding the socially acceptable way. For example, sexuality is expressed through marriage instead of in a more beastlike manner, assuming a socially adjusted normal human being.

When intense conflicts between the id and the superego occur, the ego may employ any of several defense strategies to move the event out of consciousness, but the conflict still exists in the subconscious.

The ego is a construct of mind. For all intents and purposes, it puts down strong roots in each of us during our individuation process, normally at or around two years of age. Scientific literature is full of stratifications for various activities that are thought to occur or exist in the mind.

Categories of the Mind

For our purposes here, I'll refer to four categories of the mind:

1. The **preconscious** is a part of our memory or knowledge that we can call upon but don't hold in consciousness at the moment.

2. The **conscious** is that which we're fully aware of.

3. The **subconscious** is beneath our consciousness and is generally hidden from it.

4. The **unconscious** is a deep sleep or coma state and may be the part of the mind that Carl Jung, the founder of analytical psychology, thought of as participating in the collective consciousness at all times—the telephone line or conduit, if you will.

The ego's defense mechanisms include denial, repression, regression, projection, sublimation, reaction formation, and displacement. As will be made evident in the following chapters, these mechanisms, when employed as perceptual defenses, can actually hide the obvious from us. But whether or not we agree with Freud's scheme is irrelevant to our purpose here. What *is* important is that by understanding this scheme, we can make sense of why certain images, including taboos, are intentionally used by advertisers and others to manipulate us. The next chapter gives a more complete overview of defense mechanisms, the strategies they employ, and the compliance principles that are often used on all of us. For now, let's continue with the story of Edward Bernays and propaganda.

The Advertising Revolution

Bernays sought to evolve a form of communication that, to borrow his terminology, could be used to control the dumb masses. To do this, he advanced Freud's theories in ways that modern psychology is still catching up with. Bernays's approach was to apply the insights of Freud in a scientific manner. He employed behavioral scientists to study human reactions to various stimuli. Groups were tested for their response to certain words, images, and more; and from this sophisticated analysis, advertisements were built and new tests were conducted. Needless to say, his methods were very successful.

In short, Bernays revolutionized the world of advertising, merchandising, and public relations. This man, who died in 1995, was widely acclaimed as the "father of public relations." His influence spanned more than 70 years; and his clients included elite Fortune 500 companies, politicians, and publicists. In 1929, he organized the

50th anniversary of the invention of the lightbulb. Known as Light's Golden Jubilee, the celebration gave credit for the device to Thomas Edison, and it was so successful that it permanently branded Edison as the inventor when in fact the accolades should have gone to Joseph Swan.[5]

Edward Bernays wasn't popular with everyone. He changed the meaning of the word *propaganda,* formerly meaning "truthful disclosure designed to confront ignorance and disinformation," to its present-day meaning, which most people view with appropriate suspicion. His arrogance and disregard for "the little guy" also led to some public condemnation. Most important, from our perspective, Bernays managed to meld social science and marketing in ways that sometimes led to more effective psychologists with marketing degrees than counselors with psychology degrees.

According to attorney and author August Bullock, by the end of the 1950s "an estimated billion dollars a year was invested in motivational research and another ten billion dollars a year was spent on advertising in general . . . enormous expenditures considering that at the time a loaf of bread cost 17 cents."[6] In his engrossing book, *The Secret Sales Pitch,* Bullock illustrates how some of this motivational research was done. A quick look at some of the questions asked by researchers reveals their interest in unconscious reasons for the consumption of various things. For example, researchers asked questions such as "What is your earliest memory regarding a cookie?" and "How does eating a cookie make you feel?"[7] Further, as Bullock points out, "these sessions were often filmed and analyzed by teams of researchers."[8]

Bookstore shelves are full of material teaching ideas and methods that would offend most people. Merchandisers claim they know what we want, and by some standards they're brutal in the steps they take to ensure that we get it. From books such as *The Secret Sales Pitch* to Bernays's own *Propaganda,* the message from ad agencies is clear: people are ignorant, and they're best served when manipulated. In Bernays's words, "Democracy is administered by the intelligent minority who know how to regiment and guide the masses."[9]

In the book *Age of Propaganda,* authors Pratkanis and Aronson make several relevant points about how little things that are seemingly irrelevant to an issue can be used to prime a decision, including acts as great as taking a nation to war. One such discussion points out that tiny similarities can potentially link current affairs to historical actions. For example, if two Presidents come from the same state, the actions of one may be compared to the other whenever they face similar situations.[10]

After Bernays, along came George Orwell and his classic book *1984*. Orwell envisioned a future in which the masses were under the control of government, known as "Big Brother." This regime used technology to monitor and control the public. Orwell's *1984* was published in 1949; five years later, the author passed away, never knowing just how much prophetic vision his book really contained.[11]

In 1946, adman Ernest Dichter founded the Institute of Motivation Research in New York. Dichter had done work for Chrysler and Procter & Gamble and defined his use of motivational research as "qualitative research designed to uncover the consumer's subconscious or hidden motivations that determine purchase behavior."[12]

Dichter is credited with developing the in-depth interview. He was convinced that people were unwilling to truthfully disclose and/or were incapable of telling why they buy things. In-depth interviews therefore explored associations, ideas, emotions, and more. This type of consumer research is making a comeback of sorts today.[13]

The Subliminal Controversy

In 1957, a market researcher in New Jersey by the name of James Vicary claimed to have increased concession sales by flashing on the movie screen the subliminal messages "Eat popcorn" and "Drink Coca-Cola." Subliminal communication or theory wasn't new; academics had been studying it for some time. Various forms of subliminal stimuli and their influence on an individual had been evaluated since the late 19th century. What was different was the public announcement of the surreptitious use of the technology on the public for purposes of personal gain. Mind you, up until this point there was little dispute in scientific circles regarding subliminal information processing per se.

The only disagreements were about how much influence a stimulus could have, how much behavior could be shaped or guided, how long the stimulus effect might last, and so forth. Fundamentally—and this is the important point—the general consensus was that subliminal information (stimulus of an audio, visual, or kinesthetic type) was processed and could predispose both thought and action based on the nature of the stimulus.

Vance Packard's work *The Hidden Persuaders* appeared in 1957 and, although discredited by many, made it onto the required-reading list for many high schools by the late 1960s. Packard quoted from the London *Sunday Times* regarding an account of a New Jersey theater where ice-cream ads were flashed onto the screen during a movie, resulting in an otherwise unaccountable increase in ice-cream sales. The paper referred to this technique as "subthreshold effects."[14]

As a result of investigations, James Vicary denied ever conducting the popcorn, cola, and ice-cream trials in his theater. Whether he actually did or not has never been proved. We do know that he had the ability to do so, but perhaps he only made the claim to sell the equipment that his company, Precon Processing, built.

In 1990, the now-infamous Judas Priest wrongful death action in Reno, Nevada, asserted in part that subliminal stimuli in the heavy-metal band's *Stained Class* album were a causal factor in the deaths of two young men who shot themselves. The subliminal command "Do it" had been found on a track with lyrics that overtly encouraged suicide, and this song had been played repeatedly just before the boys went out and attempted to commit suicide. One was immediately successful; the other shot off the front of his face and died three years later. (For a detailed look at this case, please see Appendix 5, taken from my earlier book *Thinking without Thinking*.)

For now, the point I want to make is this: At that time, the media was flooded with assertions that subliminal information wasn't being used, and that if it was used, it wouldn't work. In fact, it was said that subliminal technology was a hoax and a fraud.

If we follow the development of subliminal theory in the context of the legal and social issues of the time, it's easy to conclude that by the 1990s, the fix was in. "The fix" in this instance was convincing the public that subliminal communications were all a big farce. Perhaps believing otherwise is paranoia. Maybe all the evidence really is just one big coincidence—and maybe not.

In the *Age of Propaganda,* authors Pratkanis and Aronson make this statement:

> Finally, a belief in subliminal persuasion serves a need for many individuals. In our age of propaganda, citizens are provided with very little education concerning the nature of persuasion. The result is that many feel confused and bewildered by basic social processes. Subliminal persuasion is presented as an irrational force outside the control of the message recipient. As such, it takes on a supernatural "devil made me do it" quality capable of justifying and explaining why Americans are often persuaded to engage in seemingly irrational behavior. Why did I buy this worthless product at such a high price? Subliminal sorcery.[15]

As you continue to examine the evidence, you'll see repeated attempts to ridicule those who suggest the efficacy of subliminal communication. In the words of a self-appointed, orchestrated debunking group, quoting writer and critic H. L. Mencken: "A horse-laugh is worth ten thousand syllogisms."[16] In other words, if you can get someone to laugh at a premise, then you no longer need to present an intelligent and effective argument.

Factually, however, scientific literature clearly shows that subliminal technology is real. Information presented in this way predisposes opinions and decisions, influences behavior, and more. Indeed, meta-analysis of the studies conducted demonstrates robust and undeniable results in favor of subliminal influence.[17] Still, the public at large remains skeptical, secure in the opinion that no one could or would treat them in the callous, cynical way laid out by Edward Bernays.

Are others intentionally manipulating us for gain? In the documentary *Programming the Nation,* producer Jeff Warrick leaves it all up to you.[18] I'll do the same.

Understanding how, when, where, and why we could be manipulated requires a closer examination of defense mechanisms and compliance principles.

Summary

Manipulation is simply a fact of life. However, certain groups of people have taken this manipulation to a very sophisticated level. An entire area of research, founded by Edward Bernays, has been dedicated to understanding the primitive mechanisms of our mind for the sole purpose of exploiting it. What are the compliance principles and defense mechanisms wired into our being that make us so vulnerable to being manipulated?

CHAPTER 3

Compliance Principles and Defense Mechanisms

"We lost because we told ourselves we lost."

— **Lev Nikolayevich Tolstoy**

We commonly do things contrary to our own values and against our own interests. You may know people with expensive experiences of that sort. Perhaps they spend too much money on cars, shoes, or other toys.

Con artists, sales agents, and others often specialize in the skills of manipulation. What principles cause compliance? How do we make decisions? What short-circuits our decision process? This chapter will examine strategies for manipulation, perceptual defense mechanisms, and systematic means to control responses.

Further, we'll consider the ethics of compliance control. When are compliance strategies necessary, appropriate, or ethical? What separates exploitation from usefully motivating people, selling products, and influencing those around us?

The opening sentence of this chapter may become lodged in your mind. You can explain yourself rather than understand yourself. Why does it take so long to understand?

You may have seen individuals who have been hypnotized respond to posthypnotic suggestion. They rationalize. They come up with reasons why they acted peculiarly, making it appear as though it was just good sense that they pulled out a wallet and used it as a baseball. Then they feel more comfortable. They rarely guess that the hypnotic suggestion occurred.

Rationalizing works! It also conceals valuable understanding. At some point, you'll do something out of character. If you bypass the pat answer for your actions, you'll find more useful understanding. You can start with what you learn from this book.

Compliance: Why Did I Do That?

Every day we experience attempts to influence us. Some of these work to our benefit; some don't. Some people can help us escape addictions; some make big money from addicting us. How much do you know about how these things happen?

We encounter compliance procedures repeatedly. The subtlest manipulations may slip under the guard of even trained professionals. Suppose someone could manipulate us into buying products, joining clubs, and even allowing strangers to put billboards on our front lawns forever and for free. Sound ridiculous?

Governments, businesses, and churches have long studied the methods of compliance. For even longer, these methods have moved the masses. Compliance principles are simply shortcuts we use to determine our behavior. For precisely that reason, they exercise power.

Misspent Youth, Sewn Up

In my teens, I sold sewing machines and vacuum cleaners door to door. My employers trained me to control compliance, and I complied with my training. I had a lot to learn about the subject.

In those days, a tactic called "bait and switch" was legal. Rather, I should say that it wasn't *illegal*. It started with an offer too good to be true. In the early 1960s, credit depended upon deposit—a down payment of 10 percent in those days. Credit was freely available. Getting the down payment became the most difficult part of making a sale, so the company I worked for designed a system to obtain this fee.

How was this done? Prospects entered contests. A drawing at the local grocery store, a "count the hidden faces" challenge in the Sunday paper, and various other media served this purpose. Someone received the first prize. Everyone else won second prize, a coupon worth $170 toward the purchase of a new sewing machine, nationally advertised for only $199.99. We could show these "winners" the ad, usually in a popular home magazine. For only $29.99, everyone in second place could enjoy the benefits of owning a new sewing machine. Such a deal!

The machine available for purchase at $29.99 was a piece of junk. In the trunk of my car, however, was a new, top-of-the-line machine, advertised nationally at $499. If you were a second-place winner, by trading in the shoddy machine you'd just purchased, this superior model could be yours for an additional $299. And you'd already paid the 10 percent deposit of $29.99. Thereafter, you'd only pay $10 per month until you'd paid off the additional $299. Even though you only spent $29.99 for the first machine, you received its full nationally advertised price as the trade-in value. Wow—what a deal!

This means of selling worked so well that it became illegal. You may have guessed that the national ads existed only for this purpose. No one ever actually tried to buy one of those machines at the inflated price in the advertisement.

Dirty Laundry

Before I turned 20, I left door-to-door sales and went to work for a major retailer. This company also used bait-and-switch tactics, but under different terms. A dryer might be advertised for $88, but we kept the appliance "nailed down"—that meant "Don't sell." If the

customer absolutely insisted, I could sell it, but let too many of these
$88 units go out the door and I might need a new job—not for selling
inexpensive machines, but for incompetence.

The retailers sold away from the cheap bait with a routine called
"selling up by selling down." A clerk showed a customer the most
expensive dryer in the house with emphasis on all the added features
and benefits, saving the $400 price tag for last. Then, in an act of so-
called honesty, he might say, "You know, I'm not paid to talk you out
of spending money, but I have a new dryer over here. It's last year's
model. Nothing changed in this year's model except that the console
looks a little different. What's more, I can save you more than $100.
The dryer does everything I just showed you, but it costs much less.
It's up to you. Would you prefer to spend the extra money and have
this year's model?"

Notice two things the sales pitch does: it positions the customer
toward compliance, and it focuses attention on less money. (Several
principles of compliance apply here, which I'll describe more on the
following pages.)

First, the seller appears honest. He might even add: "I like you,
and I didn't want to show you this dryer at first, because we only have
one left. And I didn't want you to think that I was just saying that to
pressure you into buying." The customer receives a false impression of
integrity. Few will question the lie. Why? Because we want friendship,
we like to be liked, we want a deal, he's doing us a favor, and he's giving us the benefit of his authority. Merchants plot long and hard to
pack all they can into those little speeches.

The second item the sales presentation accomplished is focusing
the customer's attention on less. Forget that this dryer is $249—$161
more than the advertised $88 dryer. No, the focus shifts to less, to
much less than the dryer capable of doing all the wonderful things the
customer wants it to do. More subtly, focus shifts to this one limited
choice. The customer could do an infinite number of other things with
his money, but now he thinks about less. He thinks more about less.

This retail organization defined three components for training:
product knowledge, enthusiasm, and motivation. They taught little
technique. My sales record quickly attracted attention. The company

promoted me, and I became a supervisor. I trained others, and their sales increased.

Unprincipled Principles

Technique suggests rules that get results. By following rules, people can be positioned to comply with requests.

Different authors use different categories for compliance principles. Robert Cialdini, in his most-recommended book, *Influence,* describes six in depth.[1] For our purposes, I'll describe those and four others. Make yourself alert to consistency, reciprocity, social proof, association, conditioning, liking, authority, scarcity, drives, and justification.

The Con in Consistency

At the beginning of this chapter, I suggested that you might let strangers place a billboard on your front lawn without compensation. Cialdini recounts just such an incident. A volunteer worker asked home owners to sign a petition to keep California beautiful. A couple of weeks later, a different volunteer approached these same people and asked each of them to place a billboard in their front yard, advertising safe driving. The chief researchers, Jonathon Freedman and Scott Fraser, discovered that 76 percent of those who signed the petition displayed the billboard, in contrast with 17 percent of home owners who hadn't been asked to sign the petition. The first act of compliance —signing an innocent petition—apparently produced significant feelings of civic mindedness and involvement. This first innocent decision led, for the vast majority, to the second decision due to the need to be consistent. That is, they said *yes* once, so they felt as though they should say it again. Thus, a small commitment led to a larger one.[2]

The Consistence Con

People like to *be* internally consistent and to *appear* externally consistent. Suppose a customer entered the appliance department of a store with a question such as "Do you have this refrigerator in the color harvest gold?"

Salespeople learn not to answer merely: "Yes." They learn to convert the question into a "close" by asking in return, "Do you want it in harvest gold?"

Of course most shoppers respond by saying: "Yes." Any other answer implies that they're simply wasting time—the salesperson's and their own. Once this decision has been made and publicly stated, the need to remain consistent leads the individual to answer the next question: "Is Tuesday or Thursday better for delivery?" The sale is made with no need to discuss refrigerators any further. The customer has never been asked to buy. Instead, every question builds upon the presupposition of purchase. The customer maintains consistency: "Yes, I want it in gold, and Tuesday would be better."

Compliance in Lie Detection

In time, I left the sales business and entered various intelligence, security, and interrogation schools. Ultimately, I became licensed as a deception-detection (lie-detector) examiner. As an investigator and as a lie-detection examiner, I employed various compliance techniques in interrogation. Why on earth would someone confess a crime that would lock him or her away for years to come? What would cause people to give up evidence that convicted them?

The following dialogue positions suspects to commit perjury. It's intentionally designed to cause them to lie. Later, it's used to control and direct their need to prove their honesty and sincerity and to justify the reasoning involved for committing a crime. Little commitments lead to big commitments.

Imagine that you've come in for a lie-detection test. The examiner looks you straight in the eye—a firm look followed by a warm smile—and asks, "You didn't come here to lie to me, did you?"

"No."

"So you intend to tell me the truth today?"

"Yes."

"Good, because you look like an honest person, and I'm on your side. We can use this test to prove your innocence. You do want that, don't you?"

"Yes."

"Okay, I'm going to trust you. You look like a good person. I'm going to cover all the questions that I'll ask you today before I ever ask them in the test. I want to review them with you carefully, and if anything about a question bothers you, let's discuss it. Now that's important, because if it bothers you, I'll see it in the charts, and it's probably some little thing—maybe some outside thing that has nothing to do with this case. So be certain: if it bothers you, tell me. Okay?"

"Sure."

"Okay now, you're not the kind of person who lies and steals. Right?"

"Right."

"So you wouldn't lie to someone who trusted you or steal from a person like that, would you?"

"No!"

"Good. Today I'm going to ask you the following question: Did you ever lie to someone who trusted you? Later, I'll ask: Did you steal anything, say between the ages of 10 and 20?"

The foregoing dialogue involves many principles of compliance. Even more than in the sales dialogue, a deviant answer would produce awkwardness. You could scarcely answer the questions differently. As the examiner knows, everyone lies to their mother, father, siblings, and spouse—someone who trusts them—at some point in their lives. Almost everyone has stolen something, if only pennies from their parents. The questioning process leaves the examinee in a position that examiners can exploit for more than one purpose.

Principles of Compliance

Why would this be the usual practice? We'll take a look at the 11 principles of compliance for the answer.

1. Social Beliefs

Social beliefs are among the strongest principles of the individual, and they often conflict with personal desires. These tenets form the very fabric of society. Politicians and profiteers play these beliefs, longings, and their conflicts like musicians. Social beliefs, selfish interest, and the tension between them form the bedrock of compliance principles.

2. Reciprocity

Studies have shown that the act of giving produces the need to reciprocate. I remember when "little green pigs" were sold by using this principle. The little green pig was a vacuum cleaner, and the door-to-door salesman would give you a one-quart bottle of your favorite soft drink if you answered the door when he knocked. The pitch began with something like this: "I have a gift for you. Which of these drinks is your favorite?" You then received your choice. While the bottle remained in your hand and the salesman in your doorway, the next line came: "Have you heard of the little green pig?" From that point on, your answers only worsened the situation . . . unless you truly desired to hear all about this vacuum cleaner to end all vacuum cleaners. Accepting the gift of the soda incurred a sense of obligation. The least you could do was give the young man five minutes of your time to hear about the little green pig.

From the so-called warm handshake to inside information and the free things offered today, a gift extended implies that there should be a gift in return. Cialdini calls it "the old give and take . . . and take."[3]

3. Social Proof

Merchants enlist testimony after testimony from faithful, satisfied users in order to sell us their wares. Carnival hucksters seed their audiences with winners of the big stuffed toy. Merchants and politicians, like preachers, often sow the seeds of mass conversion by enlisting an army of stooges to "come forth at varying intervals to create the impression of a spontaneous mass outpouring."[4] We believe that if many people agree on something, it must be true; it must be good and desirable. And not so long ago, everyone believed that Earth was flat, too.

Social proof works particularly well in a democracy. Questioning this belief calls our future into doubt.

4. Association

Association seeks to link favorable feelings with a product or aim. We see politicians with apple pie, babies, and the American flag. We see stunning men and women in the most unlikely of places, wearing the most unlikely of apparel, just to connect their image with the product.

As with all of these principles, you can look beyond the obvious. Take, for instance, a project that sought to measure the influence of major credit-card logos on buying. In this study, carried out by researcher Richard Feinberg, it was found that subjects would spend 29 percent more on mail-order items when they could see a major credit card logo in the room. Another study by the same researcher showed that college students give money to charity more often with the credit card logo in the room. Only 33 percent of the students gave to charity where there was no credit card logo in the room, whereas 87 percent gave when the logo was present—and this was despite the fact that credit cards weren't accepted. Just the association increased spending.[5]

Advertisers also use sound, which has long enjoyed renown for its affective power, particularly music. You may be old enough to remember an old Marlboro television commercial that used the theme music from the classic movie *The Magnificent Seven.* The ad associated feelings from the movie and the music with smoking the cigarettes.

Television producers use canned laughter to punctuate comedy, although many folks don't notice it. In our culture, people often consciously overlook sound.

Sound moves upon our primordial nature. Our first knowledge of the outside world comes from sounds we hear while we're in the womb.

My own work has often focused on an area I call "audio cuing." One of my research projects, financed by a Nevada company, involved the sounds a slot machine makes. Does the sound of money falling into a metal tray attract players? We thought so. Can sounds increase playing time while leaving players with a sense of fun, even if they lose money? We thought so.

Don't discount even the most innocent of features that accompany a product or advertisement. The companies behind them spend billions annually on deliberately applying skillful knowledge to manipulate you.

5. Conditioning and Association

Some authors combine conditioning and association.[6] They tend to come as a pair. The credit-card logo study assumes the association of credit cards with pleasure, a principle of conditioning, while prior negative experience with a credit card reversed the effects on spending.[7]

I separate these two principles because classical conditioning has been accomplished by subliminal stimuli. (For a complete discussion of subliminal conditioning, see my book *Subliminal Learning: An Eclectic Approach.*) The principle of association implies at least some conscious recognition of the stimuli, but subliminal stimuli violate this assumption. In other words, although the stimuli are associated with a response, as with classical conditioning, the stimuli themselves are unrecognized by the conscious mind.

For example, when subjects have pictures of people's faces repeatedly presented subliminally to them, the subjects become more comfortable with those in the images. The more frequent the subliminal exposure, the greater the liking for the individuals when they later met. This occurs even though the subjects had no conscious awareness of the subliminally presented faces.[8]

Many forms of association can bypass conscious awareness, and not all of them necessarily qualify as subliminal. We have perceptual defense mechanisms that figuratively blindfold each of us at times. As with the associations intentionally built into most advertisements, certain consciously undetected associations can operate on existing conditioning and pair with it to produce new conditioning.

6. Liking

The more we identify with and feel comfortable with someone else, the more we like the other person, and the more often we comply with that individual's requests. Discussing anything so obvious may seem ridiculous, but the liking principle has nuances unfamiliar to most of us. It has mechanical features.

The science of neurolinguistic programming (NLP) often starts with the mechanics of rapport. It breaks the phenomenon into matching, pacing, and leading. *Match* by adopting an individual's speaking style, physical mannerisms, and so forth. *Pace* by continuing to do so, and *lead* by making a new gesture or by shifting your tone of voice. So long as others follow your example, you can continue to lead them. You have rapport.

NLP is a powerful technology now taught indiscriminately to anyone from health-care professionals to sales organizations to political and religious groups. The latter have become the major market for books on the subject. This powerful technology can operate almost as mechanically as a knee-jerk reflex. (For more information, see books by Richard Bandler and John Grinder.) The ability to build rapport, increase liking, and so on is so enhanced by NLP techniques, which nearly every trained interrogator in the country has had some exposure to.

Liking often develops under conditions of cooperation. We all know that "politics make for strange bedfellows" and that there's a strategy to unite disparate groups by getting them to band together against a common enemy. Many times television commercials tell us: "It's flu season, and there's a new dreaded enemy virus. It's coming to your town! It may find you, but never fear, XYZ is here." First, the advertisement threatens us with a new enemy, and then makes a common enemy out of that threat. Next, the commercial promises relief and allegiance from the medicine.

The rewards of recovery appear to outweigh the advantages of remaining healthy. I view this as an insidious abuse of compliance principles. I believe that ads such as these actually sell sickness. In fact, I've often imagined a scenario to test this theme.

Picture going to the American people with all the tools of compliance. Have an actor who's dressed like a doctor inform the public that a new disease has just been identified. This illness must have general symptoms—fatigue, restlessness, occasional headaches, itching, an ache (especially in the back and limbs), and sometimes dry skin, accompanied by irritability and depression. Explain the disease as being formerly unknown, although very common and potentially serious. Enhance and embellish the explanation with estimates of the great numbers of people who may suffer from this condition, yet never have received a diagnosis, let alone treatment. Finally, offer the remedy with a smooth explanation—make it an affordable pill or liquid —and watch the good folks in America rush to their pharmacy.

You don't think it's possible? Recently an article appeared on **msnbc.com** entitled "Without Ads, Restless Legs May Take a Hike." The thrust of the article is in the title. Quoted in the piece is Dr. Christopher J. Early, an associate professor of neurology at Johns Hopkins University. Early puts it this way, "Restless legs syndrome is a great example of a suddenly out-of-the-blue disease." First there was a television commercial describing symptoms so general that most people have experienced some of them, and then the commercial offered relief (a cure). Immediately, there was a rush for the cure. Then with the end of the ads, there was an end to the disease, or at least an anticipated end. It isn't that there's no such condition; it's that the prevalence of the disorder and the generality of symptoms was so exaggerated as to suggest the condition to many people.[9]

7. Authority

Authority, authority, authority. That has a ring kind of like the secret of retail success: location, location, location! Everywhere we turn today, an authority instructs and informs—authority to which we come to trust our very lives. How did we survive before we had so many different experts?

In the 1960s, social psychologist Professor Stanley Milgram performed one of the most important experiments in history. Naïve volunteers received instructions to deliver electric shocks, up to 450 volts, to volunteer subjects (who were research assistants) who'd been tied to chairs with electric wires. The punishment would be given for failing some trivial task, such as a memory test. The subject receiving the shock would protest the increasing voltage with cries of pain and warnings of a heart condition.

What would you expect people to do? What would you do? The authority, the research scientist in his white coat, insisted upon more shocks. The volunteers delivered them. The authority's power was so awe inspiring as to override severe psychological conflict in volunteers. The struggle was physically evident: their faces blanched; they sweated, shivered, and wept; and they obediently carried out the instructions to deliver more voltage, even after the "victim" acted dead.[10]

No one wanted to believe that had happened. People duplicated Milgram's experiment just to try to prove him wrong, but they got the same results. The Authority Torture Experiment produced the same results regardless of the race, gender, culture, language, nationality, education, and other varying characteristics of the volunteers.

Robert Cialdini relates the similar research findings of Hofling, Brotzman, Dalrymple, Graves, and Pierce reported in *The Journal of Nervous and Mental Disease.*[11] In this study, researchers phoned 22 nurse's stations. The caller represented himself as a doctor and instructed the nurse answering the phone to administer 20 milligrams of the drug Astroten to a patient. In 95 percent of the cases, the nurse carried out the instruction, although she'd never met, seen, or spoken with the self-proclaimed doctor before the call. Furthermore, the drug prescribed by the researchers wasn't on the approved-drug list of the hospital, and the dosage was twice that of the maximum daily dose (10 milligrams) clearly printed on the container.[12] The researchers stopped the nurses before they actually administered the drug.

Somehow, this experiment doesn't make me feel too comfortable. Nurses work for years to become trained professionals, yet they blindly followed instructions. Orders from an unfamiliar, unconfirmed authority somehow subverted all their training.

Everything in the world is sold to us partly on the basis of authority. Sometimes we must rely on such expertise in a high-tech society, yet blind obedience is absolute ignorance. Fortunately, more and more people have become suspicious of authority. More important, modern technology permits any of us to check on information and so-called experts much more rapidly.

8. Scarcity

This is the last one—better take it. Act now. Limited quantity. Don't delay. Don't miss out. Time is limited. Sale ends today. Hurry—first come, first served. These are but a few of the scarcity statements we all find in ads for everything from pickles to panty hose. Why does the compliance principle of scarcity drive us? In a word, *greed!*

Rare, scarce, and similar qualities equate to value for most people. Economic theory defines value as the relationship between demand and supply—that is, scarcity. An adage applies here: "The grass is always greener on the other side of the fence." We all want what we don't have, until we have it. Of course, the greater the demand, the scarcer the product. We belief in social proof of value: the product has to be good to be so highly sought after. Doesn't it?

No one wants to miss out. Everyone has heard of some once-in-a-lifetime chance that someone missed. Scarcity drives prices up and motivates consumers to spend. However, not all scarcity is a matter of limited time, short supply, and so on. Manipulators of compliance principles also promote another kind of scarcity.

When I conducted interrogations, I often invoked the scarcity of honesty. After all, honesty knows no such thing as percentages. It either is or isn't present . . . much like fidelity. Most people aren't interested in a spouse who's 90 percent faithful. The missing 10 percent will get you every time. Promoting the idea that it's difficult for a person to be honest while remarking upon the truthfulness of the examinee positions the person to perform honestly. Scarcity, like the other principles of compliance, has many subtle varieties not easily discerned even by professionals.

Yet another tactic involving this compliance principle is the "no longer available" notion. Book publishers know that one of the best ways to sell books is for some group to ban the work.

9. Drives

Drives are the basic built-in needs of the species. In psychology, human drives are often referred to as the four *F*'s: *fight, flight, feeding,* and *fornication.* I tend to think that we've evolved with the advent of modem merchandising and deferred payment. Consequently, my view incorporates five *F*'s, or five forces. The fifth one is simple: *more!*

Add this to the first four elements and you see that no one has enough; everyone wants more. *More* has somehow become desirable in and of itself. Today, the word *more* equals power, prestige, status, peace of mind, and so on. It now means quality as much as it means quantity. Keep up with the Joneses.

Experts know how to tap into and use these drives with the principles of compliance. When compliance practitioners wish to persuade someone in a subtle way, they employ drive-related strategies that will invariably invoke vulnerability, nondominance, loyalty, and so on. If something is scary (flight), violent (fight), filling/fulfilling (food), and/ or sexual, it sells. If all of the forces can be combined, sales soar!

If a product is really none of these things, then associating it with them will enhance sales and product image. In fact, Cialdini reports a study conducted by Smith and Engel where "men who saw a new-car ad that included a seductive young woman model rated the car as faster, more appealing, more expensive-looking, and better-designed than men who viewed the same ad without the model."[13] These same men, when questioned about the ad and their response, denied the possibility that the seductive female had anything whatsoever to do with their rating of the automobile.

10. Justification

Justification is the principle that extenuating circumstances can call for radical actions. Indeed, a tenet of our system of jurisprudence system allows for just this. That is why there are such acts as justifiable homicide, self-defense, and so on. This principle is probably the most often overlooked tool of compliance. An excellent example of its power exists in an older television commercial. The viewer sees a woman performing the many tasks of an absolutely frantic day: shopping, cleaning, caring for children, banking, and so forth. At the end of the day, she (a very beautiful and seductive woman) relaxes in her bath covered by bubbles. The ad is for bubble bath, and it ends with the statement: "Let XYZ product take you away." It's an excellent commercial that employs more than one compliance principle. Still, it's the notion of justifying indulgence that makes this commercial so powerful. How else do you sell bubble bath?

History records bizarre events. From the German attempt to eradicate the Jewish people to the mass suicide of Jim Jones's followers, history shows people acting crazily. Why? They all had a reason. Any reason will do. Can you think of anything flimsier than the excuse for torture in Milgram's authority experiment? Human beings need reasons to act, and that truth does have a good side. Victor Frankl, who survived a Nazi death camp, quotes philosopher Friedrich Nietzsche on the subject: "He who has a *why* to live for can bear with almost any *how*."[14] We must make our own reasons—our own *why*—or someone else will.

11. Informed Compliance

Being informed doesn't necessarily remove us from the power of these principles. They obtain most of their strength because they operate automatically. They don't happen as a result of thinking a matter over. Rather, Cialdini refers to the response as a mechanical one: "click, whirr."[15]

He and other social scientists regard this automation as necessary. Normally, we benefit from sticking with people we like, those who have done favors for us, who have authority, and so on. What would happen if we simply reversed all these patterns? Think about it. We use these responses in our lives because they work, and sometimes we need ways to react quickly and with incomplete information.

These patterns, called *judgmental heuristics,* have only recently acquired systematic attention. They include a reflex to protect our knees, they help emergency medical technicians make snap decisions, and they enable diplomats to reach decisions at the U.N. (The last example may seem as though it doesn't work so well, since the U.N. involves people who actively use these patterns against each other and the rest of us.)

Simple knowledge won't help you avoid the grip of a compliance operation. It may only give you the opportunity to know too late what happened. Cialdini suggests that if you feel manipulated, assume that you are and leave. Then do your analysis.

Tells

Interrogators are trained to read many things and to listen to language with a slightly different twist than most people. They spend many hours in special training sessions, learning the various methods that are employed (and, indeed, often introduced) in a court of law with more credence than lie-detection findings. You can count on those who would manipulate or sell you to know this same technology.

Just as you saw with some of the compliance principles, there are countermeasures that you can take to avoid being manipulated.

One is to "watch your tells." A *tell* is a giveaway. Some tells are found in body language, such as the subject who nods his head while you point out why he or she committed a crime.

NLP teaches that you can actually pace these tells by mirroring and matching what the subject is doing. You might be questioning someone while copying his body posture and nodding your head up and down when you begin to express your empathy for why he might have committed the crime. Of course, if the subject is innocent, he's much less likely to fall into your cadence and nod his head up and down.

Another type of tell is commonly known as the Freudian slip. There's a less well-known version of this slip that's equally good in communicating. For example, while in California during the 2008 race for the Democratic presidential primary, Senator Barack Obama stated that "small town folk become frustrated and get bitter, . . . cling to guns or religion or antipathy to people who aren't like them, or anti-immigrant sentiment or anti-trade sentiment as a way to explain their frustrations." It was widely believed that Obama's comments were aimed at the people of Pennsylvania.

There was much discussion by the political pundits regarding Obama's comments and whether they were an innocent slip of the tongue or a "Freudian slip" indicating an elitist mentality. He publicly stated, of course, that he'd misspoken—mixed up his words—and it wasn't the first and probably not the last time this would happen. However, while in Pennsylvania later on, Obama challenged the campaign tactics of Senator Hillary Clinton by calling them "kitchen sink" tactics. He described this as throwing the kitchen sink, the china, and the buffet at you. What Obama didn't realize was that this statement was a real *tell*. If he was truly trying to relate to steelworkers, farmers, and other rural Pennsylvanians, then what did his adding "the china" and "the buffet" mean? Indeed, it's not the sink, the melamine, the coffee mugs, or the pots and pans that are flying in Obama's kitchen; it's the china and the buffet. This isn't to say that rural Pennsylvanians don't have nice china, but you're not likely to find them in the kitchen except on special occasions. My point here is the disconnect between the kitchen described by Obama and the blue-collar rural homemaker's kitchen.

Content and context can mean everything. As we've seen, methods exist to persuade us, and they're in the hands of many people we wouldn't want to have such power. Knowing this makes it even more a matter of self-interest to guard against not only our own tells, compliance responses, and psychological mechanisms but also to acquire a protective lens, like special sunglasses, that can filter the responses that others show us.

When we become alert in this manner, we're less likely to be beguiled by some flimflam artist, new mortgage scheme, or any other matter that's likely to leave us asking ourselves, *Why did I do that?*

Defense Mechanisms

Earlier, I mentioned the role of defense mechanisms in exploitation. These serve our self-interest as well as the interest of humanity in general. They've proven to be so valuable that they accompany the human condition in much the same manner that genes do. They've evolved with us, and they join the compliance principles in order to help conceal their operation.

The academic study of defense mechanisms began earlier than that of compliance principles. As a result, most researchers use categories similar to those presented here.

— **Denial** is, simply, a mechanism of denying. We can see this at work when insincere compliments are accepted as genuine. Because each of us has a basic desire to be liked, we may deny that we're being flattered. People who think ill of themselves may even reject a sincere compliment. In either case, we can simply take the news and test the truth of it elsewhere. Often, denial occurs through projection (discussed further on). We can project blame or fault onto another to escape recognition of our own culpability.

— **Fantasy formation** creates a perceived reality out of fantasy. Sometimes we can't satisfy ourselves in the objective external world. We can always play make-believe and create a perceived reality in a dream world. Much of our entertainment satisfies our desire for fantasies of adventure, affection, and security.

— **Introjection** allows placement of blame upon oneself. Self-directed blame or punishment defends against disappointment, disillusionment, and insecurity. For example, when a parent pays no attention to a child, the child feels unworthy of attention. The child scarcely dares consider the possibility that the parent just doesn't care. Often, this mechanism perpetuates the acceptance of authoritarian guidance even when it has persistently erred in the past. A subtle yet pervasive form of this mechanism goes like this: "I'm not smart enough. I must have misunderstood something."

— **Isolation** involves avoiding associations that produce anxiety. One set of data is isolated from an associated set: people isolate victory in war from suffering and death, nuclear arsenals from murderous horror. Think back to the model and the automobile reviews, where the men rated the car pictured with an attractive woman as being faster than the car pictured alone, yet denied being influenced by the model. The men rating the automobile had isolated the woman from the formation of their rating; to admit otherwise would feel threatening. This mechanism can also be used in associations that have no immediate relationship, such as birth and death.

— **Projection** places our intention, attitude, blame, or responsibility onto another. Consider the numerous television clips where an actress in a short skirt is able to enlist the aid of nearly every male passerby. What do you think their fantasy formation projected onto the actress had to do with their willingness to heft heavy packages for a great distance? A fine line divides normal and pathological projection. Many rapists have the attitude that the victim "really wanted it."

— **Regression** involves returning to an earlier age, usually as a dependent, where one felt safe and comfortable. The individual returns to an earlier stage of development in which someone else assumed responsibility and where fewer, simpler, and more primitive demands existed. This mechanism commonly occurs during illness. The bubble-bath commercial, where the overworked mother relaxes in the tub at the end of the day, and other similar approaches intimately involve this mechanism. It's also present in the ads for flu medications, as well as some gusto advertisements. (For those of you too young to remember the "go for the gusto" television ads, they were designed to sell you on the idea that you only go around once so make sure that you do so with maximum joy, zest, and gusto). Pampering, spoiling, carefree desires, and other childish elements of ad campaigns appeal to this mechanism.

— **Repression** censors or conceals memories, associations, and adjustments from conscious awareness. Like an invisible filter, this mechanism prevents the conscious mind from seeing painful memories and stymied motives. Personal experiences ranging from embarrassment to cruelty are often blurred under the lens of repression. Here again, social enculturation plays a significant role. For example, one of the reasons a person fails to see a large penis in a bourbon ad is probably related to the "dirty mind" argument. To see the penis means admitting, even if only to ourselves, to having a dirty mind. So we don't see it, or we at least repress the awareness of it.

— **Sublimation** redirects basic drive mechanisms. It means substituting acceptable behavior to satisfy basic motives that might be met equally well in a primitive sense by some form of unacceptable behavior. Sports often sublimate aggression. This mechanism is most useful in associations, especially those of a sexual nature. A sports car, for example, can be made into a socially acceptable sexual expression.

Some theorists consider several miscellaneous escapes and defenses as contributing to these eight basic perceptual defenses. Each serves the purpose of concealing from us what we don't want—or can't psychologically afford—to know about ourselves and the world around us.

Compliance professionals are very aware of both the principles and the perceptual defenses. In fact, these experts are most often employed in the field of advertising for that very reason.

Altered States of Consciousness

It would be a gross oversight to leave the subject of compliance without discussing altered states of consciousness, which include what professionals call states of heightened suggestibility. Indeed, the first book on NLP as a distinct field came from studying the superb hypnotic research and therapy of Milton H. Erickson, M.D. Music rhythms, eye elevations and fixations, and flashing sequences of a light intensity difference, among other techniques, can have hypnotic effects. In my work *Subliminal Communication,* I outlined some of the ways in which advertisers, religious organizations, popular movements, and the like employ suggestibility techniques that were discovered and developed in hypnosis. Suffice it to say that if you feel as though you entered a light trance while you were watching television (for example, if you didn't hear your spouse speaking to you), you probably did.

Indirect Suggestion

Many hypnotherapists favor indirect suggestion, which can bring about compliance. This technique operates chiefly through internal decisions. A very simple form exists in alternative-decision closes. For example, a salesman never asks for the sale. He simply turns the contract around and asks, "Do you want to use your pen or mine?"

A hypnotist may have the subject imagine a magnet on his forehead and another in the palm of his hand to produce an arm levitation, a common induction procedure. The hypnotist asks the subject to sense the magnets and decide: "Is the magnetic force stronger from the hand to the head or from the head to the hand?" In other words, which is the strongest magnet? The answer doesn't matter. The point is that the question presupposes a magnetic force, and internal consistency requires that it will pull the hand to the head. Voilà—the hypnotist has control of the subject's body. Does this seem like any of the sales dialogues you've read about or experienced yourself?

Ethics and Exploitation

Use of these techniques and principles is inevitable and valuable, although I oppose their misuse. To level the playing field, so to speak, I feel that the consumer, voter, or novice on the receiving end of the technique is entitled to the same knowledge that compliance professionals have at their disposal.

I suggest that defense mechanisms and judgmental heuristics form the building blocks of compliance principles. Society plays the architect, while our families and acquaintances lay the bricks and nail the boards.

Defense mechanisms, like compliance principles, are essential and necessary elements in individual and social well-being. How they're employed determines whether they're good or bad. An ethical imperative requires skillful and well-intentioned use.

Compliance principles are appropriate in marketing, provided there are no misrepresentations. Advertising moves products, which drives the economy, and that has given us the physical capacity to feed and clothe everyone on earth, however poorly we manage it.

Employing these concepts to sell products while surreptitiously using subliminal imagery that may increase hostility is unethical and irresponsible. Our sensitivity to violence has declined dramatically in this decade. I even argue that the continued tweaking of the psyche and manipulation of the human condition could eventually erode the very fabric of our social order. Do you think that you've never turned down the request of a friend because someone who felt like a friend took advantage of you?

All of this information adds up to a brief overview of the data available. It can facilitate our understanding of some manipulations and protect us from them. It can suggest the ethical use of the patterns of compliance and denial of them.

Summary

Compliance principles can influence decisions and activate automatic processes that incline a person toward compliance. Professionals use these precepts to gain their ends, sell merchandise, or evangelize to prospective converts.

Defense mechanisms can inhibit or prevent the recognition of information. Their existence explains why so-called subliminal print advertising can present blatant sexual material that goes undetected.

Awareness helps defend against these principles and mechanisms. I sincerely hope that you're now a lot more aware.

■ ■ ■ ■■■■

CHAPTER 4

Marketing Techniques

"Money is a new form of slavery, and distinguishable from the old simply by the fact that it is impersonal—that there is no human relation between master and slave."

— Lev Nikolayevich Tolstoy

> **Warning:** This chapter includes sexually explicit material and isn't intended for younger readers. However, I believe that it's important to include actual transcripts of the objectionable material to demonstrate the thinking of some advertisers and so preempt the argument that the embedded material is there accidentally.

Advertising is big business. Take a look at certain items in the next television or movie scene you view. From the cars to the computers, this so-called casual placement is, in fact, not casual at all; it's very effective advertising.

Consider this: A promoter of the Manchester Midnight Walk, a charity walk organized by St. Ann's Hospice in Manchester, England,

arranged for a poster advertising the event to be placed in a prominent position during an episode of *Coronation Street,* a top UK soap
opera. The scene in which the poster appeared was a particularly dra-
matic one, critical to the plot. According to the *Manchester Evening
News,* this "PR stunt" resulted in an unusually large increase in inquiries to the fund-raisers at St. Ann's.[1]

Not long after my book *Subliminal Learning* was published, an
anonymous reader sent me an advertising training manual. This little
"smoking gun," as some of my colleagues have called it, sets out the
how and why behind subliminal advertising. It's complete with actual
advertisements that have appeared in mainstream media. Despite the
evidence, however, many people just continued to sing the same old
tune: "We don't use it and wouldn't use it, and besides, it doesn't
work."

The marketing world is well equipped to address the psyche
behind human nature. Recently, I heard on Fox News that the advertising industry spent $149 billion in 2007 on market research. Just so
you get the full picture, this equates to $500 per person! Advertis-
ers have employed the best psychologists and sociologists, provided
them with the ultimate in research laboratories, devised and used
equipment that measures unconscious thoughts, and much more, all
in their zeal to know what makes us tick. Using sophisticated biofeedback devices, they've monitored reactions to a panoply of stimuli in an
effort to uncover the minutest details underlying choices and behavior. Not all of this has been limited to marketing research, as you'll
see when it comes to various brainwashing techniques explained in
the next chapter. For that matter, it's known that during the 1960s,
several radio stations used subliminal advertising. In fact, KTLA-TV in
Los Angeles "signed a $60,000 contract in which it agreed to insert
subliminal *public service* messages in television programming."[2]

In 1972, Canadian professor Wilson Bryan Key published his hotly
debated book *Subliminal Seduction.* Key exposed ad after ad full of
images that were hidden or disguised from normal perception. Key
and his students at the University of Western Ontario had discovered
so-called optical illusions and more devices in advertisements that
were appearing in the most popular print media. Key's work remains

somewhat controversial, but his book *Subliminal Ad-Ventures in Erotic Art* points out that the international scope of U.S. advertising agencies means that they control the media "to a great extent throughout the noncommunist world." Key continues, "Consumer advertising media educates the poor into the acquisitive value systems of the rich . . . the never ending orgy of conspicuous consumption for which they have been subliminally programmed."[3]

If you're interested in subliminal advertising per se, I strongly recommend reading both *Subliminal Ad-Ventures in Erotic Art* by Wilson Bryan Key and *The Secret Sales Pitch* by August Bullock. Both authors have taken a great deal of time to pull apart many ads and illustrate their subliminal content. Of course, some people disagree with their findings, using the so-called dirty-mind argument. In other words, they believe that if you find taboo images in an ad, you'll probably also find them in the clouds as well. A sort of Rorschach test is applied by the pundits who assert that subliminal information is a hoax and a fraud, that no one uses it, and that it wouldn't work if it was used.

Rather than showing you ads and giving *my* interpretation, I'll show you what the advertising world shares with its trainees, at least through the manual sent to me. I've shared some of this training manual in earlier books, but I've never before reproduced so much of the explicit descriptions of the why, what, when, and where of everything in the ads that follow.

Excerpts from the Advertising Training Manual

The training manual begins with a color rendering of what will become a liquor advertisement. Boldly written underneath this drawing are the words: "Sometimes you have to go above the written law." The accompanying image is in black and white here, but you can see the color version online at **www.eldontaylor.com/mindprogram ming.html**.

Figure 1

After a cover sheet marked "Top Secret," the manual begins:

> The gravy train is over for millions of Americans. Don't become naively caught up in the "it can't happen to me syndrome" that so many are, as ample research will substantiate. The breadlines and soup kitchens are filled to bursting with those poor souls who thought they couldn't be replaced, only to awaken too late to the grim realities of life without money.

The manual offers a guaranteed job to those completing their art school, which is designed to teach the art of subliminal manipulation. At the time the document was printed, the 60-day course had tuition of $2,578 (probably much more today) and further promised "adventure into mental frontiers that challenge even the most stalwart individual."

Continuing, the course offer reads:

> You'll learn the hows and why of taboo imagery, group motiva-
> tion theories based on collective animus-anima symbolism, how to
> slow thought waves and enter the Alpha, Theta, Delta levels of the
> mind, the emotional meaning of colors, shapes, and patterns plus
> basic illustration and airbrushing techniques . . .
>
> Initiation into the psychological concepts and manipulative
> stratagems of the art course often comes as a shock to those naïve
> individuals the computer mispicked.

The material is sold to the potential student as both secret and
shocking, two approaches that in and of themselves have great sales
appeal. The manual continues to boast of its secrecy and shock by
saying things such as "36% of all previous candidates dropped out in
disgust within the first 3 days." Further, get this macho appeal: "Since
there is *no* refund, we try to stress that certain squeamish types of
people aren't suited for the psychological demands of this fast paced
secret business." Note how this positions and challenges simultaneously.

Their goal? "To produce artists and idea personnel dedicated and
obedient to the advertising necessities involved in regulating America's production-consumption cycle."

The manual continues with statements about the advertising
industry, its revenue generation, and so forth. Then, just before analysis of the picture from its cover, the manual adds:

> Man lives in an environment of symbols, and it is extremely
> important to understand something about the symbol-making pro-
> cess because symbols are the raw material of human thought and all
> communication. Superficially we think that words are the only form
> of communication, because we live in such a highly verbal atmo-
> sphere. Yet in actuality there is a far greater amount of nonverbal
> communication going on all the time through the use of other sym-
> bols than words.

You might ask why I'm quoting so much of this manual. The answer is simple: I could interpret the material for you but then, as in a court of law, that's hearsay evidence, or I could put the testimony on public trial and let you be the jury. My experience dictates the latter approach because many people would otherwise dismiss all of this as just another *conspiracy theory*. You're not just reading my interpretation of the information—this is all from the actual training manual itself!

Sexual Embeds

I'd like to make one other point before continuing with the manual. Remember that the agencies and market makers have done the research to see exactly how and to what people respond. They've shown erotic and semierotic pictures to individuals while monitoring bodily functions such as galvanic skin response (skin conductivity), heart rates, and so forth. As such, they know exactly how certain symbols, colors, and images are interpreted emotionally and from a general cognitive perspective as well. Furthermore, understanding the Freudian psychosexual scheme should prove to be of great value as we continue with the manual.

In their words, then:

> The enclosed photos [see Figures 2 and 3] provide an excellent example of some of these "advertising necessities" and they visually sum up what our school is all about.
>
> One photo shows a sexy blonde woman holding a cocktail glass. "Just another pretty face in the crowd," is the visual impact most observers have. . . . Let's take a close look at the artistic strategy we've used to enhance the emotional triggering power of the advertisement.
>
> First off, the woman has sex appeal. Do blondes have more fun? The connotations are that blondes are more sexual, more easily seduced, and enjoy sex more than the other hair colors. Since blatant sexuality is the subliminal theme of this ad, the blonde hair helps to act as an emotional catalyst in insuring [sic] a sexual interpretation

by the viewer's subconscious.

The satyr on the woman's collar or choker further enhances the subconscious theme of the ad. A satyr is an age-old symbol for man's baser instincts, his primitive lustful dark side. This satyr identifies its wearer as being associated with instinctive eroticism.

The choker around her neck is a visual indication of her submissiveness to the eroticism of the satyr. Since a choker closely resembles a collar its submissive symbolism (in this context) is much the same—she will be as obedient as and docile as a dog in obeying the erotic desires of her master (the viewer). She is a sex slave.

If we look closely we see that this blonde woman is holding the cocktail glass in an odd and dissonant way. Her right hand is folded except for her index finger. Her index finger is extended and is pointing to the "ice-cubes" in the cocktail glass.

Airbrushed into the "ice-cubes" are several erotic symbols. These symbols are designed to activate socially taboo thoughts and emotions in the viewer. By activating these deep instinctual thought processes we guarantee our client the emotional involvement of the viewer or potential consumer. We create desires that can only be satisfied by product consumption.

The symbols in the "ice-cubes" may seem invisible but hypnotic research has shown 95% subconscious pickup. The subconscious can take in an astounding amount of information. This information filters its way up to consciousness by way of what is socially acceptable. The rest is to remain in the subconscious where it later emerges in the form of desires and wants that are satisfied only through acts of consumption.

For some individuals, these urges can be—and sometimes are—acted out. Rather than simply seeing and processing the input, they act upon it in socially unacceptable ways. It would be interesting to determine just how many colds are produced as a result of cold medication ads or how many school shooters are acting out urges planted by unconscious means.

However, continuing with the manual:

The "ice-cubes" which her index finger points to form an erect penis. These two cubes have been flesh colored and can easily be seen from a distance of several feet, once pointed out. Note how the penis angle is correct for proper virile erection. Since a penis in a glass is considered taboo, this image would be immediately repressed. People only see what they expect to see.

The woman's lips are in close proximity to this erect, flesh-toned penis. This idea of fellatio is reinforced by the satyr blowing on a flute or phallic-shaped object. Oral sex is a commonly desired quest and fantasy of males of all ages. By retouching and airbrushing in this symbolic sexual message we've elevated a mere glass of whiskey into a potent aphrodisiac.

Next to this erect penis is a red cherry. Red is a hot, loud and active color. On the right of this red cherry is a happy fornicating rabbit. This rabbit is an apt symbol for love and sex. It's common knowledge that the logo for *Playboy* magazine is the promiscuous rabbit. Male boastings of sexual prowess often include emphasis on the partners ability to "f— [my substitution, and I will substitute in this way throughout] like a rabbit." Note that the ice-cube area surrounding the rabbit's engorged penis is a creamy white. The ice-cube area above the cherry is also creamy white rather than a see-through clearness. In this ad's blatant sexual context, this creamy white color correlates with the creamy whiteness of sperm. Obviously ejaculation by fellatio will be successful, enhancing the virility appeal of this product.

Below the fornicating rabbit is a happy smiling human face to symbolize a drink that tastes good and will make one happy. It also correlates with love for oral sex—licking her lips in anticipation.

Is this material shocking to you? Unfortunately, it's so shocking to many people that they deny the possibility that anyone could be using such symbolism against them. Remember, all I'm doing is quoting from a training manual of a very prestigious advertising company. To choose to ignore this information is to give such organizations tacit consent to use it—and they're using it against you every day!

Let's look a little closer at the graphic in question before we go on. The initial picture we looked at was the conceptualization. The actual ad looked like this:

Figure 2

A close up of the glass reveals this:

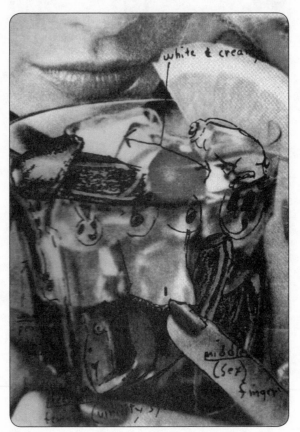

Figure 3

Closer examination of the tracing provides the real picture:

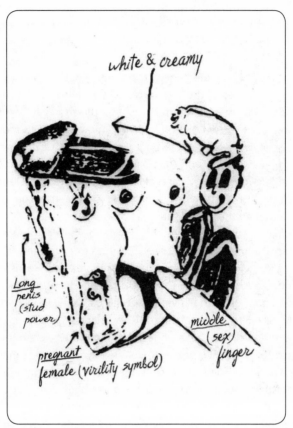

Figure 4

Now, with the visual fully unmasked, let's continue with the explanation set out by those who actually created this image. When you're finished, I trust that you'll be convinced that nothing in this ad is just coincidence, as some might insist. Nor are my observations just the result of some "inkblot" dirty mind.

The manual continues:

Below this smiling face are several other penises in varying stages of sexual excitement. To the left of these aroused penises are several female shapes with large breasts. The large breasts help activate instinctual maternal sucking impulses associated with the pleasure principle. The female shapes visually stimulate any repressed sexual desires in the viewer.

The model's middle finger on her left hand is visually touching the genital area of the large breasted female shape. The middle finger is associated with sex and sexual gestures such as "F— you;" f— being a sexual connotation implying intercourse. This touching of the genitals by her middle finger is subconsciously interpreted as being bisexual or impish (game for anything) in character. Since male fantasies often include acts of lesbianism, we took the liberty to airbrush this visual enticement into the sexual repertoire our impish host is tempting the viewer with.

Earlier it was stated that the satyr and choker indicated the model's willingness to be sexually submissive to the viewer's own fantasies. To help aid in this submissive interpretation we instructed the model to look upward. This looking upward visually places her in a lower position than the viewer. In this context it would subconsciously be interpreted as being on her knees or at a level convenient for oral sex. The large white areas of her eyes were retouched to match the exact hue of the white, creamy ice-cubes. Exhaustive research indicates the subconscious reads this as "she has eyes" for spurting sperm, she loves climactic pleasures, she's voyeuristic.

Even the copy of the ad must correlate with the erotic theme. About midway through the copy the wording goes, "the *smoothest* thing since *skin.*" This correlates with the smooth skin of the penis that she's pointing to.

The rest of the copy is quite sexual when placed within the subliminal sexual framework of the ad. "It brings out the *Imp* in all of us" refers to the releasing of primitive sexual desires and *imp*ulses found in every human.

The manual continues, but by now the point should be clear.

Fearful Embeds

In still another ad detailed in this same manual, the discussion regarding the selling of fear is worth examining, because fear is as powerful a sales tool as sex. The ad in question this time is for cigarettes. Here are both the artist's rendition and the finished piece, using professional models, as in the liquor ad we just examined.

What a good time.
What a good taste.
What a good time for a XYZ

Figure 5 (The cigarette brand has been removed from the photo on the right for legal reasons.)

The manual introduces this ad by referring to an alleged recent dropout rate among their new students of 99.7 percent. They claim that this led to an investigation of why people were leaving the program. The manual picks up here:

> The findings of this investigation indicated that the majority of the new students exceeded their *traumatic overload threshold* during Theta level ambiguity bypass. It is during this nauseatic necessity of indoctrination that the squeamish are weeded out. The recent exceedingly high dropout rate tells us that many were unprepared for the *violent* aspect of 20th Century salesmanship. Sex and violence

are two sides of the same coin and are used without hesitation in a meticulously coordinated way to nurture the Even-Keel psychic growth of *consumer* qualities. Qualities deemed necessary for future corporate growth. Violence, as a manipulative force, is an integral part of this Even-Keel approach.

The manual continues with further positioning statements asserting that the company doesn't rest on its laurels or morals, but uses what it needs to for its clients. It then explains the cigarette ad in this way:

> The ad itself seems innocent enough to conscious interpretations: a couple of young lovers enjoying a quiet lakeside sunset and a cigarette. Hardly enough emotional pull for one to risk the dangers of cancer.
>
> Since its conception in the early 1960s, the subliminal selling strategy for XYZ [my substitution] cigarettes has been based on a variation of our top-secret Hell-Sell theory. To visually promise the viewer salvation from death, and loss of one's very soul to the devil, is an emotional hook that we've cast over and over again, in varying forms for a variety of clients. Religious beliefs and feelings about death stir deeper emotions than the frequently used sexual strategies.
>
> Enclosed [see Fig. 5] are two photos illustrating one variation of our Hell-Sell technique. One photo is of the actual cigarette advertisement while the other photo is of an illustration that emphasizes the subconscious emotional meaning of the advertisement (minus the flower).
>
> In the photo of the actual advertisement note that the sky is a dull, dreary, lifeless gray. Had we so desired we surely could have chosen a more colorful and romance-inspiring sunset. This dull, lifeless sky surrounds a weakly glowing sun that is setting. Darkness is fast approaching. Further statements about the sun and its symbolism will be explained later in more detail. Just keep in mind that it's dreary and weakly glowing.
>
> The couple sharing this dismal, insipid sunset are seen clearer in silhouette than in inner body detail. The man's facial silhouette has sharp features. His hair comes to a *point* above his forehead. His nose is sharp and pointy rather than round or piggish. The man's chin is

visually extended by his thumb. This chin area has been retouched so that the chin and thumb are one.

Figure 6

The placing of the hand and the thumb near the chin area projects the idea that this long chinned man is *thinking.* His head is slightly tilted forward to aid in this thinking interpretation. Verification of this interpretation is readily available through our research department.

At this point please direct your attention to the visual center of the advertisement and focus on their joined hands. Note that their hands form the silhouette of a devil's face very similar in shape to the man's facial silhouette. His pointy hair tip coincides with the devil's horn (man's left thumb). His long chin, with its retouched oneness with the thumb, coincides with the long chin (lady's index finger) on the devil's silhouette. The man is facing to the right with a slightly *downward* (towards Hell) tilt to his head. The Devil's face formed by their joined hands (pact of evil) is also facing to the right with a downward tilt. Note that the female's head is also tilting slightly downward towards the man's. It is very close to the "thinking" man's head. In this ad's controlled context, the combination of the man's "devilishly" *long-chinned* silhouette, his *thinking* position, the devil's face silhouette of their joined hands, and the closeness of their fore-heads, tell the viewer, at their subconscious level, that they are in the act of observing some type of eerie mind-over-matter situation.

The following representation of an actual page from the manual as delivered to me may be helpful. Some of what you see is ahead of this discussion, but we'll catch up.

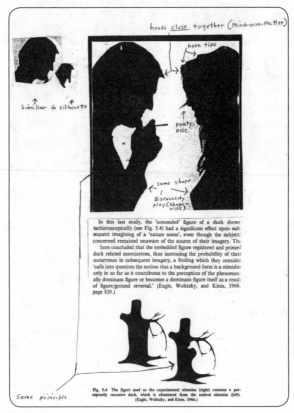

Figure 7

The manual continues:

To further aid in this interpretation we've placed this devil's head-hand combination directly *over* the sun. The devil's head is visually in a superior (winning) position over the sun. Near the lower portion of this *weak glowing* (about to go out) sun is a *horizontal* line that ends up at the sun's left edge. This simple line, placed *below* the blurred background horizon line, indicates that the sun is setting *into* the lake, rather than behind the lake. The death of the sun, due to satanic mind-over-matter powers, appears imminent! Of course, this is a physical impossibility at the conscious level. The sun symbolizes Life itself. All life, as we know it, cannot survive without the sun. To visually witness the end of life comes as such an overwhelming emotional jolt that the viewer's mind searches for a way to repress such matter. To provide a *way out* for this disturbing thought we've provided a distinctive weed directly below the horizontal sun-sinking line. This weed makes conscious *lock-on* relatively easy. It's easier for the conscious mind to interpret the horizontal line as part of the weed rather than to deal emotionally with the death of the sun (conscious reality correlation is nuclear winter).

This evil couple, with the dying sun *trapped* between them, are wearing the same color and style pants. Her *black* leather belt is very wide and masculine appearing; it is not thin, dainty or feminine. By giving her subtle masculine traits we've changed their gender in a subliminal role reversal. Several of these role reversal subtleties will be brought out as the ad is gradually explained.

The fact that their pants are green is no coincidence. Green is the color associated with witches. Research based on Halloween studies readily verify [*sic*] that most children who choose to be witches choose green makeup. Children's stories often portray green witches.

The green of their pants blends in with the green wild weeds they're standing in. Unkept or uncut weeds represent (in this context) the wild, uncontrolled, uncivilized natural element. Their shoes or feet have been retouched to blend with this wild, weedy, *green* ground area. Feet are often symbolic of one's foundation, of being the cornerstone upon which their lives are based. Devils are often portrayed as hoofed or cleft footed. Dastardly villains in movies, plays, and TV programs often walk with a limp or crutch of some type. This symbolizes a crippled, weak, twisted foundation, on which their lives are based. By blurring the couple's feet into the weedy and wild foreground area, then airbrushing in devil faces and horror faces, we've visually shown that their lives are based on evil and death . . . their *soles* (souls) are evil. To further enhance this evil foundation interpretation, the male's knee areas have been artistically distorted and warped. They bend inward at a dissonant distance, implying a weak-kneed and warped structure. The female has a dissonant wrinkle in the knee area. Both their pants are full of deep wrinkles and creases, which further enhance a weakened, warped, twisted interpretation. (They're not the types to wear pressed, neat, socially acceptable clothing).

Airbrushed into the lower leg area of the female's pants is a giant spider. Another giant spider is airbrushed below it, lying upside down on the ground. (Because of the size reduction of the photos these spiders and foreground horror faces may be difficult, if not impossible, for the unschooled to see at the conscious level. However, the reader can rest assured that these two arachnids are there).

See the close-up that follows, or view the color version online at: www.eldontaylor.com/mindprogramming.html.

Figure 8

These two spiders are joined at their abdomens, implying that they are mating. Since small spiders are high on the Phobia Index for fear arousal (2nd to snakes), it only stands to reason that larger, f—*ing* ones will provide the emotional *jolt* necessary for conscious repression. The dissonant cues are the thin, lightly etched, almost vertical lines that form the top spider's legs. These ultra-light leg lines are much higher than any of the surrounding wild weeds, and thinner than any wrinkles or creases. The spiders' round bodies provide yet another dissonant cue that *can't be missed* by the viewer's subconscious, according to Durffstinckles Law on Fabric Sensitivity and Fold Formations.

When I tried to research "Durffstinckles Law on Fabric Sensitivity and Fold Formations," I came up empty. It may be that this is totally made up so as to look impressive to the prospective student, so we'll continue with the manual:

The habitat this evil couple are in is favorable for spiders. Spiders often lurk around cracks and crevices. This would correlate with the deep folds and creases in their wrinkled pants. Spiders stalk through the *weedy* areas in search of prey and often spend their entire lives among the weeds. Spiders are often green or are capable of changing their colors to blend in with their habitat (the green pants). Spiders are often more active at night (the setting sun).

Note that in the man's pocket is something long and hard, as evidenced by the telltale bulge and crease. This is very close to his genital area. The devil's head silhouette is in front of both their genital areas. This "mind-over-matter" evil situation picks up sexual powers of procreation with the interplay of the following elements: larger than life fornicating spiders, hard phallic object (knife) in male's pocket, and the devil's head created near both of their genital areas.

The giant spiders also imply usage of hidden webs and snares . . . being snared by Satan . . . being caught up in a web of death and despair. Spiders often paralyze their victims in order to suck them dry at their convenience. A painful and gruesome death. Not the type of thing one would want to deal with at the conscious level . . . easy repression material.

Both individuals are wearing red tops. Red is the color associated with Hell and the devil. Red and green are also color opposites. Since both of these individuals are wearing just red and green, it signifies the joining of opposites and correlates with the devil's pact theme. The union of the devil (red) with a witch (green) to forge a superior evil force capable of overpowering Life (the sun).

By meticulously positioning the couple, we've given their silhouette many sharp and angular features. Pointy shapes act as catalysts for early infantile experiences of pain, brought about by sudden contact with pointy object (bumping into table corners). In the man's lower back area is a spike or pointy shape dissonant to the round form a sweater wrinkle would normally form. His spine appears warped. A long, pointy spike shape is also formed by the space between his lower legs. A wisp of hair has been airbrushed into the woman's nose area. This visually gives her a long, witch-like pointy nose. Her belt-buckle top forms a pointy shape. Two small points have been airbrushed along the top edge of her head, suggestive of horns in this controlled context. The two individuals are pointing their cigarettes towards each other. These two cigarettes are thinner than actual cigarettes. This thinness implies that these objects are needle-like and pain producing. Rather than smoking, these two are actually caught in the act of jabbing each other. This is indicative of their sadistic love to inflict, as well as experience, pain.

This pain-loving female is the same height as the male, rather than being smaller. He's wearing a long-sleeved turtleneck while she sports a thin, short-sleeved top. Usually the female is smaller than the male and dresses warmer than the male, in chilly situations. Wearing a turtleneck with long-sleeves during the summer weather (the green weeds) is dissonant in respect to the short-sleeved female and implies a desire to be overly warm; in this evil context . . . a love for heat, a love of Hellish warmth. These dissonant elements in height and clothing are another subtle way to also convey gender role-reversal; she's taller and "hardier" than most females while he comes off as shorter and more weather sensitive than most males. Several advertisements in this particular series used a "wool sweater" in the summer ploy more obvious than the subtle one used in this selected advertisement. Again, the reader will have to take our word (what little that's worth) on this matter.

Note that this devil's pact takes place at the water's edge. This symbolizes being on the edge of a new experience (death). The water's edge is where one form of matter (land) meets another form (water). Two *opposite* forms meet and *join*. This correlates with the joined hands and joined spiders. A matrix of joined opposites adds power to the subliminal horror theme. Water often has spiritual and religious associations (used in baptismal ceremonies, etc.) because of its ability to change form. It can be either vapor, liquid or solid. This adds a mystical ambience to the evil mind-over-matter situation *confronting* the viewer. The viewer is on the edge of a new experience in pain and horror. Lifeless matter often washes ashore to gather and collect at the waters edge. Creatures of prey (of both water and land) prowl shorelines more frequently than inland areas.

By now it should be obvious, to the most casual observer, that the viewer is in a BAD situation. A situation where eternal darkness, a pain filled death, and loss of one's soul to Satan are imminent! By placing the viewer in such a Life and Death situation, we've activated subconscious instinctual self-preservation channels to the max (all within a matter of seconds . . . the turning of a page). Very few people desire to die painfully only to spend eternity in Hell. In fact, most people would do just about anything to avoid such a Hellish situation. This is where XYZ (brand of cigarette) comes in.

Note the top copy of the ad stresses the word Good. The word is aligned above itself 3 times. This visual emphasis on Good makes it stand out and be associated with the XYZ cigarettes. By placing the viewer in a Bad situation, while promising them GOODness with XYZ, we've elevated the image of XYZ from mere "cancer-sticks," into portable packs of protection magically endowed with soul saving capabilities.

In today's violence saturated world, where muggings, murders and molestations happen every few seconds, GOODness and protection (self-preservation) are subconsciously sought incessantly. Every day, getting about entails contact with strangers and the placing of one's Life on the line . . . on the *edge*. These are times of stress and anxiety. What we do is promise salvation and protection, through product consumption from the very anxieties we instigate. By "tapping into" the fear of the new, of the unknown, of dying, of going to Hell, we struck *emotional* gold. Variations of the Good versus Bad strategy sell a variety of products for us, as well as our competitors. This Hell-Sell strategy is reinforced by the Church. Religious attendance by the consuming public reinforces the spiritual reality of Hell. This indirectly embellishes the emotional believability and "pulling power" of our Hell-Sell strategies. When one considers that the "average American" sees or hears over 800 advertisements a day, this "pulling power" is awesome.

Since drinking and smoking are such "high-stakes" items, we cannot let them be driven off the marketplace by health crazes or civil disobedient do-gooders. The high rates of Alcoholism and Lung Cancer provide statistical proof as to the effectiveness of these simple but emotional selling strategies. Let them also stand as proof of our willingness to fight like Hell (pun intended) for the rights of our well-heeled clients. It's quite frequent in the advertising field to create "leeching techniques" that allow us to ride the crest of current Religious, Social, and Economic movements at little, if any, final monetary cost. The true beauty of this is that the consumer actually pays to be "brain washed," while we corporate "fat cats" laugh all the way to the bank.

Disgusted? There's a tone present that's somewhat akin to the conversations criminals have where they openly plan a crime, justify it, and mentally relish the activity—laughing all the way.

If you've ever smoked a cigarette, how does this make you feel? I smoked two to three packs a day for more than 40 years before I saw through the message, but that's another story. The manual continues with more detail regarding this particular advertisement; as well as more ads, more pictures, further themes behind them, and more descriptions regarding every last detail incorporated (airbrushed and posed).

When you finish reading, there's no doubt that the ads have been thoroughly thought out. One might question the assumptions, but the research that these ad agencies possess isn't publicly available. The millions and millions of dollars in private psychological research owned by private companies, ad agencies, and the like isn't in the public domain and isn't generally available to the community of behavioral science. Even the trained professional is left to test the assumptions or work from what's already known through more public research.

In an upcoming chapter, I'll review what's in the public domain in terms of psychological research regarding persuasion techniques, subliminal effects in particular. I can unequivocally state in advance that it's my belief—based on hard science—that the techniques and strategies employed by advertisers are well grounded in proven, albeit private, research. (That is, it's held only by those who paid for the studies.) Not only is the evidence there to support the assumptions laid out earlier in the training manual, but the funding that's allowed some of these ads to be repeated over and over again, sometimes spending millions of dollars on a single ad, demonstrates either the effectiveness of the campaigns or the stupidity of the advertiser—you decide.

One last note before we leave this chapter. There's an entirely new kind of research being carried out today called "neuromarketing." It utilizes sophisticated technology such as functional Magnetic Resonance Imaging (fMRI) and electroencephalography (EEG) to monitor brain activity during ad exposure. Already, a new $7 million neuromarketing study has revealed information such as the fact that the warning label on cigarettes increases "craving," thus generating the opposite effect from what was expected and desired.[4]

In a recently released book titled *Buyology*, the author, Martin Lindstrom, repeatedly refers to his work with a team of researchers in Oxford, England, and their findings that consumers are driven by subconscious motivations.[5] Lindstrom, CEO and Chairman of Lindstrom Co., studied responses from some 2,000 people in five countries. He had this to say to *Advertising Age* about his work and findings: "Neuromarketing is like a hammer. It depends on whose hand you use and how you use it. You can use it to destroy or hang up a beautiful painting on the wall."[6]

Summary

For years, many people have discounted the use of sexual "subliminals" in advertising, putting them all down to the dirty mind of some viewers. Yet the evidence from the advertising moguls laid out in front of us fully refutes that argument. There can no longer be any question about quite how far some people will go to manipulate our thoughts and desires.

While using subliminal embeds in advertising is considered unacceptable to most people, the new technique of product placement isn't much better. Truth may not make for exciting television, but it would assist us all in making choices based on rational input.

This chapter has been all about the use or misuse of psychological persuasion techniques to sell goods. Understand that in selling goods, ideas and beliefs are also communicated. Repetition of these ideas means that they're reinforced to the point that they're incorporated in various ways at differing levels of consciousness. In time, as a result of repeated exposures to these themes, beliefs emerge within a culture. Sometimes they find their way into entertainment and then become a conscious part of our modeling procedures. We not only begin to take on these ideas, such as the "GOODness" of a cigarette, but we incorporate such themes as the now-popular notion that it's okay to get even ("I don't get even, I get evener"). These notions or constructs don't reflect who we really are, nor are they true to our highest potential. In short, in very many ways we become the product of the merchandising we've consumed.

Although I've spared you some of the more graphic content available, it's clear just from the few pictures I shared that the real gravity and extent of the education behind the efforts to manipulate all of us has been grossly unrecognized. I hope that this journey into the thoughts of those who would sell you everything from health care to lipstick has been truly informative.

CHAPTER 5

Everyday Brainwashing

*"Television to brainwash us all and Internet
to eliminate any last resistance."*

— Paul Carvel

Merriam-Webster defines *brainwashing* as: (1) "a forcible indoctrination to induce someone to give up basic political, social, or religious beliefs and attitudes and to accept contrasting regimented ideas" and (2) "persuasion by propaganda or salesmanship."

Let us look first at "persuasion by propaganda, or salesmanship." My earlier book *Choices and Illusions* is about how we learn or acquire the language we speak and the beliefs we hold dear, and the alternatives we might consider—indeed, it's about the box within which most minds think. In this book is a story about a female eagle, Nina, who's brought up by chickens. Nina works hard to be a good chicken even though she's aware that she has some traits that aren't very chickenlike. Eventually, when another eagle attempts to show Nina her true potential, she prefers to deny this truth and continue to live as a chicken, digging in the dirt rather than soaring in the sky.

The moral of this story is obvious. Most people have been enculturated to accept and believe certain things that may, and likely do, betray their real potential. Like the chickens in the coop, we've all been *imprinted.* Behavioral scientists use this term for the process whereby animals seek to be accepted by imitating their peers. An eagle or a duckling raised in a chicken coop will behave like a chicken, and so on. For many, unlike the ugly duckling in the story by the same name, there's no swan that comes along. If there is, then perhaps they get the treatment that Nina gave the other eagle.

The point is simply that humans are socialized in ways that produce limited thinking—or rather, *trained* thinking. Indeed, this is done so well that a certain blindness exists in most of us. This unawareness is sometimes well illustrated by what cognitive theorists refer to as *context-bound thinking.*

Context-Bound Thinking

Ellen Langer of Harvard University uses a couple of analogies with regard to this concept. The first invites thinking of the saliva in one's mouth. It tastes good as one moves it around the tongue, and it feels good, especially compared to a dry mouth. So, Langer says, imagine spitting the saliva into a glass in front of you and then drinking it down. Something changed in how you thought of that spit—right? In context, within the mouth, it's great. As a drink, however . . . for most people this is rather disgusting. Why?[1]

Before sharing Langer's second analogy, let me point out something. If a product is placed in a context that by definition is desirable, then we're typically blind to seeing the alternative context. Most smokers think of a cigarette as their friend. It assuages anxiety and relieves stress. It's always there, it tastes good, and it helps the smoker think clearly. It gives the hands something to do and makes it possible to endure many things that otherwise would be difficult, such as sitting and listening to long conversations. Indeed, the cigarette may make conversations last even longer (ask any waitress who has served smokers).

All of this is, of course, nonsense—but the smoker doesn't think so. Why? Because the tobacco industry has carefully framed (developed the context) in such a way that we know this image hasn't just appeared; it was created. When the smoker changes the context—"the spit in the glass"—smoking becomes easy to give up.

That statement may shock many smokers, but it's true. I smoked for more than 40 years, but only when I could see through the context in which the cigarette was framed was I able to quit. Tobacco is addictive, but the physical addiction is much easier to break than the psychological one. Cigarettes really don't taste good when one focuses on every drag, they make a slave out of the smoker, and so forth. I could go on in much greater detail, but the point should be clear. Cigarettes are a perfect example of deployment via context. Like the spit in our mouths, it's fine in one context but not another.

Langer's second example goes like this: Imagine a knock at your door one evening, say around 9 P.M. You answer the door, and there stands a friend. He says, "I'm in a scavenger hunt and if I can find a piece of wood that's three feet by seven feet, I can win $10,000. I'll split the prize with you if you have the wood." You think for a moment and then say, "I'm sorry, I don't have a woodpile or anything like that. I can't help you." And you close your 3-foot-by-7-foot wooden door.

Langer is right: We don't think of doors as slabs of wood. We also often don't think at all. We're bound by definitions, contexts, and other beliefs that limit our very perceptions. Some people think that if they see a thing, it exists, and that the opposite is also true. The fact of the matter is quite different. In *Choices and Illusions,* I show just how false this assumption really is, and the hard research is equally clear: "Our perception is based more on expectation and belief than on independent interpretation."[2]

Buried Prejudice

There are many things about the human condition that are truly glorious and only a few that most would choose to deny. One of those "hide-it" facts that we all share is a buried prejudice. It isn't the same for all of us, but everyone has biases, many of which we're embarrassed to admit. Jesse Jackson, the African-American civil rights activist, once said, "There is nothing more painful to me at this stage in my life than to walk down the street and hear footsteps and start thinking about robbery—then look around and see somebody white and feel relieved."[3]

Studies have demonstrated that prejudices are often implicit rather than explicit. That is, many of them may exist without formal conscious awareness. Most people recognize biases they may have against Hitler and other tyrants of history; toward organizations that have been labeled reprehensible, such as the Ku Klux Klan; and even toward those in the political arena who hold views they disagree with. That much is obvious, but what isn't so apparent are strong opinions we're unaware of. For example, the reaction Jesse Jackson described must have really startled him when he discovered it.

In a study designed to look for biases, white preschool children were shown angry faces, which they tended to color black rather than white. Just as interesting is the fact that in this study, happy faces were colored white.[4] Both are good examples of unconscious bias.

After plain-clothes police officers shot and killed unarmed west-African immigrant Amadou Diallo, researchers wanted to discover whether the outcome would have been different if the young man had been white. They devised a computer game where volunteers were shown 100 images of people holding guns, wallets, or phones. Half were white, half were black, and the game measured reaction time before either shooting or not shooting them. The research showed robust evidence of racial bias in decisions to shoot.[5] You can try this game out for yourself at **http://backhand.uchicago.edu/Center/ShooterEffect/**.

Take everything that you've read to this point and think about the television stations in Middle Eastern nations such as Saudi Arabia and Iran, which show Jews and Americans in a light that casts them as the evil villains. (This well-documented practice has gone on for years and continues as of the date of this writing.) Long after conscious conflict has been extinguished, deep-seated explicit and implicit prejudices will remain and affect all sides. Indeed, it's difficult to imagine that similar biases aren't being created at this moment throughout the world by and between religious and political groups.

Some of this is just obvious; some isn't. The important point is how easy it is to make a judgment based on an implicit bias. As with most things, knowledge is the best preparation for defense.

The Effects of Television Viewing

Children's entertainment, ranging from television to computer games, can have far-reaching consequences. Research reveals that children not yet in school are watching TV approximately 60 hours a week, while those attending school typically view 25 to 30 hours per week. When you crunch the numbers, this translates to some 20,000 commercials viewed per year. By their mid-teens, some 200,000 commercials have been stored in their minds. In addition, they've seen an estimated 33,000 murders!

There are many known effects associated with this intense television intake by children, to say nothing of the impact on their self-image and expectations. Here's a quick rundown of the possible negative effects: TV can impact sensory development in a negative manner, increase aggression and hostility, and diminish the development of hearing in young children. It displaces physical activity and thereby impacts health negatively. It overdoses kids with artificial light and can cause sleep deprivation. It's implicated in poor cognitive and intellectual development, can slow language acquisition, and is associated with poor reading abilities. Television also negatively impacts social development and perceptions of reality. [6]

Everything a very young child sees is perceived as real. Adults know that they can play peekaboo by simply hiding behind a sheet of paper and then popping out from behind it, to the total amazement of a young child. To the child, the face (person) has disappeared and reappeared magically. It's reasonable to believe that to this same child, everything on television is also real. This includes the violence, monsters, and depravity that so many programs contain. To the thinking person, television should be as tightly controlled for children's interests as one might control access to the Internet.

Indeed, TV is a powerful tool when used correctly. The opportunity to enhance learning, to explore the fine arts, and to enrich education is absolutely awesome. Given the choice, why would people choose to watch some nasty reality show or violent movie when they could take in an opera, view a nature channel, see the latest in astronomical discoveries, or even watch a historical undertaking such as an ongoing archeological dig?

Ask yourself, *What do I choose to watch and why?* Are you addicted to a particular form of entertainment, or do you use TV for some purpose like assuaging anxiety? Is it the family gathering place for food, film, and more food? Do you gather around the TV instead of the fire and let others tell you stories? Are they the tales you truly want to fill your mind?

Who Are You, Really?

At this juncture, it's easy to see just how far away from ourselves we might have gone. Our beliefs, taboos, desires, and interpretations may all have been manipulated and foisted upon us in much the same way that we acquired our native language. Our consumption habits, movie icons, contemporary mores, appetites, and even illnesses have been implanted in our psyches even more surreptitiously. And by whom? Why, the vendors of course. Purveyors of goods, services, government, and even religion—all of them and more had a part in this.

What, then, is authentic? Who are you, really? Does it matter? If this is brainwashing, hasn't it always happened in some way or another? How would individuals go about discovering who they really were or escaping these impositions? What's left if a person does get past the blind thinking and goes beyond the limits of the box?

In part, this book is about these questions. In Book Two, I'll deal directly with the how, what, when and where of becoming authentically oneself. Indeed, I'll explain such tools as hypnosis and neuro-linguistic programming, with subliminal communication, brain-wave-entrainment methods, and much more—all in a positive light. The same tools often misused to disempower, as you'll see shortly, can be used to empower.

Deliberate, researched, planned propaganda is part of our culture. It occurs wherever consumption is desired, whether that consumption is of ideas or merchandise. Often symbols, stereotypes, and more are used to eliminate words. This technique is also intentional and has its own underlying philosophy designed, once again, to bypass critical thought—in fact, to make it appear unnecessary. In his must-read book *Public Opinion,* Walter Lippmann describes this practice this way:

> This philosophy is a more or less organized series of images for describing the unseen world. But not only for describing it. For judging it as well. And, therefore, the stereotypes are loaded with preferences, suffused with affection or dislike, attached to fears, lusts, strong wishes, pride, hope. Whatever invokes the stereotype is judged with the appropriate sentiment. Except where we deliberately keep prejudice in suspense, we do not study a man and judge him to be bad. We see a bad man. We see a dewy morn, a blushing maiden, a sainted priest, a humorless Englishman, a dangerous Red, a carefree bohemian, a lazy Hindu, a wily Oriental, a dreamy Slav, a volatile Irishman, a greedy Jew, a 100% American.[7]

I might add that you see a door, not a piece of wood. You see vile spit—not warm, mouth-bathing saliva.

Hark back to Edward Bernays. Modifying psychoanalytic concepts for consumer research has led to a very sophisticated use and development of symbols, stereotypes, and more, including such things as ideas turned into moral attitudes. One such belief of our time can be said this way: "It's okay to get even." This is but one example of an idea that became so popular as to be accepted into our value system. Lippmann had this to say about our values, and it's as relevant today as it was then, more than 80 years ago:

> Morality, good taste and good form first standardize and then emphasize certain of these underlying prejudices. (The prejudice is stated earlier as, "Neither justice, nor mercy, nor truth, entered into such a judgment, for the judgment has preceded the evidence.") As we adjust ourselves to our code, we adjust the facts we see to the code . . . for a moral code is a scheme of conduct applied to a

number of typical instances. To behave as the code directs is to serve whatever purpose the code pursues.[8]

What does the notion of "It's okay to get even" serve? As I mentioned earlier, "I don't get even—I get evener" is the theme of at least one bumper sticker that serves this code. Where does this come from? What does it encourage?

Escalating School Violence

In a paper I presented several years ago regarding school violence, I predicted several things, none of which should surprise you. The first was that the violence would increase. Second, and the reason for the first, the media would continue to increase the amount of violence and other stimuli of arousal they showed as a means to sell their product. Third, this would further desensitize the threshold of arousal, forcing ever more explicit violence, sex, and other methods of stimulation. Last, not only would the threshold of arousal become so elevated as to allow individuals to look upon death, dismemberment, and worse without emotion, but it would lead to desensitizing our young people to the meaning of death and values in general. It didn't take a soothsayer to see this coming.

Today we see much more violence everywhere. Young children not yet in their teens blow people away. Sometimes they do this from a hillside, demonstrating their marksmanship, a skill they've practiced over and over again in some arcade game. Just as a terrorist can learn to fly a plane in a simulator or with sophisticated software on a laptop computer, so too can a child learn to shoot a weapon and kill fellow human beings.

The popularity of first-person-shooter games (FPS) has grown since 1993 when Senator Joe Lieberman headed Senate hearings investigating violent video games. Those reviews led to software ratings, but the ratings, as with cigarette warnings, only tease young people into finding ways to obtain the games. Another symbol is twisted to become another attractor for consumption.

For now, it's noteworthy that we acknowledge the depth and breadth of what Webster defines as "persuasion by propaganda or salesmanship" before we continue with the first definition of brainwashing: "a forcible indoctrination to induce someone to give up basic political, social, or religious beliefs and attitudes and to accept contrasting regimented ideas."

Summary

Certain learned and self-imposed tendencies have short-circuited our true thinking. Human beings have been socialized to such a degree that our mental processes have become limited. Many so-called choices are between alternatives that have been scripted during our maturation. As such, we choose to do A instead of B or C but never consider that there's an entire alphabet of possibilities. We're blinded by our labels, definitions, thinking patterns, and so forth. It's as if we live in thought boxes that limit our alternatives.

CHAPTER 6

Forced Brainwashing: Interrogation and Thought Control

*"We know now that men can be made to do exactly anything.
. . . It's all a question of finding the right means."*

— Jules Romains

At least one thing our culture shares with the entire world is con-spiracy theories. There are so many of them, and some are so blatantly stupid (I hate to use that word, but no other is as accurate) that if you have any self-respect, denouncing them is almost required. With that said, however, not all conspiracy theories are bunk. A well-known idea in political science and philosophy circles is: "A good lie begins with a kernel of truth." Whether on purpose or as a beginning for exag-geration, some conspiracy theories contain more than one element of truth.

This isn't to suggest that all of them are lies, but rather that turn-ing our back on a conspiracy theory may lead to ignoring some truth. Most people will be surprised (and horrified) to know that the epi-graph for this chapter was taken from a quote found in a 1960 CIA study on brainwashing. The full quote is: "We know now that men can be made to do exactly anything. . . . It's all a question of finding the right means. If only we take enough trouble and go sufficiently slowly, we can make him kill his aged parents and eat them in a stew."[1]

In this context, then, this chapter explores forced or coerced brainwashing techniques, including a brief review of some of the best known. Later, we'll examine some of the tools allegedly employed in these techniques, such as hypnosis, brain-entrainment methods, frequency resonance, subliminal communication or commands, and the combination of these technologies.

Public Education

It will probably surprise you to know that one of the most important starting points in any discussion of brainwashing has to be our public-education system.

There's no shortage of conspiracy theories regarding education in America. The Internet is chockablock full of articles, commentaries, first-person accounts, historical documents, extolled evils, and so forth. I'll leave it up to you to review them if you so desire. What I choose to focus on is the obvious—the enormous power and influence the education system in America has over the way we think, the way we behave, our expectations, and so much more. In my book *Choices and Illusions,* I dedicate a great deal of time to illustrating just how "in the box" our thinking is conditioned. Taking a brief look at how public education began is fruitful in understanding how and why many believe this potentially invaluable tool has been subverted for purposes of the power elite.

The first public compulsory-education system originated in Prussia in 1819. The system was divided into three tiers, which afforded three different levels of education (not to be confused with grade levels). The tiers were designed to serve three different classes of children. According to retired school teacher and author John Gatto, tier one was for those who would become the rulers; tier two was for those who would become the rulers' assistants and professionals, such as doctors, lawyers, and the like; and tier three was for those who were to be ruled. This last group would receive the necessary education involved to guarantee obedience to the authority (rulers). The subjects constituted more than 90 percent of the population.[2]

This lower class, the ruled, would be educated, but it would be led away from thinking and reasoning. Variations on curriculum and methods would expose the masses to math, social sciences, hard science, language, and art—but once again, in a manner that created what I've called, "in-the-box thinking," and I use that word loosely, for this really isn't thinking at all.

Over time, this system was copied and exported to many other countries. By the late 1800s, it had fully arrived in America; and under the tutelage of a few, it prospered. One of the most influential men of the period, philosopher John Dewey, believed that the purpose of public schools was to "take an active part in determining the social order of the future . . . according as the teachers align themselves with the newer forces making for social control of economic forces."[3]

Another influential individual in the history of American public education was Edward Lee Thorndike. For Thorndike, teaching was:

> The art of giving and withholding stimuli with the result of producing or preventing certain responses. In this definition the term stimulus is used widely for any event which influences a person . . . for a word spoken to him, a look, a sentence which he reads, the air he breathes, etc. etc. The term response is used for any reaction made by him . . . a new thought, a feeling of interest, a bodily act, any mental or bodily condition resulting from the stimulus. The aim of the teacher is to produce desirable and prevent undesirable changes in human beings by producing and preventing certain responses. The means at the disposal of the teacher are the stimuli which can be brought to bear upon the pupil . . . the teacher's words, gestures, and appearance, the condition and appliances of the school room, the books to be used, and the objects to be seen, and so on through a long list of the things and events which the teacher can control."[4]

It's clear that the opportunity to control/train the thinking of students is present and that at least some of the most notable and influential of those involved in the creation of our educational system intended for schooling to socialize rather than educate. They even thought that it should subjugate the student to a philosophy that emphasizes a social-order doctrine over the development of intellectualism. It's also worth noting that men like Dewey and Thorndike were instrumental in establishing the direction of the Teachers College, part of Columbia University, and according to Jim Keith, author of *Mind Control, World Control:* "By the 1950s, the Teachers College was indisputably the most powerful force in education in America, with approximately one third of all school presidents and deans, and one fourth of all American teachers accredited there."[5]

The next time you drop your child at school, think about this: When you buy your child pencils and so forth and learn that they were collected by the teacher, together with those of other students, and placed in one common holder for everyone to use, ask yourself, *Why? Does this promote individuality and property rights or . . . ?* The next time you hear of some seemingly outlandish this or that going on in a school, you might ask yourself, *What am I doing to see that does not go on in schools near me?* The next time you hear that the Pledge of Allegiance will be recited omitting certain words, ask yourself, *What will the Pledge be like in years to come?*

Psychological Predispositions

Now, as mentioned earlier, let's take a quick tour of some of the psychological predispositions that give rise to ease in brainwashing. Many people remember when Patricia Hearst was kidnapped in 1974. Not long after she was abducted, the newspaper heiress was photographed with an automatic rifle in her hands assisting her kidnappers, the Symbionese Liberation Army (SLA) in a bank robbery.

The Stockholm syndrome, simply described, is the propensity for a victim to loyally bond with the kidnapper, hostage taker, or even abuser, in some instances, in an attempt to join that person and avoid additional pain. A variant of this syndrome is known as psychological identification with the more powerful abuser. Victims of this disorder often defend the very family member who hurt them. This appears to be the case with Patty Hearst.

One psychological predisposition that catches many people and makes it easy to con or brainwash them is something known as *psychological arrogance*. This condition essentially leads to the notion that whatever one thinks must be right. As a result, rational efforts to find out the truth are ignored. In a way, this is a form of self-brainwashing.

Our very social fabric and our need for acceptance underscores many of the reasons we can be so easily persuaded. I may be biased, but I find it interesting that throughout human history there has been a belief in a spiritual reality or God. The artifacts of ancient burial sites attest to the fact that people have always believed in life after death. On a more modern note, neuroscientists have demonstrated the existence of religious centers in the human brain.[6] In other words, we're built to believe. It takes an act of society and an orchestrated effort by educators to produce an atheist. In this sense, atheism is a product of brainwashing.

We've already seen the impact that mass-marketing groups, sales organizations, politicians, and even the *news* (if there still is news in America, rather than commentary and editorials) can have on everyone's mind-set; but what may not seem so obvious are the themes sold to all of us. Take the myth that vegetarians tend to be intellectuals, or the beef industry's answer—that to be a real man, you must eat beef! Think of all the themes you hold dear and true. How many of them are myths, distortions, exaggerations, or just plain old lies?

Group Behavior

Group behavior is still another force that must be added into the equation. Scientific literature is full of documented cases of group hysteria. Sometimes this actually leads to physical symptoms. In one instance, a high-school teacher noted a gasoline-like odor in her classroom. She developed a headache, nausea, shortness of breath, and dizziness. Students began complaining of similar symptoms. The school was evacuated, and emergency personnel from several counties responded. That day, 100 people went to a local emergency room with symptoms reportedly related to exposure at the school. Physical examination and laboratory testing, however, revealed no evidence of a toxic cause for the symptoms.[7]

Philip Zimbardo's Stanford Prison Experiment in 1971 was a classic example of the effect roles and groups play in individual behavior. This well-known study separated student volunteers into guards and inmates. In a very short time, the guards—who were given ultimate authority and power over the inmates—were behaving in ways often described as simply monstrous. As for the inmates, their roles demeaned their humanness in ways that Zimbardo fears negatively effect our prison systems today. In his words: "Prisons are evil places that demean humanity. . . . They are as bad for the guards as they are for the prisoners."[8]

Mind Control

Mind control and so-called *psyops* (psychological operations) are often the stuff of science-fiction movies. They're also, as a matter of fact, the subject of billions of dollars spent by governments of the world. Attributing a motive to this, especially the clandestine activities involving citizens who did *not* volunteer, is something I'll leave to you.

The well-known movie *The Manchurian Candidate* depicts the use of posthypnotic suggestions to activate programmed behavior. The behavior involves sabotage of American interests. When this film was originally released, a great deal of concern was voiced concerning the brainwashing possibilities suggested in the movie. Professionals were quick to point out that the movie was fictional and depicted impossibilities. A common statement repeated over and over again simply asserted: "You can't get a person to do something under hypnosis that's against their will!"

Since the movie's release in 1962, the argument has remained the same, even though there are many people who believe that our government and others continue to program individuals in covert operations for sinister purposes. In 1987, the American Psychological Association (APA) Board of Social and Ethical Responsibility for Psychology (BSERP) dismissed brainwashing theories with the explanation that they "lacked the scientific rigor and evenhanded critical approach necessary for APA imprimatur."[9]

Part of what feeds conspiracy theories is a disagreement among professionals or the so-called experts. Many professionals today believe that aspects of brainwashing are truly possible, and this agreement further feeds the theorists, who see denials by organizations such as the APA or sectors of government such as the CIA as cover-ups.

Brainwashing and the United States Government

Let's explore some of theories and then discuss the possibilities by beginning with a short history of the whos, whats, and whys behind the alleged perpetrators of brainwashing within the U.S. government. President Franklin D. Roosevelt authorized the creation of the office of Coordinator of Information (COI) to serve as America's defense against psychological warfare ("winning hearts and minds," as we call it today). The COI evolved into the Office of Strategic Services (OSS) and eventually into the Central Intelligence Agency (CIA).

According to official records, "All plans for projects to be undertaken by the Office of Strategic Services will be submitted to the Joint U.S. Chiefs of Staff through the Joint Psychological Warfare Committee."[10] Published accounts show that the Office of Strategic Services spawned Operation Mind Control, and "it developed psychological warfare into an effective weapon against the minds of civilian and military populations foreign and domestic alike."[11]

According to Walter Bowart, as quoted by Jim Keith in his book *Mind Control, World Control,* George Estabrooks of Colgate College proposed the use of hypnosis early in World War II to train spies and assassins. Keith continues:

> Estabrooks became loose-lipped on one occasion, when in 1968, he chatted with a reporter for the *Providence Evening Bulletin.* According to the article that resulted, "Dr. Estabrooks said that the key to creating an effective spy or assassin rests in . . . creating a multiple personality, with the aid of hypnosis," a procedure which the

good doctor described as "child's play." Estabrooks even offered the suggestion that Lee Harvey Oswald and Jack Ruby "could very well have been performing through hypnosis."[12]

The OSS (Office of Strategic Services) was not limited to hypnosis in their methods or research. Keith recounts one such top-secret study designed to find a truth drug:

> This project was to break down resistance in spies and POWs. The project was run in conjunction with the Freemasons, and supervised by Superintendent Winfred Overhulser, the Scottish Rites chief psychiatrist at St. Elizabeth's Hospital in Washington, D.C., along with a research team composed of Harry J. Anslinger, head of the Federal Bureau of Narcotics, and Dr. Edward Strecker, then president of the American Psychiatric Association. The study assessed the uses of mescaline, scopolamine, peyote, and barbiturates, but settled upon a mixture of marijuana and tobacco, attempting to perfect a concoction that would stimulate a "state of irresponsibility." OSS scientists then came up with a potent extract of marijuana called TD. Its results were noted in an OSS report: "TD appears to relax all inhibitions and to deaden the areas of the brain which govern an individual's discretion and caution."[13]

The OSS ceased to exist on September 20, 1945, when President Franklin D. Roosevelt signed an executive order terminating it. Allen Dulles took over the new CIA.

The Manchurian Candidate

This early history in psychological warfare is fertile ground for many conspiracy theories. Experiments that were conducted during and after wartime by our government and others seem to heighten the odds that there's more truth than fiction to many of these hypotheses. For example, James Jesus Angleton of the CIA, chief of the CIA's counterintelligence section, defined three goals for their Manchurian Candidate Program (named after the book and movie). The goals involved research with hypnosis: "(1) the speedy hypnotic induction of unwitting subjects; (2) the ability to create long-lasting amnesia; and (3) the implanting of long-lasting, useful hypnotic suggestions."[14]

Estabrooks had already demonstrated to the CIA that young privates with low education could be programmed to retain complex verbal information. Researcher J. G. Watkins did some subsequent testing with Estabrooks's low-rank, low-education subjects. As Keith reports, Watkins showed "that these men could be, contrary to popular wisdom on the topic, hypnotized to commit acts that violated their own moral codes, not to mention military codes. One experiment that Watkins carried out involved hypnotizing army privates and then telling them that an officer who was in the same room was an enemy infiltrator. Watkins told the hypnotized subjects that the officer would try to kill them. Without exception, on command the soldiers violently attacked the officer."[15]

One of my hypnosis mentors was Harry Arons, who spent much of his early career working to understand how the North Koreans had been so successful in brainwashing American POWs during the Korean War. Since then, many more experiments have been conducted on human subjects with the intent to manipulate or control them and their beliefs. There's no shortage of books on the subject, so let's talk about some of the more well-known experiments.

Project Bluebird

According to Anton Chaitkin, writing in *British Psychiatry* in an article entitled "From Eugenics to Assassination," a man named Morse Allen researched the idea of disposable assassins under what is known as Project Bluebird.[16] According to materials contained in the Bluebird book, we find that:

> A declassified CIA document dated 7 Jan 1953 describes the experimental creation of multiple personality in two 19-year old girls. "These subjects have clearly demonstrated that they can pass from a fully awake state to a deep H (hypnotic) controlled state by

telephone, by receiving written matter, or by the use of a code, signal, or words, and that control of those hypnotized can be passed from individual to another without great difficulty. It has also been shown by experimentation with these girls that they can act as unwilling couriers for information purposes."[17]

According to Chaitkin, the CIA backed a study by Alden Sears at the University of Minnesota that sought to install multiple personalities in subjects. This work was conducted simultaneously with the Bluebird project.

Project Artichoke

Project Artichoke followed—some say replaced—Bluebird and was a collaborative effort between the CIA and the Federal Bureau of Narcotics. "The scope of the project was outlined in a memo dated January 1952 that stated: "Can we get control of an individual to the point where he will do our bidding against his will and even against fundamental laws of nature, such as self preservation?"[18] The project studied hypnosis and such chemicals as morphine in forced addiction and withdrawal situations.

Many other projects followed Artichoke. Some of them include Project Chatter, Project MKDelta, Project MKNaomi, Project MKUltra, and the HAARP project. MKUltra and HAARP are probably the two most written about today. We'll look at both of them briefly.

MKUltra and HAARP

MKUltra was the code name for a secret and covert CIA operation researching mind control and chemical interrogation. During Congressional hearings on the Senate floor in 1977, Senator Ted Kennedy said:

The Deputy Director of the CIA revealed that over thirty universities and institutions were involved in an "extensive testing and experimentation" program which included covert drug tests on unwitting citizens "at all social levels, high and low, native Americans and foreign." Several of these tests involved the administration of LSD to "unwitting subjects in social situations." At least one death, that of Dr. [Frank] Olson, resulted from these activities. The Agency itself acknowledged that these tests made little scientific sense. The agents doing the monitoring were not qualified scientific observers.[19]

The project's intentionally oblique CIA name is made up of the digraph "MK," meaning that the project was sponsored by the agency's Technical Services Division, followed by the arbitrary dictionary word *ultra.*[20] (Note that it was the Technical Services Division of the CIA that hatched the plot to assassinate Fidel Castro during the Kennedy administration.)

A recent review by Paul J. Norton entitled "Investigative Report: MKUltra and Nazism in the U.S. Government" calls for anti-propaganda measures. Norton flatly asserts that the CIA continues its project work. According to Norton, speaking out in the *Freedom of Thought Public Journal,* "Rape, murder, mayhem, illegal surveillance, wars of aggression, pretty much anything that you can imagine the enemies of the people would do, the CIA has done and more."[21]

Declassified documents regarding MKUltra are revealing, to say the least. I quote from the Joint Hearing before the Select Committee of Intelligence and the Subcommittee on Health and Scientific Research of the Committee on Human Resources, 95th Congress, First Session, August 3, 1977:

> Over the ten-year life of the program, many "additional avenues to the control of human behavior" (this is in addition to chemical and biological means) were designated as appropriate for investigation under the MKUltra charter. These include "radiation, electroshock, various fields of psychology, psychiatry, sociology and anthropology, graphology, harassment substances, and paramilitary devices and materials."[22]

Many think that MKUltra or a derivative is still operating globally, not just in the United States. Indeed, it's a common belief in Canada that the U.S. has used subliminal messages in their Radio America broadcasts and other psychological means elsewhere in the world. When Lynn Schroeder, author of *Super Memory, Super Learning,* and *Psychic Discoveries behind the Iron Curtain,* wrote to me regarding my book *Thinking without Thinking,* she included an article that was sent to her anonymously.

The information was easy enough to verify. It seems that a top FBI scientist admitted to proposing a mind-control device to alter David Koresh's behavior during the Waco, Texas, standoff. Dr. Igor Smimov of the Moscow Medical Academy "demonstrated to 10 American military, intelligence, and law enforcement officials in Washington a device they claimed could subliminally implant thoughts in people's mind, and thereby control their actions."[23] Indeed, the only reason the FBI did not use the equipment is that the Russian scientists would not guarantee that it might not "back-fire and trigger more violence."[24] They did, however, deploy loud sounds 24-7 and use other mind technologies.

Skull and Bones

Behind most of the conspiracy theorists is an undertone not yet discussed. Essentially, this is the Skull-and-Bones argument that insists a "New World Order" is behind the scenes, orchestrating a careful plan to produce not only the world's leaders but also the world's agenda. The Order of Skull and Bones, originally known as the Brotherhood of Death, is a secret senior society based at Yale University. It has been asserted that the society began primarily to smuggle drugs, chiefly opium, from China. "The society's alumni organization, which owns its properties and oversees all the organization's activity, is known as the Russell Trust Association (R.T.A.), and is named after one of Bones' founding members."[25]

This theory argues that many world leaders have been willing cohorts of the CIA, MI5, and other such agencies in a covert effort to control the masses. The theory draws on many specific examples, the scope of which is outside the purpose of this chapter, but which can easily be discovered on the Internet. The bottom line is that the propaganda, the secret brainwashing projects, and even some real-world scenarios (tragedies) were the products of those who sponsor and support a New World Order.

This thinking isn't limited to the Skull and Bones Society. Indeed, many believe that the Illuminati, a secret society thought to run world affairs from behind the scenes, is ultimately behind this attempt to control humankind. Because these conspiracies depart too far from our purposes here, I'll leave it at that.

Suffice it to say, I think you can understand why there's a reasonable concern about brainwashing. And I'd drop that matter as well, except for HAARP and where that leads us.

HAARP

HAARP stands for High Frequency Active Auroral Research Program. It was made to "beam 1.7 gigawatts (billion watts) of radiated power into the ionosphere—the electrically-charged layer above Earth's atmosphere."[26]

An online article explains:

> The High Frequency Active Auroral Research Program (HAARP) is an investigation project to "understand, simulate and control ionospheric processes that might alter the performance of communication and surveillance systems." Started in 1993, the project is proposed to last for a period of twenty years. The project is jointly funded by the United States Air Force, the Navy, and the University of Alaska and Defense Advanced Research Projects Agency (DARPA).[27]

There are many concerns about HAARP, including, as Dr. Nick Begich puts it, "the boiling of the upper atmosphere," but we'll leave weather management, global hazards, and the like to others.[28] Our concern is different.

HAARP is really a reversed radio telescope—it transmits instead of receives. It has a growing network of transmission antennas that look much like the satellite antennas used for cell phones. HAARP theoretically has the capability to transmit information of all sorts on a carrier frequency. These are frequencies that can seriously affect the health and well-being of individuals, as well as being able to entrain brain-wave activity. The transmitted information also could be subliminal messages delivered in so-called dead zones of our perceived hearing ability. Theoretically, by using high-frequency carrier waves, a truly silent subliminal message could be delivered.

A few years ago, I had dinner with Pat and Gayle Flanagan. Dr. Pat Flanagan is best known today for his Neurophone, which inputs audio information directly to the brain, bypassing normal hearing channels. It was patented as a device for the hearing impaired and was soon thereafter seized by the U.S. National Security Agency. For 25 years, the inventor was unable to access his own device.

Pat is truly a genius and pioneer. As a young boy, he built the first early-warning device that could detect a nuclear detonation. Our government acquired this technology, and he became known as a child prodigy overnight.

Years before we met, I'd conducted some research using hypnosis, subliminal affirmations, and the Neurophone. At our meeting, we began by discussing my earlier work with Pat's Neurophone, and soon the subject of HAARP came up. He'd visited the general area where the program was under way and knew of the security surrounding it. By the evening's end, we concluded that without a doubt HAARP posed an opportunity for someone to carry out real human experiments, using our knowledge of frequency patterns and subliminal information. Every day on the way to my office, I pass a suspicious antenna that reminds me of this conversation.

HAARP can be used to output a continuous or pulsed carrier wave on which many things can be piggybacked, including an electrical current. That's important because research has shown clearly the effects of electrical stimulation on the brain. Indeed, as a slight departure, the technology exists today to capture the distinctive frequency of different things, ranging from pharmaceutical to electrical signals. This "signature," if you will, is capable of producing effects in the human body comparable to what's known as resonance. In other words, vibrate the signature or deliver it through a liquid, and the body responds.

HAARP, according to one source, "broadcasts at the same frequencies as the human brain, and can be attuned for specific applications on entire populations. The technology also could be used for projecting words and images directly to the minds of entire populations."[29] HAARP is a capable entrainment tool as well. It possesses the ability to generate a signal that paces brain-wave activity.

This technology is the mechanism behind what Jerry Smith calls radio intracerebral mind control.[30] According to Smith in his book *HAARP: The Ultimate Weapon of Conspiracy,* much of the work set out for HAARP is in response to Soviet advances in mind-control technologies. One of those technologies, known as Woodpecker, bombarded our embassy in Moscow, arguably causing illness and death. This microwave bombardment went on for 15 years before being confirmed by the U.S. government. Former embassy employees and their families recalled suffering strange ailments during their tenure in Moscow, and a number were diagnosed with cancer. A full-scale medical investigation was launched.[31]

But back to our immediate concern. In Dr. Jose M. R. Delgado's book *Physical Control of the Mind: Toward a Psychocivilized Society,* the manipulation of behavior is demonstrated in animals by delivering an electrical current.[32] Delgado, a Yale professor, managed later to produce the same effects without implanted electrodes—establishing control at a distance without apparatus. Following up on this research, neurosurgeon Dr. Robert G. Heath of Tulane University managed to further manipulate human behavior via electrical stimulation. *Angels Don't Play This HAARP,* by Dr. Nick Begich and Jeanne Manning, tells us that "like Dr. Delgado, the neurosurgeon [Dr. Heath] concluded that ESB (Electrical Stimulation of the Brain) could evoke hallucinations as well as fear and pleasure. It could literally manipulate the human will at will."[33]

It's worth noting that some people find it more than coincidental that the frequency band used by cell phones is the same as the one discovered by Wilhelm Reich to affect thought transmission. One writer, describing the effect of Reich's second order of waves (used today by cell phones), puts it this way: "Reich worked on this project secretly for the CIA for over 5 years, from 1947–1952, until he realized who the CIA was planning to use the mind control on—the American people."[34]

Neuro-Electromagnetic Mind Control

Another key device, the Persinger Helmet, gets its name from its creator, Dr. Michael Persinger. He was a neurologist at Laurentian University of Ontario, Canada, when his research using electromagnetic frequencies led to the discovery that different results are produced by stimulating different areas of the brain. Persinger was also later involved with Operation Black Beauty, according to author and conspiracy theorist Glenn Krawczyk, which was all about creating a freezer-sized, electromagnetic broadcasting appliance to be used during riots and other mass civil disobedience.[35] According to Jim Keith, author of *Mind Control, World Control*, "The device is said to employ time-varying fields of extremely low frequency energy, broadcast at frequencies between 1 and 10 hertz, that cause vomiting in whomever the unit is trained on."[36]

In the 1990s, I spoke with Dr. Robert Beck, who had worked with the Soviet Woodpecker signal and had extensive experience with Extremely Low Frequency modulation (ELF). He shared a story in which he and a friend used one of the devices he built to control behavior outdoors near a stairway leading into a class building on a California university campus.

If you think neuro-electric or neuro-electromagnetic weapons or mind-control methods are far out, consider this. If you Google "Voice-to-Skull device" the U.S. Army's Website appears. However, when you click on the link, you discover that the page has been taken down. Still, a description remains on the Federation of American Scientist's Website. The device is described there as:

> Nonlethal weapon which includes (1) a neuro-electromagnetic device which uses microwave transmission of sound into the skull of persons or animals by way of pulsed-modulated microwave radiation; and (2) a silent sound device which can transmit sound into the skull of persons or animals. Note: The sound modulation may be voice or audio subliminal messages. One application of V2K is use as an electronic scarecrow to frighten birds in the vicinity of airports.[37]

This microwave-sound transmission has another name: Medusa. This project was funded for a period by the U.S. Navy and designed to be a microwave-sound weapon. This type of transmission is a silent audio form that essentially puts noises in a person's head.[38] It's been suggested that it might be used at low power to produce a whisper that was too quiet to perceive consciously but might be able to sub-consciously influence someone.[39]

There are many other projects and additional implications and applications beyond those discussed here. There's also no shortage of conspiracy theories or personal testimonies to account for alleged abuses arising from these projects.

Mind Manipulation

I'm no conspiracy expert, nor do I indulge in secrecy and mind-manipulation theories. My work has at times led me to people and places that are much better informed on some of these matters than most. What I can say with certainty—and what should be clear to you after this little tour through such ideas—is that certain facts are worth bearing in mind.

First, as with the advertising world, a lot of research has been designed and carried out to determine how and under what circum-stances human behavior can be best manipulated; it's also examined what ends this can be used for. Second, the technical capacity exists to control people using a variety of methods, ranging from the direct and overt to many covert possibilities. Third, there remains a lot of secrecy around all of this research. Indeed, in some instances, much of it has come to light only during investigations as the result of a whistle-blower or an internal agency leak. Fourth, the experts disagree about what's known and what can be done. Certain information has been declassified, but the blacked-out areas on those documents, together with everything that remains sealed in secrecy, leave room for an awful lot of discomfort. Add this all up, and there are definitely the makings of several conspiracy theories.

Summary

We've now traveled to the end of the spectrum, exploring the lengths to which some people will go in order to learn how to manipulate us. Persuasion, manipulation, and brainwashing are all a reality, whether they're performed by our loved ones, salespeople, or the government itself. The purpose of this chapter has been to inform and further our insights into the art of persuasion. Knowledge is power. Information is critical to managing choices, and it appears that many people and groups would like to make those decisions for us.

■　■■■■■

PART II

TRANSITIONING: JOURNEYING INTO THE BRIGHTER SIDE OF PERSUASION

CHAPTER 7

Subliminal Communication

*"Trickery and treachery are the practices of fools
that have not the wits enough to be honest."*

— Benjamin Franklin

We've now seen how easy it is for others to manipulate our very thoughts and beliefs. Of all the methods discussed, it's subliminal communication that I've focused my research on for almost 30 years. Subliminal communication could be used against us every day, but it also holds the greatest promise for assisting us in achieving our goals and dreams. For this reason, I believe it's most beneficial to look at this area in greater depth.

Subliminal technically means any form of communication that isn't consciously perceived. For our purposes here, the following definitions and distinctions of word usage and meaning apply:

— **Supraliminal** is used to mean *perceivable,* although generally not perceived by the conscious mind. Associations, such as a politician and a baby, and contextual inferences, such as those we draw from seeing the politician with the baby, are examples of supraliminal communication.

— **Subception** refers to something ordinarily *not perceivable* by the conscious mind because of the operation of one or more defense mechanisms. An example is a taboo embed.

— **Subliminal** is that which isn't assessed by the conscious mind because of some technical application that masks its accessibility (unless technical unmasking capabilities are first applied) or in rare instances of certain altered states of consciousness.

— **Supraliminal communication** covers ordinary discourse that may have unconscious elements inherent to it, and **subception communication** covers manipulation of the kind sometimes used by advertisers in print media. Both of these forms of communication are accessible to the trained observer without the technical assistance of special equipment or instruments.

— **Subliminal communication,** then, refers to communication created with technical assistance (that is, with equipment, instruments, or technology in general) that can't be perceived directly by the conscious mind, irrespective of the observer's training or sophistication about such matters. For example, a sound engineer can backmask (play a word, lyric, or phrase backwards) a spoken message in a heavy-metal recording, creating a subliminal stimulus to the listener. In this case, the engineer doesn't possess the conscious ability to perceive the subliminal message in the finished product any more than any other listener without technical assistance from special instrumentation.

The earliest research into subliminal communication may be that of M. Suslowa, who in 1863 demonstrated a discrimination threshold relative to subliminal electrical stimulation. In 1894, W. R. Dunham, M.D., wrote a fascinating commentary on the subliminal mind and subliminal communication that, more than 100 years later, some people still perceive as though it were science fiction.[1]

Current Research

In my earlier books *Subliminal Learning, Subliminal Communication* and *Thinking without Thinking,* I discussed a great deal of the research that was carried out in the area of subliminal communication before the "Judas Priest trial." With the controversy around that case (full details of it are in *Thinking without Thinking* and *Choices and Illusions;* it's also explained in Appendix 5), scientists hesitated to explore this field further. In fact, in a vetted, or refereed, journal article that appeared in *Annals,* the *Journal of the American Psychotherapy Association,* I argued that many academics prevented ambitious young students from researching subliminal-communication theories because of the disinformation that surrounded the Judas Priest matter.[2] I further pointed out that—also contrary to popular opinion among academics and laypeople—no laws prohibit the use of subliminal methods on the public. Additionally, some very different technologies can underlie a subliminal stimulus.[3]

Very recently, however, there's been a resurgence of research in this area, and it's reverifying earlier discoveries. In 2007, the findings of cognitive neuroscientist Ken Paller at Northwestern University demonstrated that facial expressions that aren't noticed consciously do register subliminally. At the time of this writing, these results are scheduled for publication in the *Journal of Cognitive Neuroscience.* In the words of Paller's colleague Wen Li, as quoted by Charles Choi in *Live Science:* "Our results show that an unconsciously perceived signal of threat, such as a brief *facial expression* of fear, can still bubble up and unwittingly influence social judgments and how we act."[4]

According to an article that appeared in *New Scientist* and was posted on **NewScientist.com,** Johan Karremans of the University of Nijmegen in the Netherlands subliminally induced subjects to like a particular drink. Karremans used both thirsty and what one might call regular-thirst subjects and flashed before them the 23-millisecond subliminal message "Lipton Ice." When later asked to choose a drink, both groups significantly favored the Lipton Ice brand beverage; and of the thirsty group, 80 percent chose Lipton Ice. This outcome suggests that the presence of the subliminal message is made stronger or acted upon sooner by a congruent drive (thirst).[5]

A CBC News report from Ontario, Canada, appearing on February 26, 2007, reported the removal of slot machines that allegedly flashed subliminal winning images: "The games flashed winning jackpot symbols at players for a fifth of a second, long enough for the brain to detect even if the players are not aware of the message, some psychologists told CBC News." The company Konami, which produces the slots, claims it's clearly only a "software glitch." CBC News added, "Problem gamblers complain that the machines affect how they think, electronic gaming specialist Horbay said. They can't pinpoint the problem, but 'this may be a part of what they believe is messing up their heads.'"[6]

Researchers at the University of Jerusalem also tested the subliminal impact of flags as symbols. They reported their findings in the *Proceedings of the National Academy of Sciences* in 2007. They found the subliminal "presentation of the Israeli flag was sufficient to make people adopt more moderate views."[7]

Headlines everywhere in March 2008 touted the almost magical effect the Apple logo had on creativity. Professors Gavan Fitzsimmons and Tanya Chartrand of Duke University joined with Grainne Fitzsimmons of Waterloo University, Canada, in this experiment. Subjects were presented subliminally with either the IBM or the Apple logo (the rainbow version) to test the influence of both on creativity. The researchers assumed that the Apple logo would have more creative impact because of the brand's association with creativity, and that's just what they found. In an *Information Week* article, author Thomas Claburn noted: "The findings are sure to spark a resurgence of interest in subliminal marketing because a follow-up test showed that imperceptible exposure to other well-known brands also produced a response in subjects. When shown the Disney channel logo, for example, participants behaved more honestly than those shown the E! Channel logo."[8] (A resurgence? As if the merchandisers had ever stopped using subliminal technology!)

In February 2008, Channel Ten in Australia was investigated for allegedly using subliminal advertising during a music-awards program. Purportedly, "during the October telecast, frames of sponsor logos lasting 1/25 of a second (standard visual subliminal time frame) flashed onto the screen part of the way through each award category. The logos of the programs sponsors—Chupa Chups, KFC, Toyota, BigPond and Olay—also topped and tailed each segment."[9] At this juncture, it's easy to see the advantage that advertisers seek in doing this.

In the UK, a team of researchers from University College in London used brain scans—visual images and functional MRIs—to watch subliminal information as it was processed by their seven subjects. They observed activity in the primary visual cortex when delivering the subliminal information under "easy task" terms (such as picking out the letter *H* from a list of letters). However, they found that in circumstances defined as "more difficult," the findings weren't as pronounced.[10] The article then pointed out that subliminal advertising was banned in the UK but is still permitted in the United States. It closed with comments that essentially assert the following: Okay, now we have absolute physical proof that subliminal messages are processed in the brain—but that doesn't mean they'll influence behavior. (Really, now—do you believe that?)

In two studies carried out in 2000 and 2003, researchers found that sexual response may be caused by unconscious cognitive processing. This may suggest an extra power of the unconscious nature of information processing where subliminal stimuli are concerned. If so, it would only bear out what the ad agencies' research apparently discovered long ago. According to researchers Both, Brauer, Everaerd, and Karsdorp, writing for the *Journal of Sex Research,* "In men, subliminally presented sexual primes facilitated recognition of sexual targets. Without the need of conscious evaluation, sexually competent stimuli activated sexual implicit memory and set up sexual responding."[11] In nonspecialist language, the researchers found that the subliminal presentation of, say, a woman's breast resulted in a sexual response in men.

The study tested the female response to subliminal stimuli as well. The findings were somewhat different, as was the conclusion drawn by the researchers: "It is possible that although implicit information-processing is qualitatively similar for women and men, there is a quantitative difference. Men do seem to be more strongly motivated sexually than women."[12]

In March 2007, Jagdish Sleth, president of the American Psychological Association's Division of Consumer Psychology, stated, "The controversy has always been over changing people's attitudes. That you can't do! What you can do is trigger a prior attitude or disposition." This statement of Sleth's is quoted in what appears to be an Internet advertorial (an advertisement that imitates editorial format). He seemed to be answering whether or not subliminal advertising and subliminal antitheft techniques (termed *gimmicks* in the article) might really work.[13] My question is: What is there about attitudes that says they can't be manipulated?

In his book *The Secret Sales Pitch,* August Bullock reports a study conducted by Gerald Gorn in 1982, in which he demonstrated that pairing music with a product could predispose the consumer's choice.[14] Bullock effectively makes a case in his book for consumer conditioning in a classical-conditioning fashion thoughtfully carried out by advertisers. He puts it this way:

> Naturally, advertisers long to secretly condition us to purchase their products. In an article in the Wall Street Journal, a "communications research manager" working for Coca-Cola was quoted as saying: "We nominate Pavlov as the father of modern advertising. Pavlov took neutral subject and, by associating it with a meaningful object, made it a symbol of something else . . . that is what we try to do."[15]

Subliminals in Politics

I'm sure that I don't need to remind you of the efforts advertisers have taken to exploit subliminal-research findings. However, you should also remember that it's not just products per se that are being sold using these techniques. In the 2000 Presidential elections, there was a great outcry over a Republican commercial that was found to contain the subliminal word *RATS* over Al Gore's face. Many explanations were given, ranging from "It was an accident" to "The RATS was just the tail end of the word DEMOCRATS." The whole incident was made much more of a joke when George Bush wasn't even able to say the word *subliminal* correctly, and the entire matter was put to bed by a comment that went something like: "What's the big deal? It was only one frame of the entire commercial!"

You may be interested to know that during the same time frame, I was approached by a representative of a prominent politician from another country and asked about the use of a subliminal advertisement. After some discussion, I advised the politician to employ subliminal messaging only if the audience was informed. The campaign could use the technique to get attention and place the subliminal message "Be sure to vote" in the ad. This text only encouraged voting, not choosing a specific candidate. The politician chose not to use any subliminal content, or at least not to have my assistance in creating such a program.

But back to the RATS ad, which was selling a President—or selling away from a candidate, if you prefer to see it that way. A follow-up study was conducted to determine how effective the TV spot may have been. Psychologist Joel Weinberger from Adelphi University in Garden City, New York, and his colleague Drew Westen of Emory University in Atlanta developed a questionnaire, which they placed on a Website. In it, they asked visitors to evaluate potential candidates from their pictures. The experimenters flashed one of four sets of letters on the purported candidate's face: *RATS, STAR, ARAB,* and *XXXX.* Subjects were divided into groups by the letter set they received subliminally.

Sid Perkins reported on this study in *Science News Online* in an article titled, "Dirty Rats: Campaign Ad May Have Swayed Voters Subliminally." He stated, "Exposure to RATS had the same negative effect among men and women in the study. In addition, participants who identified themselves as Republicans responded to RATS just as negatively as Democrats did." Further, this study showed that the subliminal influence was stronger when statements that accompanied the candidate's photo were negative.[16]

Similar things are in the news as I write this book. KMSP, a Fox Television affiliate in Minneapolis/St. Paul, showed Barack Obama's face in the background during the story of a terrorist sex offender. The station claims it was some sort of mistake. Also, pictures of John McCain and his wife, Cindy, were recently found embedded in the

Fox News logo. In my opinion, this combination of images can't be an accident—rather, each case is a clear example of subliminal priming. Take a look for yourself and see if you agree. Go to **www.youtube .com** and search for "Who's That Hiding In My Fox 5 News Logo?"

In his book *Subliminal Ad-Ventures in Erotic Art*, Wilson Bryan Key reports several instances of politicians using subliminal techniques, including embedding profane words on candidate posters.[17] The value of pairing (association) is obvious, as is the hazard.

In March 2008, during the hotly contested Democratic-candidate selection process, daily headlines ranged from the hurling of innuendos to character assassinations and other dirty politics between Senators Obama and Clinton. During this month, *Newsweek* published an article titled "The Political Psychology of Race and Gender," a conversation with two men who'd just coauthored a *Law Review* article by the same name. The authors, Cornell law student Gregory Parks and Professor Jeffrey Rachlinski, both hold doctoral degrees in psychology. The article covered a number of issues, but of relevance here is a study cited under the title "American Equals White." Here is Rachlinski:

> And what it (American Equals White study) showed us was that at the implicit level people tend to correlate whiteness with American-ness as opposed to blackness with American-ness. What's more, studies of the 2008 election have shown that when you prime individuals with the images of the American flag—at a subliminal level, so you just flash it for a millisecond—it has a tendency to make white individuals show less liking toward Barack Obama. This harkens back to the question of Obama not wearing the American flag pin and the accusations that he failed to put his hand over his heart during the singing of the national anthem. This stuff is tricky for him especially considering that some opponents are questioning his patriotism.[18]

On the other side of the fence, there was a lot of talk about Republican contender Mike Huckabee and the so-called subliminal cross that was in the background of one of his commercials. In that instance, the cross wasn't actually subliminal, although when viewers focused on his face and his message, it certainly seemed to be. There were many comments from the media pointing out that considering Huckabee's well-known attention to detail, it was unlikely this was just an accident.

Homeland Security

Amidst all of the public denial by various naysayers regarding the use of subliminal technology and other mind-probing or controlling technologies, the public learned in 2007 that the U.S. Department of Homeland Security was testing and perhaps even negotiating to purchase the Mindreader 2.0. This device was developed by a Russian organization through the pioneering work of the late Igor Smirnov and his wife, Elena Rusalkina.

Rusalkina heads the Psychotechnology Research Institute in Moscow. According to Sharon Weinberger, writing for *Wired,* Rusalkina claims that her device is "faster than a polygraph and can be used at airports" to screen terrorists. The device flashes subliminal images behind an apparently innocent computer game. "The underlying premise of the technology is that terrorists would recognize a scrambled terrorist image without even realizing it, and would be betrayed by their subconscious reaction to the picture."[19]

Smirnov was the lead Russian to give recommendations to the FBI during the Waco standoff with David Koresh (see Chapter 6). Weinberger is quick to point out that there are differing opinions about Smirnov's work, the Waco matter, and the Mindreader. Although the writer was unable to obtain comments from the Department of Homeland Security, she pointed out that the contract is imminent, according to those involved. Quoting Geoff Schoenbaum, a neuroscientist at the University of Maryland's School of Medicine, there are doubts as to whether the technology really works. While "there is no question that your brain is able to perceive things below your ability to consciously express or identify," that doesn't mean that there's evidence we "can produce the specificity and sensitivity to pick out a terrorist."[20]

This said, the future of U.S. antiterrorism efforts might be linked—at least in part—to subliminal cues that uncover unconscious motives.

Subliminal Denial

There are literally hundreds more instances that could be cited. (Visit **www.progressiveawareness.org** for over 800 more examples, even though that database hasn't been updated in several years, or have some fun and simply search **www.youtube.com** for *subliminal*.) Yet even with all of the research, many people still argue that subliminal-information processing is a joke. In one such article that appeared in an online issue of *Real Magick,* author Todd Stark said, "Clearly, the published empirical data show that subliminal audio influence is either extremely weak or non-existent. And most of the theoretical rationales for the effect are questionable at best."[21]

Stark's article is just one among many that punctuate the Internet whenever a search for *subliminal* is done. Subliminal—emperor's clothes? Subliminal—just another hoax. Subliminal—a pseudoscience appealing to those with diminished faculties. Once again, I quote the words of Pratkanis and Aronsons, the authors of *Age of Propaganda:* "This time it was linked into New Age beliefs that claim there is a powerful hidden force in the human personality that can be controlled for good by magic, crystals and subliminal commands."[22] What a marvelously well-put positioning statement this is—crystals, magic, and subliminal commands. If you believe in one, by association you must accept the other—at least that's what's implied. This is death by implication—or is it the death of intelligent inquiry by ridicule and laughter?

Perhaps, at least historically, the *Skeptical Enquirer* is the most ardent of the pundits who insist that subliminal communication doesn't work, advertisers don't use it, and self-help applications of the technology are a hoax. But even this science journal, which has a history of debunking many things that were later proven to be true, now admits evidence for behavior changes due to subliminal stimuli. However, this only occurred after the Judas Priest trial.[23] Remember this when you read the next chapter.

Summary

We've looked at just a tiny fraction of the research regarding subliminal communication. I've covered the history of research in my earlier books. The profusion of material that exists today in support of subliminal efficacy claims continues to accumulate. In the next chapter, we'll explore the attempts by some to pass legislation to control the misuse of subliminal communication, or at least to require informed consent.

Controversy continues over this subject. Clearly, motives are attached to nearly all of the various positions, even if the reason is just defense of one's research. The subject of subliminal stimuli isn't always well defined, nor is it linear, which would lend it to a direct in-and-out examination. No, it's more like consciousness itself. The subject is dynamic—a process, a continual process that sometimes lends itself to direct inspection and sometimes acts in a delayed manner. Nevertheless, it should be clear that it's *real*. Subliminal commands aren't the fodder of nonsense, magic, New Age crystals, or the like.

CHAPTER 8

Legal Status of Subliminal Communication

"Punishment is now unfashionable . . . because it creates moral distinctions among men, which, to the democratic mind, are odious. We prefer a meaningless collective guilt to a meaningful individual responsibility."

— Thomas Szasz

Most people assume that laws are in force to protect them against the misuse of subliminal communication. Unfortunately, that's not the case.

Part of the reason for the absence of laws rests with confusion about definitions. In the 1984 congressional hearings on the matter, the only real consensus that was reached suggested that any law written would have to approach the matter as Judge Whitehead did in Reno during the Judas Priest trial—that is, from a standpoint of "informed consent."[1]

Subliminal Perception

Congress called a number of experts to testify in the 1984 hearings. Among the many questions was one that addressed the human "mechanic" involved in processing subliminal information. The prominent assumption was largely based on the work of Benjamin Libet, a researcher at the University of California–San Francisco, who was a pioneering scientist in the field of human consciousness. It's enlightening, to say the least, to look at some of that testimony. In a paper delivered by subliminal researcher and expert Howard Shevrin, who also testified in the Judas Priest case on behalf of the plaintiffs, the nature of the unconscious/subconscious mind was addressed. Shevrin first distinguished the nature of the unconscious as belonging to psychoanalysis and not necessary to the rest of psychology. Moving that construct out of the way, he took a more direct, verifiable approach to the matter. He began with Libet's work:

> In 1967, Libet et al. reported that a somatosensory evoked response can be obtained at the cortex when the subject is stimulated by a sub threshold electrical current to the skin. Although the subject consistently reported no sensation, the evoked potential revealed a decided cortical response. The brain could show cortical responsiveness in the absence of awareness.

Shevrin continued with a lengthy technical discussion based on cortical-response experimentation (the brain responding to stimuli—processing information), showing that research clearly suggested the following:

> If we combine Libet's two findings, the first showing that a cortical primary response is present for a subliminal stimulus and the second that a cortical pulse train is necessary for conscious experience, we conclude that somatosensory stimuli can register cortically without consciousness and that conscious experience itself is a function of some additional system having its own properties.[2]

The Influence on Behavior

Later, before the House Committee on Science and Technology, Shevrin voiced his opinion regarding the potential influence on behavior that subliminal information could have; his answer essentially asserted none. Later, in the Judas Priest matter, Shevrin reversed this position.[3] It is noteworthy that Shevrin had a decade more of research and other findings upon which he could base the testimony he gave in Reno, Nevada.

Dr. Lloyd Silverman, New York University psychologist, also testified before Congress in 1984. Silverman accounted for the processing of subliminal information by drawing on the models from psychotherapy of a dynamic thinking unconscious. His work with symbiotic messages (merging messages) convinced Silverman that subliminal information could and did directly influence behavior.

Although there was divided testimony regarding the effectiveness of subliminal messages, the abiding problem for the legislature was one of the legal and constitutional issues—chiefly the First Amendment.

Legal Definition

In a prepared statement presented at the hearings, the *Southern California Law Review* addressed this issue in context. The authors began by discussing the alleged usage of subliminal messages to sell concession refreshments in 1957 during showings of the movie *Picnic*. From the public outcry that followed to the moral dilemmas of dealing with various forms of behavioral control, the article stated differing points of view. Moral, social, and ethical issues, together with constitutional and legal matters, were eloquently laid out. The writers recognized the difficulty inherent in defining "subliminal perception" and settled on this definition as a general one:

> The process whereby individuals and groups can be presented with the visual and auditory information without their being aware of exposure to this information but to which they make a selective response.[4]

It's key that the definition includes the term *response.* In other words, without a *selective response,* information isn't considered to be a subliminal stimulus.

Legal Conclusions

The testimony continued with a review of scientific literature, ranging from extensive references to the work of Norman Dixon and his research, which clearly demonstrated the influence of subliminal communication on behavior, to the public availability of equipment designed to deliver subliminal content. The legal experts stated that the use of subliminal devices was increasing, and moreover, "recently invented devices were specifically designed not to be detectable."[5]

Their conclusion and suggestion are worth quoting:

> Considerable controversy centers on whether the techniques are capable of inducing behavior or only strengthening behavior to which an individual is predisposed. Nonetheless, several generalizations can be made about the existing research findings.
>
> (1) Individuals are capable of receiving information presented at levels of which they are unaware, and will unconsciously evaluate and react to the content of the information, resisting negative content and more readily accepting positive content. This might suggest that an individual censors subliminal information in the same manner that he censors or evaluates supraliminal information—responding in a predisposed manner so that he is no more easily manipulated or changed than if he had consciously perceived the information. If this is the case, subliminal communication would not be an effective brainwashing technique.
>
> (2) Individuals can be taught new responses at preconscious levels of awareness, and can use subliminal information for more efficient problem solving.
>
> (3) A predisposing behavior or response is not always necessary for effective subliminal suggestion, and certain new responses may be induced. This finding supports the concern that subliminal communication may cause people to do something they otherwise would not have considered—that it "manipulates" rather than "reminds."[6]

The opinion continues with three more points:

(4) Individuals do not react uniformly to subliminal messages presented at the same level of intensity and duration.

(5) Certain personality characteristics may predispose some individuals to be more easily influenced by subliminal suggestions than others.

(6) The effectiveness of subliminal communication may be somewhat dependent upon the motivational and emotional states of the receiver.[7]

First Amendment

In the end, the conclusion pointed out that the central issue was one of protecting autonomy and privacy and further that there existed a First Amendment right to the freedom of thought processes. Case law was reviewed, especially regarding the nature of "ideational content as an aspect of privacy." Finally, the proposal was made to require "full disclosure of the use and content of message"—informed consent.[8]

That's the overview. If you're interested in the full transcript of these hearings—and it's fascinating reading—please see Subliminal Communication Technology, produced by the U.S. House of Representatives.[9]

Informed Consent

Not long after these hearings before the U.S. House of Representatives Committee on Science and Technology, an informed-consent law was introduced in Utah. The year was 1986.

Twenty-two years later, although several states and even the United States Congress have introduced legislation to prohibit subliminal information in public-communication media, no legislation has ever been enacted. In 1986, Representative Frances Merrill of the

Utah House of Representatives initiated legislation to prohibit subliminal communication without informed consent. In other words, just as restaurants used to be required to post notices regarding microwave use, a retailer using antitheft "subliminals," for example, would be required to inform those who might hear the audio programs. Obviously, heavy-metal-music groups using subliminals would also be required to display appropriate notices, as would all other users of such communication.

I was involved in this legislative process, as was my business. I cohosted a radio talk show at the time, and my staff and I took the argument to the airways. In my opinion, not only did an informed-consent law make sense, but it appeared then and now to be the only legal measure likely to be enforceable and not infringe on constitutional freedoms. Perhaps I shouldn't have been as surprised as I found myself on the day we addressed the Utah House committee, but I do remember being almost shocked by the number of professionals representing various interests, including advertising agencies, who showed up to speak against the legislation. What we thought was a local decision apparently had national and even international interest. Speakers from New York argued that the legislation wasn't needed—no one used this technology, it was too expensive, and it didn't work. The committee heard both sides and was pressed by my office and others to at least send the issue to the full House for a vote.

The committee narrowly approved the proposed legislation to go to the House floor, but the House voted it down. To this date, there still exists no legal protection against subliminal invasion of privacy.

Subliminal Patents

There's no limit to the devices of subliminal communication that might be the subject of regulation. More than 100 patents have been approved by the U.S. Patent Office, and my patent is just one of them. Some of these devices add subliminal content to ambient background sounds; some track specific sound patterns or sound tracks; and some inject visual or audio material and project it through similar media, such as the television set. There are devices to add subliminal content to in-store music systems and devices that flash images onto anything and can be controlled according to light strength, such as wattage output; others automatically adjust to the candlepower in the room, delivering subliminal information at a slightly lower candle watt power, and on and on. There are tools for your computer, to record audio and video media, to impress print media, and more . . . so many devices, and no laws to punish irresponsible use of them.

A Federal Communications Commission (FCC) codification does prohibit subliminal content. It essentially is a warning to broadcasters (and I'm told by the powers that be that technically the FCC could pull a broadcaster's license for violation), but then there's the whole matter of discovery. For example, when a television station broadcast a toy advertisement with subliminal messages that were delivered slightly out of sync, the hidden directive became obvious: "Tell Mom, buy now." Concerned citizens complained, but everyone denied creating this message.

Without the power of discovery, where to next? In other words, without a punitive description in a penal code, it all comes down to cooperation. What technically *might be* pursued and what practically *is* pursued are generally not the same. We do know that in the case of the ad just mentioned, nothing happened. For that matter, when the Bush campaign admitted to the RATS in DemocRATS as a deliberate act, no legal action was taken.

It may make you feel warm and cozy to think that laws prevent the invasion of your private thoughts, but the fact is quite different— at least in practice.

Summary

Worries regarding the misuse of subliminal communication have varied since 1953. Concerned individuals have pushed for stringent controls, and many bills have been proposed. None have been passed.

Despite the efforts of many people over five decades, no laws exist to control subliminal communication. Not until 1990 was there a proposed precedent to protect subliminal communication as free speech under the First Amendment. This catch-22 interpretation of our 18th-century document seems to have been defeated. It could still cause obstacles to future regulation.

Many problems are inherent in regulating subliminal communication. Enforcing such regulations could prove both cumbersome and expensive, and attempts at regulation have generally failed.

---CHAPTER 9---

The MIP Paradigm and Reverse Speech

*"Research is to see what everybody else has seen,
and to think what nobody else has thought."*

— **Albert Szent-Györgyi**

One reason so much controversy surrounds subliminal communication is that various methods are used to create it. There are also many subliminal audio self-help programs on the market that simply don't work because of gross errors in how they were created, ranging from affirmations in the second person (rather than first person) to embedding the affirmations so far beneath the primary carrier that they are, for all practical purposes, not there.

Because I do believe that subliminal self-help programs are some of the most powerful mind-training tools available, I'd like to share with you some of the theory behind the development of my InnerTalk programs.

My own research has evaluated audio subliminal messages using the particular method I originally patented in 1988. Known as the "Taylor Method" (or, in the patent, as the "Whole Brain Subliminal

Method") and now more commonly referred to as InnerTalk, it differs some from other audio methods. This isn't to say that there are no other audio methods that could work; rather, I only mean to differentiate the technology from those in the "Effect of Labels" study designed by Eric Spangenberg and presented as proof that subliminal audio messages didn't work during the Judas Priest matter. I'll give you a brief overview of the study here; full details may be found in *Choices and Illusions*.

The Spangenberg Study

In this study, a doctoral student set up a research project using subliminal audiotapes from five different companies. There were two kinds of tapes, one to improve memory and one to build esteem. The labels were switched, however, so that the esteem tapes were labeled "Memory," and vice versa. After the testing period, subjects were evaluated for actual improvement. Those who thought they were playing memory subliminal messages reported an improvement in memory, and those who believed they were listening to esteem messages reported an increase in esteem. The instruments failed to identify a statistically meaningful change in either. It's fair enough, at this point, to state a definite label influence, but how about a real effect regarding subliminal communication?

The five tape companies all claimed different methods and messages for their programs, including messages in both the second person and first person. Audio analysis failed to recover messages on any of the programs. Some companies used questionable affirmations and in other ways produced material that differentiated one product from another. All shared the label "subliminal," but that certainly didn't mean they were the same.

So we're not looking at a scientific study with a single variable. We're mixing multiple variables and coming up with a single conclusion —and that simply isn't good science!

InnerTalk®

But back to InnerTalk. Briefly described, this method masks itself with forward spoken messages on one channel and reverse spoken messages on the opposing channel. The channel differentiation is directed at hemispheres of the brain according to their primary information-processing task. This means using a device that converts an audio signal into an electric one and tracking two audio signals as electric signals and locking them into a precise gain ratio. In this way, the signal strength of the subliminal message can be made much stronger than in typical *burying* procedures, where the subliminal may be as much as 60 to 80 decibels beneath the primary carrier (the outer sound pattern, such as ocean sounds, music, a babbling brook, and the like).

Employed in the aforementioned way, the signal strength is hardier, and indeed, most listeners report hearing what sounds like voices off in the distance, but they're unable to tell exactly what's being said. This is the reason why some critics have referred to what I do as "un-subliminal."

Using channel differentiation makes it possible for a dichotic delivery, which typically delivers one message in forward speech on the right channel, aimed at the left hemisphere; that message is permissive, such as "It's okay to be good." At the same time on the left channel, aimed at the right hemisphere (for most right-handed people), is the authoritarian message: "I am good."

I originally theorized, and research has borne out, that if people simply tell themselves: "I am good," the left hemisphere, home to logic, reason, and many defense mechanisms, will come back with something such as: "Yeah, sure. Good for what?"

The idea behind subliminal messages is to bypass critical consciousness and prime self-talk. That is, we want the messages/affirmations to come from the inside out. Because we tend to give more credibility to our own thoughts than to the thoughts of others, this method can ultimately teach optimism and put an end to the self-defeating self-talk that so many people allow to limit their realities.

That basically sums up the InnerTalk technology, but let's look at some of the research from which I derived my conclusions. If you aren't interested in the technical aspects of the research, you may choose to skip this section and pick up on some of the independent research and the results obtained using InnerTalk as outlined at the end of this chapter.

The Taylor Method

InnerTalk delivers forward and reverse speech simultaneously, distinguished by channel differentiation and delivered at a level of sound within the bandwidth of liminal sound information. The delivery of information is out of phase. (Both speakers are not *pushing* together but may be *pushing* and *pulling*. Full technical details are available in U.S. patent number 5,170,381.) This method allows the easy detection of the subliminal on home-stereo equipment. The same information goes unreported by the listener when played normally. Many independent researchers have demonstrated this method as being effective in a variety of settings, as you'll see toward the end of this chapter (Roche, 1993[1]; Plante, 1993[2]; Ashley, 1993[3]; Isaacs, 1991[4]; Pelka, 1991[5]; Kruse, 1991[6]; Galbraith & Barton, 1990[7]; and Reid, 1990[8]). To this I can add my own studies, double-blind and clinical (Taylor, 1986[9], 1990[10], and 1991[11]). It has been called the "un-subliminal" method (Moore, 1990).[12] Others have used it to support subliminal theory (Urban, 1992).[13]

The method evolved from work in my lab that began in 1982. Many of the concepts derive from studies of brain laterality and hemispheric function, viewed through the holographic models of Karl Pribram.[14] I published my first description of the method and then patented it in 1987. Professor Peter Kruse of Bremen University dubbed it the "Taylor Method," so as to differentiate it from other subliminal technologies and stated: "The Taylor Method works!" [15]

In an unpublished paper, I proposed mirror-image processing (MIP) as a working model to describe a key element of my patent.[16] Research has shown that the brain can process information presented in reverse.[17] The original theory behind InnerTalk viewed the perception of information reversed in any way as analogous to "up-righting" visual information that was presented upside down.

What follows is the history behind the development of InnerTalk, and a complete discussion of the theoretical and mechanical nature of the method.

History

My study of information processing actually began with sales, and my first look into the mechanics of the brain came with required courses in college. My personal interest grew when my oldest daughter, Angela, entered school.

Angela had some difficulties, and her first-grade teacher called her dyslexic. Her dyslexia seemed mild and something she might outgrow. We worked with her to help her overcome it.

She copied letters and integers from a written example, often producing various mirror images of these symbols. That struck me as something that I could only do with difficulty. The S's especially intrigued me because they were perfect.

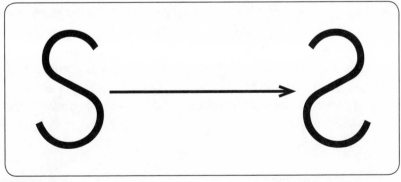

Figure 9

As I worked with Angela, it became apparent that both her choice of hand and eye altered, if only slightly, the nature of reversed characters in her writing. Closing an eye or changing hands resulted in different writing, different kinds of mistakes. In time, she outgrew her dyslexia, and I basically lost interest in the issue. I kept some of my notes, but I went on with other matters in my life.

Subconscious Cerebration

In 1981, I attended a hypnosis course in Chicago led by Harry Arons. Harry emphatically maintained that the brain processed information, in part, by a sort of tumbling. He maintained that this must actually take place in some physical part of the brain, and he compared the action to a dice tumbler. He described the tumbling as part of a process he called "subconscious cerebration." Hence, words— and even letters of words—became mixed, reversed, and jumbled. This mixing would normally occur entirely unconsciously.

Words could, as a result of the tumbling process, recombine into other sentences, which could alter the meaning of the statement entirely. Sentences required careful construction to avoid unwanted transformations. This notion was particularly interesting to me.

Arons used the example of affirmations. An affirmation for reducing cigarette smoking could go something like this: "I find 10 cigarettes a day more than enough for me." Arons suggested that this seemingly helpful phrase could recombine to state: "I find more than 10 cigarettes enough for me."

This idea seemed odd. I had no reason to disbelieve the man. Nevertheless, how and why the brain functioned in this process puzzled me. I began listing related correspondences between accepted theories and anomalies of the models of information processing and the observed world.

Hemispheric Mirroring

By 1984, I'd become convinced that the hemispheres of the brain functionally mirrored each other in many unexplored aspects. These certainly included learning processes relative to the development of logic and reason (especially affective orientations) and language and mathematical propositions (especially three-dimensional math models).

In 1985, I encountered the book *The Holographic Paradigm and Other Paradoxes*. The work of Karl Pribram and David Bohm attracted me.[18] The physics of the world appeared to match the mechanics of the brain and even metaphysics. Suddenly—for me, at least—the model of hemispheric mirroring came into focus. Within me grew a certainty and intuitive clarity that I didn't have a clue how to demonstrate objectively. In 1987, with reckless abandon, I put the idea of holographic information processing in my book *Subliminal Learning: An Eclectic Approach*.

The Holographic Brain

As stated earlier, many of the theoretical underpinnings for the Taylor Method derive from hemispheric laterality and function studies viewed through the holographic models of Karl Pribram.[19] He's proposed that the brain stores memory holographically through resonated modulating frequencies. The holographic model of the physical universe suggested by David Bohm has a similar structure.[20] The holographic MIP model could explain anomalies in memory storage, as well as failure to retrieve or access memory. This seems obvious in cases of overstimulation, such as those demonstrated in the classic B. F. Skinner "maze bright rat" experiments.[21]

The interface of parallel processing models observed from positron-emission tomography (PET) scan analysis, which I discussed as holonomic information processing, also applies here.[22] PET-scan analysis appears to accurately trace the epicenter(s) of stimuli events. From these epicenters, which correspond with and form a part of the hemispheric asymmetry observations, stimulus information spreads out via frequency modulation. It's possible that this storage system spreads even beyond the brain to what's called the "zero-point field." Theoretically, this field is the unifying force that underlies the potential and existence of the universe. (For an interesting read and more information, see *The Field* by Lynne McTaggart).[23]

Hemispheric Laterality

The MIP model itself also derives from work in hemispheric asymmetry. Early work with split-brain patients demonstrated marked differences in cerebral cortical hemispheric functions relative to dominant (D) and nondominant (ND) hemispheres.[24]

By the early 1980s, psychological literature proliferated with task-relative functions differentiated by D and ND delineations. The lists generally label D as the left hemisphere and ND as the right hemisphere for typical right-handers. They attributed a host of tasks to primary hemispheric functions. Typically, the tasks divided as linear-deductive versus gestalt-holistic processes. The brain hemispheres show a distinct anatomical separation, and they demonstrate equally marked functional separation, as E. Zaidel concluded.[25] The dichotomies just mentioned display that separation.

Zaidel portrays the speech and language functions of the two hemispheres with D as adult brain and ND as a three- to six-year-old child's brain.[26] S. Blumstein and W. Cooper demonstrated that the ND side's activity increased when intonation was increased in human speech.[27] E. Ross asserts that the posterior ND hemisphere is responsible for the comprehension of intonation, and the anterior ND hemisphere controls the production of speech.[28]

One of the pioneers of hemispheric functional specificity is Robert Ornstein, who has studied hemispheric asymmetry and its relationship to consciousness. He believes that the highest functions of the human condition come about only with the development of both hemispheres. He suggested that Western society placed so much emphasis on the D hemisphere that its ability to grasp "wholes" had given way to fragmentation.[29] (It should be noted that many of Ornstein's original ideas regarding hemispheric specialties have changed over time but more in the strict sense than in the generalized perspective).

In other words, we lost the forest for the leaves and gave up the whole world in favor of reductionist examination and evaluation of the parts. Ornstein originally identified this dichotomy as comparable to the differences between thinking styles of the East and the West.[30]

Dyslexia

A discovery reported by M. Ferguson demonstrated that auditory laterality played a role in childhood dyslexia. Ferguson reported from the work of Kjeld Johansen that "reading-disabled youngsters showed much weaker than normal bias toward the right ear, which is connected to the verbally dominant left hemisphere."[31] This information isn't new. Still, Johansen used it to confirm earlier work. He suggested that concentrated follow-up in this area of understanding is long overdue.[32]

Dyslexia was one of the first areas studied through dichotic (one or the other) listening procedures.[33] It was also a candidate for subliminal presentations that were lateralized through tachistoscopic technology (this employs an apparatus that briefly exposes visual stimuli and is used in the study of learning, attention, and perception). Although this work remains controversial, it still led S. Springer and G. Deutsch to conclude that some peculiarity of hemispheric asymmetry did play a role in dyslexia.[34]

Springer and Deutsch also reviewed the data regarding anatomical asymmetries in dyslexics, and they found a positive correlation between handedness, hemispheric asymmetries, and dyslexias. They cautioned against overgeneralization, however, and suggested, "The reversal (of brain-asymmetry) interacts with other factors to produce dyslexia."[35]

Samuel T. Orton suggested a model of reading disability (dyslexia) as a "failure of dominance" by the D hemisphere.[36] He assumed that weak cerebral dominance caused dyslexia. Although his original model didn't hold up under scientific scrutiny in its generalization about the cause of all dyslexias, it nevertheless offers a functional mechanical model that hasn't yet been proven wrong. Some of Orton's assumptions may have strayed, but the viability of the model itself remains. This key distinction becomes even more important in the context of the MIP paradigm.

Orton studied hemispheric asymmetry largely in the areas of dyslexia and stuttering. He thought that hemispheric competition for control of speech caused this dysfunction. His model of information processing and hemispheric asymmetry assumed that we represent visual information in "opposite orientations in the two hemispheres."[37] Orton proposed the upside-down to right-side up visual correction as being mechanically a mirroring process (see Figure 10).[38]

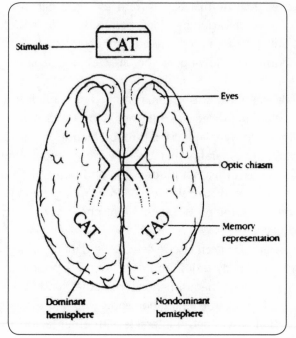

Figure 10

Consequently, a more accurate pictorial representation of the MIP holographic model is shown in Figure 11.

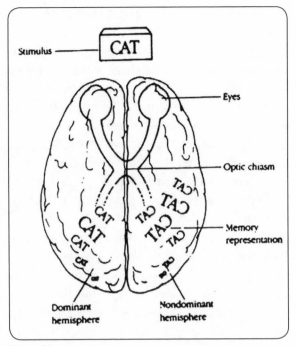

Figure 11

Orton coined the term *strepbosymbolia* to describe the condition proposed when the mirroring process seemed incomplete or absent due to a "sufficiently developed cerebral dominance . . . one normally oriented and one reversed."[39]

Reverse Speech

David Oates insists that all speech contains meaningful reversals. Apparently, the subconscious can communicate in this way. Over a six-year period, he meticulously assembled recordings and reversed them for backward-speech analysis. Repeatedly, he observed meaningful reversals, which usually complement or contradict the content of the forward speech. A statement such as "I left work and went to the grocery store" might contain a complementary message such as "loaf of bread." Such reversals add information relevant to the forward message. A contradictory message might say, "Hate it" in a forward message stating: "It's really okay."[40]

I've also come across this phenomenon. In 1984, I examined recordings from a lie-detection test that involved manually reversing audiotape across the play heads of a reel-to-reel recorder in an attempt to isolate a specific response. As I dragged the tape in reverse, I heard the word *liar*. It was spoken clearly, and later, others easily demonstrated this for themselves. In forward response, the examinee simply said, "No." In reverse, this "No" contained "Liar." The charts also clearly demonstrated distress indicative of deception. The examinee later verified this deception by confessing. If Oates was correct, this incident wasn't a fluke.

Oates also reported that in addition to the forensic applications of the reversal phenomenon, therapists had been successful at finding underpinning traumas from recordings of patients. One example offered described a woman who went to her therapist for reasons substantially different from the sexual abuse discovered in her speech reversals.[41]

Of greatest significance for us, Oates played tapes backward at about a 20 percent reduction in speed. The sounds made by a child during the stage between gurgling and meaningful speech contained reversals such as "Daddy play?" "Mama home?" and so forth.[42]

Apparently, in first learning to talk, we generate reversed speech. Most of us create this reversal in the right hemisphere. As mentioned earlier, clinical data that I assembled supported this hypothesis.[43]

I spent years doing voice-stress analysis, specifically looking at the presence of a microtremor that exists at about eight cycles per second. It persists as long as the autonomic nervous system functions relatively stress free. When distress occurs, this microtremor disappears. Many times the "giveaway voice crack" happens at times of distress. The left hemisphere attends to the rules of sentence structure, tense, word choice, logic . . . so does the right hemisphere form the affect structure of speech?

Just as speech suggests an interplay of hemispheres, graphological (handwriting) reversals require some such explanation.[44] Hypnotic and parapsychological literature have often reported backward writing. Holding this script to a mirror provides clear interpretation. Left-hemisphere activity declines during trance, and this seems to be another example of brain reversal. Is the critical mind (left hemisphere) in abeyance? During religious worship of a cathartic type, many people have spoken in tongues. How much of this actually connects with speech reversals, as suggested by Oates?[45]

The implications of speech reversals occurring without the speaker's knowledge (at least consciously) are as staggering as the list of corresponding observations is long. Prior to hearing of Oates's findings, I viewed reverse-speech information from an intake-only perspective. Did the brain make intelligibly meaningful translations of reverse speech? Some articles argued "Absolutely not!"[46]

The studies tested conscious evaluations of the reverse information. They could have tested presentation of reverse speech via an instrument, such as thematic apperception testing designed to detect unconscious *tumbling* and response (right hemisphere). Instead they chose to evaluate consciously recognized meaning (left hemisphere), immediately following the reverse-speech presentation. Given the MIP model, this type of design has little if any value, and the conclusions derived from it are invalid.

How InnerTalk Works

Now we have at least a theoretical understanding of my approach. Let's review the essentials. What happens in the average human brain? It receives sensory stimuli, and the Dominant (D) hemisphere generates a stable representation. The Nondominant (ND) hemisphere generates counter-representations. These may match previously established representations (beliefs). By resonance, in the holograph metaphor, a counter-representation could trigger matching representations in the whole brain. The combination of counter-representation and established representation could overwhelm the current D representation.

Affirmations give a simple example of how this works. When I say "I forgive . . . ," I already remember people whom I haven't forgiven yet. Affirmations seem to work well to establish beliefs that we haven't yet released. Alternatively, an affirmation also helps reveal beliefs that block us. Once discovered, we can use effective means of working on them.

In the case of reverse speech, the D hemisphere attaches no meaning to it. The ND hemisphere, as always, generates counter-representations. One of the simplest of these, reversal in time, does have meaning. This counter-representation doesn't have sufficient signal strength to enter consciousness or to stimulate counter-counter-representation. Hence, repetition can establish a representation (belief) without disturbing consciousness or generating contradictory representations.

InnerTalk applies simultaneous information of both forward and reverse speech. It delivers on the left channel (to the right hemisphere) an authoritarian statement such as "I am good," while delivering on the right channel a permissive corollary statement such as "It's okay to be good." I chose to use and subsequently patented this simultaneous delivery for several reasons. The top two are:

1. Both halves of the brain are addressed in the manner most appropriate—that is, permissive or authoritarian—the left brain being the center for logic and reason while the right brain is the creative, artistic center.[47]

2. Just as thinking is slowed down when both halves of the brain are being tasked, as seen in the Stroop effect, so the subject is less likely to hear speech, even though the messages are easily detectable on home-stereo equipment. (The Stroop test prints the names of various colors in colors that don't correspond to the name of the color. For example, the word *yellow* would be printed in green ink, the word *blue* printed in red ink, and so forth. If you'd like to try this test for yourself, please go to **www.eldontaylor .com/mindprogramming.html**.)

The recording delivers these messages within the bandwidth of the music and nature sound track, slightly beneath the peak volume of the outer edge. On a good stereo, you can reveal the subliminals: simply pan the speaker balance to full right, eliminate the equalizer bands on everything but 500k and 1k, and increase those two frequency ranges to the maximum. You can easily detect the voices speaking the messages.

I opt for a definition of *subliminal* that has pragmatic value. The value of subliminal information is, and always was, to deliver information without conscious interference. Many have eloquently argued for the advantages. I refer you to Norman Dixon (1991) for more regarding the strategies and rewards inherent in subliminally presented information.[48]

InnerTalk Research Findings

Let's now focus on the research findings and what they suggest with respect to behavior using InnerTalk. I should explain that many of the studies that follow were conducted by independent researchers in distant facilities (such as universities), and my role was simply providing a subliminal audio recording and a placebo audio recording. In most cases, the placebo audio program contained a benign subliminal message such as "People are walking," for the simple reason that using this technology often does give rise to some voice detection, albeit nondiscriminated detection. (The studies that follow are described in more detail in Appendix 1.)

One of my first studies with this technology was in the Utah State Prison. This was a life-changing study for me, for it not only launched a new career path but also marked the beginning of a new way of living. The study demonstrated the importance of forgiveness in liberating self-improvement in any sense. (This study is covered in more detail in earlier publications, and more information appears in Appendix 1.) For now, let me emphasize that not only was the intervention effective but I learned that forgiveness is the most powerful and absolute prerequisite mental shift necessary to empowering our potential. (I'll discuss this more in Chapter 12.)

From there, I moved to the influence of InnerTalk on stress. Two students (P. Galbraith and B. Barton) from Weber State University, my undergraduate alma mater, sought to test my new technology as an aid to reducing stress. The State Trait Anxiety Inventory was used as the instrument of measurement. The subjects who used the InnerTalk program experienced a significant decrease in stress.[49]

From Weber State, the material went to Colorado State University, where James Joseph Reid conducted a double-blind study with depressed subjects. The conclusion indicated no meaningful findings for subjects who used the program fewer than 17 hours. However, all subjects who used the program during the 60-day study for more than 17 hours demonstrated marked differences on the Beck Depression Inventory (an average score lowering of 10 points). This study not only demonstrated efficacy of the InnerTalk subliminal as an adjunct to therapy, but further suggests a dosage relevancy.[50]

From the university environment to the operating room: another study explored the effect of subliminal auditory stimuli in lowering anesthetic requirements in surgery. This research involved 720 patients and was carried out by Robert Youngblood's surgical team. (Dr. Youngblood is a plastic surgeon in Salt Lake City, UT). An audio subliminal program was designed specifically to lower stress levels before, during, and after surgery. Half the patients (360) formed a control group. The other 360 patients listened to the subliminal recording for three relevant hours. All subjects were advised that a "positive message" subliminal would be played pre-operatively, intra-operatively and post-operatively. The programs were used for an average of three relevant hours by the patients. Results indicate that verbal messages presented subliminally did lower anesthetic requirements during surgery by 32 percent.[51]

Perceptual instability was evaluated by Professor Peter Kruse of Bremen University in Germany. This study examined the theory of intrusion effects on cognitive processes as a mechanistic element involved in preconscious processing (subliminal perception). The study's findings suggest that one's perception along value lines can be manipulated by subliminal stimuli.[52]

Also in Germany, working from the Federal Armed Forces University in Munich, Professor Rainier B. Pelka tested the effects of subliminal messages on weight control. Thirty-four female subjects were used, aged between 24 and 49 years. Approximately 25 percent of them were under medical treatment specifically for weight problems. During the experiment, the subjects made no changes to their normal diets or to the amount of exercise undertaken. There was an average weight loss of 6.4 kilograms after an average InnerTalk usage of nine weeks. The subjects also reported feeling slim, vital, and fit.[53]

T. G. Plante, B. T. Doan, M. P. DiGregorio, and G. M. Manuel of Stanford University and Santa Clara University looked at the effect of InnerTalk on subjects with test anxiety. This study sought to examine and compare the effect of brief aerobic exercise and relaxation training using the InnerTalk subliminal program entitled *I Excel in Exams* and *Breathing* by New Harbinger Publications. A total of 52 subjects were included in the study, and they were randomly assigned to one of three conditions: aerobic exercise, relaxation training, or control (magazine reading). The data demonstrated the effectiveness of a subliminal message to reduce test anxiety.[54]

Kim Roche of Phoenix University in Arizona tested the use of InnerTalk subliminal messages on children with ADD and ADHD in a double-blind experiment. The findings indicated a significantly positive effect.[55]

In a study that I conducted, a cancer-remission audio subliminal program was designed and made available to cancer patients through consent and concurrent care of their physician. A follow-up with subjects who had received the tape was conducted by mail. Initial findings, generalized, consist of the following observations:

1. The average patient outlived his or her original prognosis in excess of 12 months (extremes were three years and 6 months), and ratings by the physicians indicated positive correlations between the audio subliminal and the patient's attitude toward his or her disease.

2. Attitudes of the physicians are suggestive of patient outcome, according to early correlations between mortality rates and physician attitude.

3. Of the patients who used the program, 43 percent went into remission.

The questionnaire developed for this study was designed to evaluate four categories:

1. Patient attitude (pre- and post-program usage)
2. Quality of life experienced by patient
3. Remission/survivability
4. Physician attitude

A number of additional studies have demonstrated the effectiveness of using InnerTalk subliminal messages in a variety of domains, including in such areas as procrastination, time management, self-confidence, anxiety, positive relationships, assertiveness, self-esteem, and more. (See Appendix 1 for more or log on to **www.progressiveawareness.org** for these and hundreds of other studies provided in the online version of the *Clinician's Desk Reference*.)

Under the Influence?

This bit of a history should make it clear that I know firsthand that subliminal information is processed and acted upon. This doesn't mean that all subliminal, supraliminal, and similar stimuli are the "same" or, as we've seen, even that everything labeled "subliminal" works. Still, it's fair to ask the big question: "How much of this stuff is influencing me now?"

The fact is that no one can be absolutely certain of the answer, for the mind is far too complicated to make this kind of calculation. We can be certain that in the aggregate, there *is* an influence. It's much easier for each of us as individuals to listen to our own self-talk, hear our own evaluations of beliefs and attitudes, pay attention to what we want and why, and notice what we want but just never seem quite able to obtain. While in some ways it's almost impossible for us to be our own psychotherapists, it's nevertheless incumbent on each of us to get to know ourselves in a much deeper and more meaningful manner than unfortunately is typical in our day and time.

I do think that most of us absolutely have the power and ability to fathom our inner dimensions in ways that can set us free. Some things may be difficult to process at first, but once we recognize them, they can be released. Take, for example, people who discover that they're truly selfish and self-centered. They generally either blame or ignore others and their feelings. Once the revelation occurs, however, a fundamental inner shift occurs, regarding how they see themselves and how they interpret others. The transformation may not be total, but it nevertheless is a change.

Evaluating what we seek—and why—is one good way to uncover more information about ourselves, as well as how much influence various persuasion devices have had upon us. Let's assume, however, that you decide to turn the tables and use these devices to train your own beliefs and expectations. So you get a subliminal program or a hypnosis recording, or you try some other self-improvement tool. What should you expect?

What to Expect When Working with InnerTalk

We are who we are in part because of accumulation. We've accumulated jargon such as "Go ahead and make my day." We add body language to this jargon, and we have potential hostility. Our vocabulary may include pickup lines, and our body language responds accordingly —it's not hostility oriented when we're using such come-ons, but something quite different. I could go on, but the point is obvious: we all have scripts that activate body language and facial expressions and otherwise set up a given possibility, even if the scenario is only rehearsed in front of a mirror. This fantasizing and practicing of scripts can almost overtake the real person. In other words, will the real you please stand up?

Given that we've accumulated, rehearsed, and otherwise practiced our scripts, jargon, actions, and so forth, it should come as no surprise that we may not be able to change them instantly. Ah, but we live in a world that seeks instant everything: instant pudding, instant rice, instant oatmeal, instant satisfaction. Instant—or faster—is fine. So we have those seeking that fifth drive, *more,* and doing so with an expectation of *instant* results. It's no wonder that so many people just keep right on looking. Nothing seems to work for them, for their need for gratification is instant; but change doesn't lend itself to instant anything.

I'll return to this notion of instant gratification in a moment, but something else about our expectations should be examined at this point. I'm reminded of a time in Mexico City that was most instructive for me. I'd just finished a presentation and opened the floor for questions when a woman stood up. I called on her, and she explained that she'd purchased a subliminal InnerTalk program (one of my products), and it didn't work. She'd played it over and over for at least an hour each day, usually for two or more hours, for 30 days without success.

I asked her for the name of the program and discovered that it was called *Creative Writing.* I then asked what she did for a living and learned that she was a writer. Indeed, she wrote a daily column for the newspaper, and she'd written several books and articles. In fact, she was a pretty well-known author.

I asked her exactly what she thought she was getting when she purchased the *Creative Writing* program. She answered, "More creativity—more writing ideas."

I asked whether she'd read the affirmations that came with the program, and she had. I then asked if there were any statements among those affirmations that she didn't already believe—truly believe deep down inside. Her answer? "No."

So there I had an instance where the program could in no way benefit the subject. Imagine that you were a devout vegetarian, and I gave you a program designed to help you be a vegetarian. How much change would you see?

Instant Gratification

The writer did understand, so she worked with a different program and enjoyed success with it, but there's something else here, which brings us back to the topic of instant gratification.

I've seen lots of people respond almost instantly to many programs. I've heard how their lifetime of headaches disappeared overnight, how little Johnny stopped wetting the bed in less than a week, how they stopped chewing their nails the first day, how others have lost weight, stopped smoking, and much more—and all very quickly. Sometimes these reports are as a result of a hypnosis program, sometimes a subliminal recording, and sometimes an audible coaching program, but my point is simple: although such things happen, they aren't typical (if there is such a thing). No, generally the change is gradual, and it happens over time.

Priming Self Talk

Let's review what an audio subliminal self-help program is designed to do and what we can expect from it. The best we can anticipate is that the affirmations will prime our inner talk. In other words, the affirmations will find themselves expressed in our thoughts, our self-talk. For example, take a weight-loss program. The affirmations might include statements such as "I like water, I drink water, I like fresh fruit and vegetables, I like exercise, I leave food on my plate," and so forth. These are obviously designed to make changes in how we view and use food, as well as what we might normally eat. Thus, it suggests vegetables, fruit, water—and lots of it, for it's both filling and cleansing, to say nothing of how much better it may be than so many alternatives—and finally, exercise.

The statements prime our self-talk, until we get the thoughts that might go something like this: *I like water. Yes, I really do. I think I will get some now.* What we observe changing first might be a subtle increase in the amount of water consumed. In short, no miracles. The weight took years to gain, and losing it responsibly and for good won't provide immediate or instant gratification. If our expectation is something along the lines that in 30 days, all that excess weight will be gone, then the expectation won't be met, for that's simply unreasonable. Alternatively, if we realize that our behaviors and attitudes will have to shift first, then we'll probably also notice that changes begin to accumulate—gradually at first, but most certainly increasing over time.

Expectations for other forms of persuasion run along the same lines. You may try a hypnosis recording and, when it's over, feel that you simply drifted off: "How boring. That will never work—I just fell asleep." The fact is that most people think they nodded off the first few times they experience hypnosis, unless it's with a therapist who takes steps both to suggest that they may feel this way and to provide so-called clinchers, such as cataleptic tests on isolated muscle groups. Good hypnotists explain everything that they know the subjects will probably experience, if only to deepen the hypnosis as a result of the subjects' experiencing exactly what they're told. Often, this form of suggestion takes on a certain double-bind characteristic that bypasses critical awareness, such as with the magnetic dialogue discussed earlier in the book.

The Influence of Suggestion

Understanding the influence of suggestion—our own via our expectations and beliefs or those of others who apply the overt and covert technologies that induce our compliance—is paramount to understanding ourselves and how much we operate under others' influence without our awareness.

You deserve at least to exist as you choose, insofar as that's possible. Your mind is yours! You can, and probably have, been played in ways you didn't even realize were possible before you read this book. Still, within you is that power and ability I spoke of earlier that can lift you by the proverbial bootstraps out of the quagmire that you may find yourself in when you stop and look at what your life has meant and what you've done with it.

In the end, we're much more than consumers, vacuuming up every little this and that while we otherwise chase our tails. So for me, as Fox News broadcaster Bill O'Reilly would say in the "no spin zone," the tail chasing stops here—and I hope it stops for you, too!

Summary

Mirrored information processing (MIP) is a model for how data is treated in the human brain. It's contributed to understanding more fully how we process, learn, remember, and create information; and its predictions about how we respond to language have passed extensive testing. It's possible that some alternative model will better explain these results. Meanwhile—and regardless of what may be learned in the future—the simultaneous delivery of reverse and forward speech for presenting subliminal information has proven itself effective for many goals in personal development.

Reasonable expectations should accompany the use of persuasion tools for self-improvement. Understanding how a technology works can facilitate judging your progress as you employ that technology. Remember, change doesn't come instantly.

CHAPTER 10

Undetectable Information

*"If the grace of God miraculously operates, it
probably operates through the subliminal door."*

—William James

The usual definition for *subliminal information* is "data that's present and detectable, although normally unnoticed." However, two forms of subliminal delivery systems present silent information. Both of these methods appear to be without sound and to be undetectable by any normal standard. Beyond that, they differ greatly in many ways. This chapter speculates on these genuinely inaudible and invisible means of information delivery.

Silent Messages

The idea of a truly silent subliminal invites some confusion. Such recordings allegedly have verbal information on them. They claim to play *frequency modulated* (fm) sound in an inaudible range. Consequently the program, when played, makes no sound. You hear exactly the same thing that you'd hear if you played a blank CD.

According to proponents of silent subliminal programs, the sub-conscious detects, processes, and acts on the information. I've heard of studies purportedly demonstrating this influence. I've tried to get my hands on them, but I've yet to see one.

What *does* exist is evidence that humans process information out-side the range of hearing. For example, silent dog whistles have been paired with electric shock to demonstrate classical conditioning. Blow the whistle and deliver the shock; and after a certain number of rep-etitions, when you blow the whistle, the hand jerks in anticipation of electric shock. Although processing a frequency isn't the same as processing linguistic information, the frequency itself may be more important than any verbal content, as you've already seen.

I decided to run my own experiment, which employed a simple "danger" subliminal message. (A subliminal audio program was cre-ated, using the message "Danger—danger—watch out—danger!" at specific intervals.) The actual study demonstrated autonomic responses consistent with the fight-or-flight responses people would expect if they suddenly heard the message audibly.

The chart in Figure 12 is from a subject who listened only to ocean sounds, whereas the chart in Figure 13 is from a subject who listened to ocean sounds with the "danger" subliminal message.

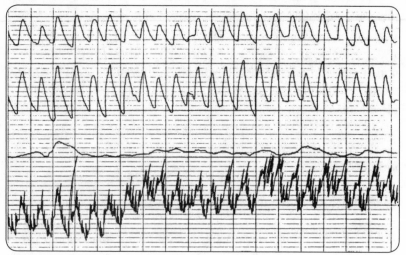

Figure 12

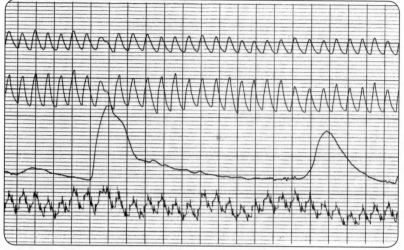

Figure 13

In addition to the charts, the subjects completed a simple questionnaire following the experiment. The answers consistently revealed thoughts of death and dying for participants in the experimental group.

Before this research, I conducted a pilot study in my offices. During this period, I made two additions to the test protocol. First, I wanted to try out delivering information via silent subliminal communication, so an expert on the subject prepared a tape with the same message, which I gave to some of the volunteers. Second, I wanted to test a delivery method using a scalar-information antenna designed by an inventor friend of mine. (*Scalar* is thought to be a new kind of electromagnetic wave that exists only in the vacuum of empty space—the gaps between the atoms of our bodies as well as the empty space we see in the night sky.) I used this method with one subject.

The polygraph recording showed no response during silent subliminal presentation (fm), but it did reveal a response for the subject of the scalar transmission. This result permits no conclusions, but it provoked me to plan a study employing only scalar-information transmission.

You may find your own interest piqued. Take care: like subliminal programs, scalar antennas differ from each other. Experience has led me to believe that few who claim knowledge of scalar potential possess sufficient expertise to build any measurably effective device.

In a conversation with Dr. Thomas Budzinski, a neurotechnology researcher, I learned that he'd also measured physiological responses to similar stimuli. He, too, tried the fm form of subliminal information delivery, and like me, he found no correlation to physiological responses. He did record reactions to subliminal delivery of words presented in both forward and reverse fashion with normal ocean-masking.

I only found evidence against the fm transmission of subliminal information in the form known as "silent subliminals." Perhaps that will change tomorrow, perhaps not.

Maybe the U.S. government has done some work with fm audio. Certainly, the most powerful governments have studied subliminal communication and manipulation extensively. Perhaps someone will use the Freedom of Information Act to find out.

The confusion over subliminal information should stop, because the field shouldn't be extended to include forms of delivery outside the scope of what's normally thought of as audio or visual subliminal information. If you acquire a subliminal self-help program, play it. Do you hear nothing? Unless it clearly states "Silent Subliminal" on the package, send it back. If you hear nothing . . . there's probably nothing there.

Enfolded Subliminal Information

Many years ago, I encountered repeated reports of the Soviets employing subliminal technology (the Woodpecker project mentioned earlier). Supposedly, they used microwave transmissions to carry *extremely low frequency* (ELF) information. The miles of nerves in the human body dwarf the largest radio telescopes. The human nervous system received the information. How would it process the information? How would it respond?

I'm acquainted with some respected individuals who have access to restricted information. A few of them insisted that the Soviets created disease among those stationed at the U.S. embassy in precisely this manner. The microwave broadcasts at the embassy have become common knowledge, although whether the Soviets used ELF or other information in those transmissions remains unknown. There's evidence to suggest that enfolded information could be used as a weapon.[1] Indeed, as we've already seen with HAARP, technologies could influence all of us without our awareness.

Summary

Some people have taken the concept of subliminal communication beyond its usual boundaries. My research has indicated that at least some kinds of silent subliminals found in self-help technologies don't work. However, testing *scalar* delivery of subliminal messages indicated that it may have some efficacy. This method also appears to be something that governments have looked into.

Because this chapter concludes Book One, it's worth noting that it appears, as is the case with the surgeon's scalpel, that there are many possible abuses for all of the persuasion technologies, including but not limited to subliminal communication, hypnosis, drugs, and NLP.

The main thrust of Book One has been the dark side; it has largely dealt with persuasion methods that are used against you. Book Two will dedicate more time to alternative persuasion methods that can be used to train your mind in the way you wish it to be trained. In other words, we'll begin to look at the more positive side of methods of persuasion in the next section.

■　■■ ■■■■

HARNESSING THE POWER OF THE MIND

*"We must be the epitome—the embodiment of success.
We must radiate success before it will come to us.
We must first become mentally, from an attitude
standpoint, the people we wish to become."*

— Earl Nightingale

PART I

THE MIND AS HEALER: PROGRAMMING FOR SUCCESS, HEALTH, AND SPIRITUALITY

CHAPTER 11

Self-Discovery/The Shift

"The greater danger for most of us lies not in setting our aim too high and falling short; but in setting our aim too low, and achieving our goal."

— Michelangelo

In Book One, we examined the idea of two brains—the left hemisphere and the right hemisphere—and we evaluated this concept from the perspective of information processing. However, there's yet another manner in which we can view the theory of two brains.

The right hemisphere is separated from the left in such a manner as to suggest that not only do the two hemispheres process information differently, but they also experience the world in entirely separate and differing ways. The right hemisphere experiences now—right now—while the left deals with the future and the past. In fact, according to Dr. Jill Bolte Taylor, a prominent neuroscientist, not only does the right hemisphere experience "now," but it does so in a spatial way in which one merges with all—"true Nirvana," in her words. In her unforgettable presentation recounting how she experienced a stroke and was able to study her own brain from the inside out, Dr. Taylor makes it very clear that in every moment, we have a choice regarding how we'll experience the world. We can choose to do so serially, with one event coming after another in time, moving from past to future; or we can opt to live in a parallel manner, in the "now" that so many people are talking about. In the present moment, we experience ourselves differently—as being one with our fellow members of planet Earth, as sharing energy in an exchange with life. (I strongly urge you to watch Jill Bolte Taylor's story on Ted Talks: **http://blog. ted.com/2008/03/jill_bolte_tayl.php** or to read her book, *My Stroke of Insight*.)

After reading the first part of this book, the concept of choosing to experience life "in the now" may seem somewhat airy-fairy, but let's digress a little and ask ourselves the big question: *Who am I?*

When I was in high school, I had a special teacher, Mrs. Foster, who encouraged me to write poetry. I loved poetry and still do. One of the things I remember most about her was her willingness to be brutally honest. I worked on a poem over and over until I was sure it was just what I wanted, then I turned it in to Mrs. Foster. She gave the paper back to me with red writing across the top: "This is so trite that Adam kicked the slats out of his cradle when he heard it." Although I was offended by her comment, I respected her too much to ignore what she had to say. As a result, I persisted with the poem until it met her very high standards.

Who am I? is at least as trite as the poem Mrs. Foster criticized, yet it remains unanswered by many people and overlooked by still more. Perhaps we should restate the question: *What does it mean to be human?*

What *is* humanness? How does it differ—if it does—from any other form of animal existence? With all our alleged potential, with all the historic merits that can be used to argue for our genius, are we humans just smarter than other animals in certain ways?

I find this to be much more than an idle question. Indeed, I believe the way in which we choose to answer points to the very future of humankind. We've seen how some people would manipulate and use us, much as we might program robots in the future. Certain social rules, habits, customs, expectations, and more appear to make us predictable. Under close inspection, we should also note that our very predictability comes from our reactions, not our thought-out responses.

As reactive human beings, we take little time to live in the now and even less time to consider our humanness. We lose ourselves in consumption, and sometimes that means consumption of ourselves. We live such fast-paced lives that there's no time to do anything other than pursue the next goal, where we'll consume something again.

We consume our time with the many idolatrous activities available, such as computer games, television, Nintendo DS, PSP, PS2, and so forth. Modern inventions all seem to favor our forgetting self-reflection. Our culture busies itself with everything from cosmetic makeovers to reality television. While we're operating in this mode, can anyone really expect the human condition to truly improve?

Being Human

What is the human potential? It's an aspect of what it means to be human. Is it limited to some finite evolution—a dust-to-dust model of being? Are we destined to be consumption robots, building wealth and power for those who would control us? I think not, and I'm certain you agree.

Most people I've spoken with find the methods of the manipulators disgusting. These same individuals, and I'd even venture to say everyone I've ever met, believe that somehow, somewhere within themselves, there rests more—an untapped potential. Oh, some folks may initially resist this admission, but once they get past the various defense mechanisms we all employ from time to time, there's an awareness of the "more" that I speak of, resting dormant within.

Defining *more* is a good place to begin when it comes to answering the question *What does it mean to be human?* To that end, let's list some of what we might think of as the "more" within—the attributes of being human. I think the list would look something like this:

- Compassionate
- Patient
- Accepting and forgiving
- Loving
- Peaceful
- Balanced
- Joyful
- Empathetic
- Sympathetic
- Benevolent
- Charitable

We may also want to add qualities such as "spiritual."

When we seriously ponder the nature of being human, we look at ourselves through a lens that expects more of our species than it does of the rest of the animal world. Somehow, whether rightly or wrongly, most attribute to humanness a special quality that transcends mortal existence. You can think of this as spirit, soul, or simply our quintessential selves, but for most people throughout history, being human includes life after death.

Whether we're atheists, agnostics, or believers, the point is simple: we all *do* expect more from humans than from our monkey relatives and our canine or feline friends. At the same time, it's glaringly obvious that some of these animal companions possess more of what we think of as the highest human qualities than many people do. For example, I recently lost a very dear friend, Balto, who was a German shepherd. She'd been a member of my family since she was just five weeks old. During the ice storm that hit the Spokane, Washington, area in 1996, most people were without power. As a result, during the first few weeks that Balto was with us, she spent most of her time either tucked into my jacket so that my body would keep her warm or curled up with the family as we huddled in front of the fireplace.

Balto turned out to be the finest dog ever. She was our friend, guard dog, and companion. Regardless of what went on, she was always there, showing us how much she loved us. As she got older and developed arthritis, she never complained, even when my kids accidentally fell on her as they played. During the last few years of her life, she developed chronic dry eye, which had to be medicated twice a day. She never gave any trouble over this either and just loved us all the more. In her last two weeks, she developed kidney failure. She was in great pain, yet she still never complained and simply loved us. Putting her to sleep was one of the hardest things I've ever had to do. Balto exemplified unconditional love. So what exactly is humanness?

The problem with defining *humanness* is that it's a dynamic experience with shared characteristics that the human mind often extrapolates or anthropomorphizes from the rest of nature. Perhaps that's the place to focus our attention. When we witness an act that produces a warm feeling, a joyful tear, a smile, goose bumps, and so forth, it's automatically a human feeling and therefore a part of being human. The dog that's injured while pulling a young child from a burning house elicits wonderment, awe, and love. We anthropomorphize the animal and realize that both the dog's courageous act and our emotion as we process the story are part of being human.

Humanness is more a matter of what inspires us, rather than what we can list in some narrative. It's emotion, but it also transcends the more primitive drive-related feelings. The stories that touch us, the creativity that excites us, the adventures that motivate us, the passion that drives us to do better, the joy and awe that lead us within—all of these and more are humanness. As with the dog that risks itself for the child, the highest aspect of our species is recognizing that being human calls upon each of us to reach higher, do better, and give more of ourselves. We're committed to being true to our highest and best selves. This is the dictum of the day, whether or not we recognize it.

Aiming High

I assert that reaching for our individual highest and best is the only way we'll ever find ourselves. This is a world of action, despite those who teach that it's a place of inaction. Such fatalists suggest that whatever happens is supposed to be that way, so do nothing. They might argue that if you see someone being attacked, then you should pass by and not try to help. They use the simple statement that "everything happens exactly as it's supposed to" as an excuse for refraining from acting—for holding on to inaction. These same people might tell us that our feelings and passions are from the ego and should be mastered. I've heard arguments that attack the ego as evil and something that must be overcome. These individuals would have us meditate and do unselfish acts in order to train us away from being involved in the world.

Language can trap us. A simple statement may lead to many interpretations and reinterpretations. At some point, whether or not everything happens as it should, each of us must choose our actions in response to what we see going on around us. In light of this, intervening in an attack may in fact be exactly "what's supposed to happen."

From the perspective of science, I may understand how to pole-vault. I may have viewed hundreds of pole vaults and calculated trajectory, speed, and the precise angle the pole should be placed in its cup as the launch begins . . . but all of that doesn't make me a pole-vaulter. I have to actually perform to know what pole vaulting is. Life works that way as well. If I don't wish to be manipulated, I must do something to see that manipulation is stopped. If I believe that humanness deserves better, then I must speak out or in some other way step up and make a case for something better.

A Primer for Living Awake

In generations past, the affairs of humankind were thought to be controlled by the gods. The idea of self-improvement or self-empowerment is relatively new, yet today it's a multimillion-dollar business. The acceptance of modern theories in psychology, together with advances in our definition of *freedom*, have led to a mobile society like no other in history. We're upwardly mobile in terms of where we live and our expectations, and we truly believe that members of our society can be almost anything they really want to be.

Oh, there are admittedly a few holdouts. There are those who believe that the mind should never be interfered with; those convinced that hypnosis, psychotherapy, and so forth are of the devil; those who essentially believe that humans are faulty and as such must beg their way to salvation. Still, for the most part, Western culture accepts that humans can create their destinies—or at the very least improve their lots in life.

We hope that our schools teach children to be responsible, eat properly, exercise, train their minds, and imagine success without limitation. When we find a teacher who betrays our trust by informing our children that they're limited creatures unable to accomplish their dreams, we oust the teacher. So not only is the notion of self-empowerment relatively new in the history of humankind, but it has become a value that most of us cherish and pass on to our children.

First Principles

Why does this matter? History is a great teacher. The struggles that led from the 13th-century Magna Carta to today's concepts of liberty and justice for all are of no small consequence. A glance at the world today and its socioeconomic and political relations informs us of the divide that still exists over what one might refer to as agreement on first principles.

What's a first principle? In this sense, it's what I like to think of as a starting place for peace in the world. Take, for example, the idea that life is sacred. We might think that everyone could agree on at least this idea—a sort of moral imperative that applies to all. We'd state our first principle this way: "Every human being has a right to life."

In science, a first principle is held to be a premise or hypothesis that can't be proven. As the great mathematician Kurt Gödel put it: "All first principles are inherently un-provable."[1] However, what can be done with a first principle—say, the one that theoretical physicist Dr. Stephen W. Hawking made famous, the big bang—is to test the principle by testing theories the principle implies.[2] For example, a big bang implies an expanding universe. Test this, and if verified, it tends to support the first principle.

To apply a first principle to humans may be something of a departure from traditional applications. However, I submit that it's both needed and appropriate. Here's why: First principles do at least two things for the communities involved with its application. The first is to lead the communities in exploring the implications and developing methods to cross-pollinate between disciplines such as chemistry and physics. The second is to provide a visual landscape, if you will, that can be embraced by all—laypersons and specialists alike.

Okay, so say that we have a first principle, and we call it "Life." We assume that all human life is precious, and that all human beings have a right to life. We can't prove this principle any more than we can prove the big bang theory, but we can work out a number of ways to test the principle, especially in the disciplines of political science, sociology, psychology, and the like. We can also create a visual framework that most will at least initially embrace. Therefore, as simple as this may seem, its elegance is in the agreement that "All human beings have a right to life."

If the world would accept this one simple premise, then wars could be ended. But the fact is that it doesn't. No, indeed there are many who believe that it's their duty to kill. For them, the lives of others have no special meaning or value if those other people fail to believe a certain thing. Given this sad state of affairs, how and where do we begin to reach that simple accord: *All human life is sacred.*

Self-Empowerment

Self-empowerment begins with self-reflection. The question *What is humanness?* is obviously a part of any serious self-reflection. For Sigmund Freud and others, humans simply occupy a position on the evolutionary ladder, a position with more "gray matter" and therefore more inhibitory ability. Humankind's marvelous brain was not only more sophisticated in terms of its ability to reason but more powerful in its ability to inhibit impulses. The latter is critical because, according to Freud, the unconscious is a seething cauldron of animalistic desires that have to be held in check. No higher self, per se, inhabited the unconscious or anything else about the human being. To the contrary, humans were beasts separated from other beasts chiefly by their ability to hide their beastliness and engage their intellect in unique ways.

Philosophers have long discussed humanness. In a day and age faced with so many possibilities and opportunities (or problems, to some), we might think that the basic tenets of what makes us different might again be a subject of great interest. It's easy to be cynical from a historical perspective and agree with statements such as: "Mankind educates his children to become absurd and thus normal," and "In the name of God, mankind has killed . . ." However, if we choose to become awake citizens, then settling for such forecasts is simply unacceptable.

The world changes one person at a time. I believe that within every human being is the capacity for such specialness that one day the question *What does it mean to be human?* will be as trite as trite can be, for the answer will be as obvious as obvious can be. Perhaps we'll all learn to stay a little more in our right hemisphere. We may know more of "now" and the interchange of our collective energy and know a little less about the particulars that we use to set ourselves apart from everyone and everything else.

The bottom line for me is this: I believe in you! What's more, I know that when each of us believes in the others, a fundamental shift will result. This is the big change that holds the promise of a world at peace.

Summary

In this chapter, we looked at what it means to be human and whether or not people deserve to be treated better than the way they have been by certain merchandisers and covert agencies—and for that matter, the way they may continue to be treated.

The vast majority of us believe that some untapped potential lies within us, and I believe that reaching for our highest individual best is the only way we'll ever find ourselves.

In the next chapter, we'll look at what I personally believe is the single most powerful aspect of humanness and perhaps also the most difficult to manage—forgiveness.

■ ■ ■ ■■■

CHAPTER 12

Forgiveness and the Happy Heart

*"Holding on to anger is like grasping a hot coal
with the intent of throwing it at someone else;
you are the one getting burned."*

— Buddha

In nearly everything I've written or recorded for the past two decades is the construct of forgiveness. I must tell you frankly that this has been one of my most difficult lessons; perhaps that's why I keep coming back to it. You see, I've learned that forgiveness isn't just about forgiving oneself or someone else; it's also about forgiving and letting go of a way of life.

First, let me share with you one of my early insights. For years, I've used subliminal communication theory and technology for various self-help purposes. Sometimes this required a custom recording.

When scripting a subliminal program, one of the uncovering methods I've used in determining relative emotive content is the administration of a simple, self-designed, adjective-relevant test with interpretation by means of a psychological stress evaluator (PSE). The list of adjectives includes such words as *mother, father, love, hate, forgiveness,* and *blame.* The PSE was developed by two military intelligence colonels to test the veracity of a subject's statements without needing physical attachments. Essentially, it measures the muscle-microtremor activity that accompanies voluntary muscle movement, ordinarily between 8 and 14 cycles per second. The microtremor originates from the interaction between the sympathetic and parasympathetic divisions of the autonomic nervous system.

The PSE is an extremely sophisticated instrument that I used for years as a licensed lie-detection examiner on criminal matters ranging from homicide to theft and in civil applications ranging from preemployment screening to executive personality profiling. The sensitivity of the instrument in subtle measurements of stress (as opposed to gross distress) makes it a valuable uncovering device. Many psychologists employ it for this purpose, and some interesting findings have come from using the PSE. For example, three statements that always produce stress are the forgiveness set.

The Forgiveness Set

Every subliminal program I've created for the past several years has incorporated what I refer to as "the forgiveness set." I'm convinced that using only these messages with the symbiotic messages would enhance every dynamic of human activity. The forgiveness set consists of three messages: "I forgive myself. I forgive all others. I am forgiven" (or in some instances: "We are forgiven"). I believe—and my research has borne out—the idea that to the precise degree we displace responsibility for anything in our lives, we reduce the possibility of freeing ourselves from whatever limitations we experience. (See *Choices and Illusions, Subliminal Learning,* and *Thinking without Thinking.*) When we assume full responsibility, we empower ourselves for change.

All of my testing with the PSE and other measurements demonstrates the direct connection between fear and anger, blame and shame, and forgiveness. By displacing this self-defeating loop, problems ranging from weak self-esteem to self-inflicted poor health are necessarily displaced. (For more on the fear-anger loop, see the model of the mind discussed in *Choices and Illusions*.)

It's also my belief that some cellular learning replaces, or disorganizes, cellular memory. The result is disease. Paradoxically, disease is sometimes an outward manifestation of emotion, which itself is generated through a lens normally dependent on false interpretations of the acceptance and rejection issue or forgiveness.

Now, all behavior comes from choice, even if it's self-destructive (as is much avoidance behavior). In that sense, as we choose actions, we educate our cells to relearn (disorganize order). In a very real sense, we choose our diseases. What we create in our lives, therefore, is often what we fear most. What we resist, we become; what we dislike in others, we imprint on ourselves. Interestingly, the adaptation process (avoidance of rejection) paradoxically could be said to operate from a law of the mind we could call defiance (the need for unique self-expression). We could also say that the strategy of manipulation toward this end is a law of our psychology.

Thus, the law of the mind is defiance, and the law of psychology is the strategy of manipulation, and chief among the victims of both is usually ourselves. The value of a paradox to the philosopher is inherent in the circularity of its relative values. Thesis followed by antithesis provides insight into synthesis. The paradox of much of the human condition is that many of its preservation mechanisms work to extinguish rather than to preserve.

With that in place, allow me to share a couple of clinical cases. The first is the story of a young boy who was considered terminally ill. The second is my own story and that of what I think of today as a happy heart. I could share other cases with you, as I have in my earlier books, but these two express the point I wish to make now.

Intervention

I still find this first case absolutely fascinating. It was initially published some 20 years ago in my book *Subliminal Learning*. In my mind, it still represents a most intriguing aspect of being human and gives rise to the promise of a potential that rests within all of us. It's a perfect example of mind as healer/mind as slayer. It also directly addresses a positive and beneficial application for subliminal technology.

VW was a 14-year-old boy with a long history of physical disorders. He was born with vocal-cord paralysis, which affected his swallowing and digestion. This was corrected with a tracheotomy, and by two years of age, he was functioning normally. Shortly after this, his parents had another child. VW began displaying symptoms of major illness, which was diagnosed as muscular dystrophy. By the time he had reached the age of 14, he was restricted to a wheelchair, with minor mobility to dress and bathe. In addition, he'd developed an extreme case of scoliosis (lateral curvature of the spine) and severe pulmonary problems. Attending physicians felt that the scoliosis was increasing his pulmonary difficulties and that surgery, using fusion and metal bars to correct the curvature of the spine, was required. Yet the doctors, while recognizing the value of the procedure, also felt that VW's pulmonary problems were such that he probably couldn't withstand the operation—catch-22, if you will.

VW's father came to Progressive Awareness Research to meet with members of the advisory board and discuss having a specialized program created for his son. A review of VW's history pointed to several significant factors. The first was that the severity of VW's illnesses and symptoms increased or decreased in proportion to the attention he was receiving. Second, he was using illness to control his sphere of influence (family and friends). Third, there was intense sibling rivalry within the family as a result of these illnesses. Fourth, parental inconsistencies and dissension had developed with regard to the young man's treatment and care, which he manipulated to serve his purpose.

I created a special subliminal program using male, female, and child voices, recorded in round-robin fashion with full echo and reverb and using hemispheric processing. Affirmations were presented with authoritative and permissive dialogue targeting the following areas: self-esteem, self-responsibility, wholeness, wellness, the ability of the cells to replicate perfectly, acceptance, love, and specific messaging directed at the affected areas of VW's body. In addition, the forgiveness set and the mommy/daddy symbiotics were employed.

Because of VW's confinement to a limited area, different record-ings were created by mixing the affirmations with multiple primary carriers. One primary carrier was mixed ocean and nature sounds to allow VW to study, watch TV, and conduct other activities using the recording as a noncompeting background. Other primary carriers selected were based upon his and other family members' personal music preferences.

At the time these programs were created, VW had been removed from school and was receiving instruction in his home because of the complications of his illnesses. For six weeks, he listened to these audio programs continually. At the end of this period, VW was administered pulmonary tests that showed incredible improvement. The attending physicians were so encouraged by the test results that they felt VW was then strong enough to survive the spinal surgery. However, within two weeks of the pulmonary tests, his mobility had increased dramati-cally. His father sent to Progressive Awareness Research a picture of his son, previously confined to a wheelchair and his bed, walking up a flight of stairs.

After a few weeks, VW began having problems with carbon-dioxide retention, so he was placed on an oxygen machine to facilitate his breathing. One evening, his parents discovered that the oxygen had been turned up to more than twice the prescribed rate. He was rushed to intensive care, where he received treatment. While there, his father noticed that VW's breathing pattern was similar to that of the period when he'd had vocal-cord paralysis. The physicians verified that VW did have the same paralysis, and a tracheotomy was per-formed.

VW experienced a total recovery. I have photos of this young man standing beside his new car, ready to be a normal, healthy teenager. The physicians state that the only thing that can be said about his condition is that he has weak muscles. Is it possible that when sub-liminally confronted with the underpinnings of a maladaptive defense mechanism, VW regressed to the point in his personal history of opti-mal health and attention?

Forgive and Release

The second case I'd like to share involves me and the idea that forgiving oneself and others isn't sufficient—we must also forgive and release (let go of) ideas, thought patterns, rehearsals, and more. I'll explain, but first I'll present my case.

I learned the importance of forgiveness in the path to self-actualization or true self-responsibility in the 1980s. As I mentioned earlier, research carried out at the Utah State Prison convinced me this was necessary. I immediately took on the task of forgiving everyone I could think of and in some instances phoning and writing letters apologizing for my errors. The latter seemed appropriate if I were to forgive myself for acts that were selfish and otherwise hurtful to others.

I began lecturing and writing books about the power of forgiveness. I developed a model of the mind that illustrated how, in the absence of forgiveness, we easily displace responsibility and blame onto someone or something else. I made convincing arguments that we can't change until we give ourselves the power and permission to do so. Further, as long as we blame someone or something, we're powerless, for it isn't our fault, and therefore what is there to change?

I began including the forgiveness set in all of my recordings, and in the early 1990s decided that forgiveness was so important that my company would make the recording available at no charge. In other words, we took our number one best-selling program and began giving it away free (and it's still free—one per customer at **www.inner talk.com**).

I felt that I was doing my work. Of course, I had many things to learn, but I really believed I was getting a handle on this issue. In fact, one day a young man stole an item from my bookstore, and a friend who was in the store shouted at me to pursue the thief as he ran down the sidewalk. I was probably pretty full of myself when I think back on this episode, for I simply told my friend, "He can't steal from me. If he needs it that badly, then it's my gift." The point is this: I didn't even blame the thief stealing from me.

Forgiveness and the Happy Heart

My History

I must digress at this point, however. As you know, for years I conducted lie-detection tests, investigations, surveillance, and so forth. My father was in law enforcement, and my memories of Dad are almost all of him in his uniform with a big gun at his side. My father had joined the Army, leaving behind his previous profession of logging, and he became a WWII veteran who received a Purple Heart. He was sent back to the States, where he became a drill sergeant. He was a rather heavy-handed person, and he had his share of biases—what some today would call bigotry.

I was raised with an ethic and morality that was very judgmental in some ways. My father thought of this as a good blue-collar ethic. When television became available, our family watched cowboy or cop movies. There was always a good guy and a bad guy, and if the movie was worth its proverbial salt, we became vicariously involved and wanted the good guy to take revenge. So some of the real Western classics, ranging from the likes of *Shane* to *The Good, the Bad, and the Ugly* lived inside of me. I must also admit to having certain favorites that I've seen over and over again, such as *Pale Rider* and *Tombstone.*

All right, you'd probably like to know what all of this has to do with forgiveness. This is what I learned: my imagined villains lived within me, and my imagined hero role waited for the opportunity to step up to the plate. (In fairness, I've experienced that hero role when I returned stolen children to their mothers and when I've been given credit for saving a person's life, and I admit to feeling good about those things.) In other words, living within me was a judgment waiting to happen.

I often "read" people, and I found it easy to transfer my judgment of criminality to politics, moral issues such as human cloning or abortion, and so forth. The result? I couldn't forgive and let go of that which lived inside me as a potential anger or harsh judgment.

Another matter that I found correlations to and taught for years now comes into play. For years, in my book *Wellness: Just a State of Mind* and other publications, I spoke about illness as fitting certain personality characteristics and needs. For instance, the singer terrified of performing doesn't suffer a sprained ankle, as a dancer would, but rather develops a sore throat. Obviously, the illness manages to work as an escape mechanism and thus the performer graciously steps out of a situation full of fear. What I'd seen was some correlation suggesting that cardiac disease was more likely to be a problem for the hostile aggressive person, whereas cancer appeared to be more common in the introvert or those who held their feelings in. My point here isn't to argue for this correlation but rather to simply point out my own inner belief.

Synchronicity?

In the spring of 2007, I was going along, playing with horses and enjoying the outdoors while working a full week, as do so many people, when I discovered a burning in my left lung. It would appear when I exerted myself on the treadmill or bike, but I could work through it and it disappeared. I told my wife about it casually because it was strange, but I was convinced that perhaps I had some new allergy.

A couple of weeks passed, and one morning my wife opened a new box of cereal. As she prepared to pour from it, she noticed a warning on the box. She came to me upset. This cereal box described my symptoms exactly and warned that these can be the signs of an impending heart attack.

Needless to say, I was soon undergoing a nuclear stress test, which I promptly failed. Next there was an angiogram, and this one had my wife and younger son in tears. By this time, we were mentally prepared for a stent, but no one was thinking triple-bypass surgery.

The long and the short of it came down to my just being very lucky (or looked after). Two of the three main arteries in my heart were totally blocked, and the third was 99 percent blocked, yet my body had found ways to keep blood coursing through the entire heart. There was no heart damage.

The surgery left me with time to reflect on many things. I discovered that I initially felt betrayed, and I was angry. I'd been working out, no longer smoked, ate little salt and less sugar, consumed lots of vegetables and fruit—why me? As I went into my anger, I discovered two things. The first was that despite my belief that I'd forgiven, I hadn't. I carried all sorts of angry scripts within me, waiting for a chance to act them out. These were often the scripts of my childhood, and when they weren't, they could have been. In other words, my mentation could include being *right* over being at peace.

You see, when you live in the state of forgiveness—that is, you forgive yourself and all others—you live in a special state of inner peace. Forgiveness is the antidote to anger, blame, guilt, and so on!

To test my theory I obtained a software/hardware setup from the *Heart Math Institute* (you can find what I used on my Website: **www .eldontaylor.com/mindprogramming**). I installed the software and began working with the system. It's designed to evaluate several measures, including pulse rate and heart rhythm; but most important, it teaches the operator how to develop heart coherence. It's a simple yet powerful device, and I quickly saw a correspondence between thoughts that were angry and incoherent versus peaceful, loving, even laughing thoughts and coherence.

I tested others. My beautiful wife had a very coherent heart pattern—until I asked her to think about something that angered her. In came the anger and out went the coherence, and so it was with everyone I tested. I was learning more, not only about the power of forgiveness but also about what I termed *a happy heart.*

A Happy Heart

What does it take to have a happy heart, and why would you want one? Here's some of what I learned: Would you believe that a heavy heart inhibits your immune, endocrine, and autonomic nervous systems from optimal performance? That means that your life is in all likelihood shortened and the quality is lessened. "Life sucks and then you die" is a self-fulfilling prophecy and reflects the attitude of a heavy heart.

What is the difference between a heavy heart and a happy one? Did you know that typically in less than one minute in front of the television, you enter an altered state of consciousness (brain-wave activity) that's thought of as a state of hyper-suggestibility?[1] This is exactly what most would define as the state of hypnosis. While you're watching television, what kind of hypnotic suggestions are entering your mind and in what way will they be triggered later? Maybe you've visited the supermarket and impulsively picked up some product that you've never purchased before. Why? Could you be responding to a sort of posthypnotic suggestion (command) that has lain dormant until the trigger, an image or symbol, goes off when you spy the product in the store (even peripherally)?

Do you know what heart coherence is? It can be seen in wave patterns that are smooth and even. What you witness in watching an EKG chart or other visual method of displaying heart activity are recursive sine waves—even, smooth, sine waves. (See Figure 14.) When there's a lack of coherence, the heart is struggling (not operating optimally), and for many people this becomes the normal pace of life.

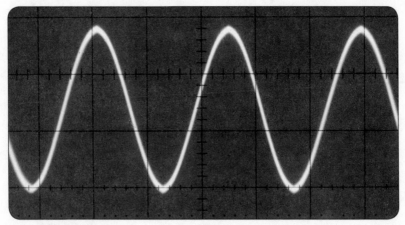

Figure 14

Did you know that your heart's coherence tells the tale of a happy or a heavy heart? Did you know that games involving "shoot-'em-up, bang-bang" themes prevent heart coherence? How about the fact that anger, excessive anxiety, and stress all bring about incoherence? Were you aware that in watching movies, you have vicarious experiences in violence and other sordid matters that are incompatible with the happy heart (heart coherence)?

Are you aware that thoughts are related to heart coherence, and that just holding the memory of something sad, evil, mean, or violent—just thinking of someone you still hold anger toward—will generate irregular and incoherent heart patterns? In other words, thoughts translate to feelings.

Do feelings last forever? It's easy to see why it's so important to protect against errant and undesired thoughts entering our minds and so important to neutralize all negative emotions. My advice, paraphrased from my book *Choices and Illusions,* is to put a smile on your face (smiling fools the brain into increasing the body's natural opiate distribution) and fake it until you make it!

Thoughts Create

Thoughts are things. Since discovering all of this, I've found comedies and uplifting viewing much more healthful. I still seem to be addicted to some good old Westerns, but much less so, and I never get personally involved. If I do, the movie just gets shut off.

I've been asked many times: "How do we avoid all of this unhealthy programming?" The answer is easy, but as with many things, speaking and doing aren't the same. Begin by turning off the television set. Consciously choose what you watch and turn off commercials, especially those that inform (suggest/sell) sickness. Guard what you put in your mind and cancel any thoughts that you have that might threaten inner peace and tranquility—you get the picture. The problem is in actually doing these things.

We're living at a time when it's appropriate for us to stay tuned to world affairs and to participate in elections as informed voters. We have freedoms and responsibilities from being in the world. However, I'm convinced that we can all live according to the dictates of our conscience and do so unattached to the outcome. If we do, we may experience differing opinions and viewpoints, but there are no true antagonists or protagonists acting on our emotions. If you think something should be a certain way—say so and let it go.

Summary

We've seen in this chapter how thoughts, conscious and unconscious, can and do affect the body in direct ways. In previous chapters, we saw how easy it is for someone else to plant thoughts in our minds that don't originate from within. With this information, it should be even clearer why protecting ourselves from unwanted thoughts is of the utmost importance.

One of the first steps in taking back control of our own minds is learning both to forgive and to release. Examples were given as to what can happen when this isn't done.

Next, we'll look at the power of belief and intention.

■ ■ ■ ▄▄■■

CHAPTER 13

Belief and Intention

*"Do your worrying before you place your bet,
not after the wheel starts turning."*

— Maxwell Maltz

There's a lot of talk today about the power of intention and belief. The latter seems to underlie our self-fulfilling prophecies, including our ability to manifest a personal reality. The power of intention is thought to be the energy we might be able to *inject* (my word) into something. For example, the intention of a group of meditators to lower the crime rate was injected into the field, or collective consciousness, of those in the city receiving the benefit of the meditation. When the meditators appeared to significantly lower the crime rate in Washington, D.C., this was evidence of the power of intention.[1]

Obviously and arguably, therefore, when a collective body prays for someone who's ill and that person is healed, that, too, is a manifestation of the power of intention. Indeed, in some minds today, the zero point, defined as the unifying force that underlies the potential and existence of the universe, may well hold memories and intentions for and from all of us that can be activated by thought power (intention).

Perhaps this might be a sort of living Akashic Record? According to many Eastern religious beliefs, the Akashic Record can be seen as a library in which there exists a "book of life" for every one of us. In our book, we'll find recorded our every action, thought, motive, emotion, and so forth.

The physics behind some of this is often question begging, but much stranger things have turned out to be true. I'll leave that to time and to the physicists (perhaps to my wonderful niece now doing her doctorate in cosmology at Cambridge University—accept the challenge, girl?). Rather, I wish to address the distinction between belief and intention.

Belief

The power of belief is pretty well documented, and moreover, it's one of those commonsense things that doesn't require the proverbial rocket scientist to acknowledge or understand. Most small children get it. For at least 60 years now, posters in public schools have promoted this idea. The Little Engine that Could—"I think I can, I think I can, I think I can . . ." is known to all of us. What most of us have rarely stopped to consider, however, is why the power of belief should be so obvious. Assuming that I'm right, and it is, why is what we believe so misunderstood or self-limiting?

The mind is a marvelous instrument when compared to any form of technology. It far exceeds the abilities of any form of so-called artificial intelligence, computer program, calculator, and the like. That isn't so obvious to many, however. It's easy to think of the computer as having a perfect memory, executing without error solutions to difficult mathematical equations, operating at incredible speed, and so forth. It's as easy to think of the organic mind as finding learning difficult, see human memory as fallible, and give little thought to our own speed. But the mind is much more than an operating system, such as software, or a memory system, such as disk space. Indeed, its highest potential in this narrow realm of comparison is in its ability to design, create, imagine, and question. Still, there's an even greater ability inherent to the mind—the ability to believe!

Belief and Intention

Believe It or Not

Belief is an interesting construct when viewed abstractly. What produces belief? Why is it so powerful? Where's the demarcation between rational and irrational belief? When does it become a weapon of self-sabotage? Can it really move mountains—that is, affect the physical world?

Social scientists have many names for the effect of belief. It has been called the placebo factor (the infamous sugar-pill cure); the Pygmalion hypothesis (the ability to take on or imitate the expectations of others, like a chameleon changing colors); the expectation factor (the influence of expectancy on outcome); and the uncertainty principle, as it's known in physics, which arguably offers evidence for the manifestation of matter according to the expectation of the experimenter. Mystics and religious teachers have often referred to this power of belief as the underlying faith by which all potential is known.

A fact of the human condition is that belief has led to virtually every advancement of humankind, including biological progress. Indeed, human consciousness is inextricably involved in the evolution of the species, for there's no evolution without intention. Some have called this intention a morphogenetic field or a type of information field both formed and influenced by conscious action.[2] Others have gathered information in ways that perhaps portend a zero-point field (the unifying force that underlies the potential and existence of the universe).[3] Some have referred to it as "selfish cells" and cell-memory memes. (According to Richard Dawkins, a meme is a unit of cell memory that is passed on in much the same way genes are passed on.)[4] Still others have looked upon this process as "liquid crystal consciousness," which is cell consciousness contributing in total to species awareness of both a conscious and unconscious nature.[5] Whatever the name of the first cause—memory, intention, or conscious thought—it's a property of the mind.

The Mind

The mind is not easily understood when thought of in terms of delimiting definitions, which tend to describe both what something is and what it isn't. The mind has thus far not cooperated with this neat little framework. In fact, it generally leads to a discussion of consciousness. Defining consciousness is akin to defining infinity. There's no simple answer—and the mind is much more than the organ brain, so the entire matter can become quite murky and controversial depending on the angle of approach.

The mind we're interested in, however, isn't quite so murky. It includes personal awareness, together with its conscious and unconscious attributes. It's the source of potential, discovery, growth, knowledge, wisdom, and creativity. What we'll work to understand is our own personal world of inner being. It's *your* mind—the home of dreams, ambitions, goals, fears, disappointments, plans, direction, and purpose. It's ultimately your best ally or worst foe. Understanding this mind of self-identification is what's of interest here.

Whatever the mind can conceive in sufficient detail, it can create. "Thoughts are things," "Mind is a causal factor," and "Believe and all things will be added" are statements that ring true to the intuitive sense of some people; yet many force upon themselves and others a law of limitation. What is this law, and where do we acquire it?

Inherited Belief

Let's imagine a scenario that may assist us in grasping mentally and emotionally the notion of self-imposed limitation. Imagine an environment that knows no hate, anger, distrust, envy, greed, fear, jealousy, or the like. Now imagine a child who's born into this environment. The child grows up knowing only support and love, never feeling neglected, abandoned, or insecure. He's raised to believe that all things are possible with patience and persistence. The child is given every tool of learning known, encouraged to explore and to be independent, and rewarded for persistence and success with praise.

Nothing happens if the child fails. Only encouragement is given. The child comes to expect to be able to master all disciplines. He succeeds and succeeds again. In time, the child is willing and desirous to test the limits of his ability.

Now contrast this with the childhood most of us knew. The environment was full of shortages of time and resources. The world was full of anger, greed, suffering, fear, and other negative emotions; and this information was reinforced over and over again via television, radio, print media, Mom and Dad, our peers, teachers, and more. Most children in this environment begin to doubt their own senses when their imagination is ridiculed at an early age—usually with imaginary friends or the like. They're laughed at and threatened. Perhaps they're physically punished as well as emotionally blackmailed by codependent nonsense such as "If you loved me, you'd do this for me," "If you respected me, you'd abide by my wishes," and on and on.

Think for a minute. What do you imagine the difference between the children would be? Would there be a difference in belief—belief in self and in the world and its possibilities? And if there would be a variation in belief, would there be a contrast in what the children produce? Please reflect on this for a moment. Imagine that you'd been raised in the first scenario. If you never expected to fail, falter, experience fatigue, be threatened, get sick, experience rejection, be assaulted with violence, be forced into a mold that never fit—where would you be and what could you do? Again, spend some time with this—really feel it—before continuing.

Most people are products of their environment. Our beliefs have been inherited in much the same way that language is acquired, and they form the lens through which we see and interpret the world. What we expect is what we get—more often than not. What we fear seems to be what we create. What we imagine is usually what we encounter.

Intention

As we've seen, the power of belief affects the believer, but is there still another power, that of intention? Can the intention of one person influence others without their knowledge or consent?

There are documented cases of believers being affected by others without direct contact, such as with some of the voodoo methods employed by so-called witch doctors. In these cases, it's rare to find someone who knew nothing at all about voodoo, the witch doctor, or the supposed curse that ends up taking effect, but it's not totally exclusionary.[6]

There's also a growing body of evidence supporting a kind of psychic specialty that connects the psychic with either victim or criminal minds in solving criminal cases. (I successfully used psychic information when conducting investigations in years past).

There's ample evidence for the statement: "Mind is not a local event." Plenty of data exists that calls for the mystery to broaden as opposed to narrow, as we might think it would under the scrutiny of recent scientific inquiry. So I ask the question again: *Is there a direct influence we can think of as the power of intention?*

Recently I read about an article, which is to be published soon, that asserted proof for the power of intention. I became intrigued and contacted *IONS* (Institute of Noetic Sciences) to get a copy or more information. The organization was delightful to work with and put me in touch directly with the lead researcher, Dr. Dean Radin. I was familiar with some of his earlier work and excited to see his paper, "Effects of Intentionally Enhanced Chocolate on Mood."

In my first inquiry, before seeing the entire paper, I asked Dr. Radin what the differential was between the placebo and the intention effect. I thought this to be the most intriguing element one might glean from an actual double-blind scientific study. For as has been suggested, the effect of belief is different from the effect of intention, but what if we add the intention of a sender to the belief of the receiver—what combined effect and what difference would we be able to discern?

As it turned out, the study didn't control for an expectation/placebo effect, as differentiated from a so-called intention effect per se. It's a nice study, but it disappointed me in that I was more interested in data suggesting the relationship (additive expected) between the placebo/expectation and the intention effects. Radin did indicate to me in our later correspondence that:

> A no-expectation group wouldn't help much in the present case because to test whether a hypothetical treatment has an effect, we need to compare expectation vs. expectation + treatment.
>
> To be clear, let's call the *control* a no-expectation + no-treatment condition, *placebo* as expectation + no-treatment condition, and *treatment* as expectation + treatment condition. The control condition vs. placebo condition might be interesting because it would tell us the effects of expectation alone, but testing control vs. treatment, I'm not so sure.[7]

Perhaps in the future Radin will isolate a differential. The bottom line for now is this that there are known effects from belief and known effects from intention, but I find "intention" in this sense to be just a little too broad. It could be a visual theme, an emotion, a verbal scheme, a random thought, a piece of voodoo work, an act of Divine intervention petitioned from prayer, and so on. Still, the collective power of many people holding thoughts of peace, balance, and harmony does indeed influence others, just as the collective absence of wisdom, holding thoughts of power, aggression, and selfishness, also influences others.

Thought power—where do you have yours invested? Like transceivers, our minds appear to be subject to the thoughts of others. As if we had radios in our heads, perhaps it's time to turn the channel and tune in to a new station.

Summary

Belief and intention have been shown not only to affect the kinds of lives we lead but also to have an effect on everybody else as well. We've all heard of the power of positive thinking, but we now see that the energy goes a lot further than that. Whatever the mind can conceive in sufficient detail, it can create. Thoughts are things, and mind *is* a causal factor!

CHAPTER 14

Altered States of Consciousness

*"Darkness cannot drive out darkness; only light can
do that. Hate cannot drive out hate; only love can do
that. Hate multiplies hate, violence multiplies violence,
and toughness multiplies toughness, in a descending
spiral of destruction. . . . The chain reaction of evil—hate
begetting hate, wars producing more wars—must be broken,
or we shall be plunged into the dark abyss of annihilation."*

— Dr. Martin Luther King, Jr.

For some, an altered state of consciousness is taboo. It means
messing with the mind, which is not to be messed with. I've always
found this assertion naïve because every human being experiences
various states of altered consciousness daily. When the typical person
turns on the television, an altered state generally ensues.

Indeed, children become conditioned to enter an altered state
within minutes after beginning to watch TV. Studies have demonstrated that even when children are hooked up to brain-wave monitoring devices, such as electroencephalographic (EEG) feedback, and
given substantial reward motivation to remain in fully alert states of

consciousness, in less than five minutes they'll fail to maintain ordinary wakeful consciousness. The children will slip into what's commonly termed alpha consciousness (more on this in a moment). When a person daydreams, falls into a light sleep or reverie, slowly wakes from a deep sleep, or fixates on almost anything, that individual is almost always in an altered state of consciousness.

So what is an altered state of consciousness? Typically, consciousness is divided into four categories. Normal awareness is called "beta," lightly modified is "alpha," deep sleep is "theta," and comatose states are "delta." These levels are thought of in terms of brain-wave rates (cycles per second). Beta consciousness is normally 15 to 30 cycles per second, alpha is 8 to 14 cycles per second, theta is 4 to 8 cycles per second, and delta is less than 4.

Now let's translate this schema into something meaningful.

Beta Consciousness

In normal, ordinary wakeful states of consciousness, the mind operates from its most critical platform. It constantly judges input from the self (inner talk) and others. It evaluates and reacts. Indeed, it chiefly reacts. For even when we believe that we're evaluating, more often than not, the judgment is made before we begin. The belief system of the unconscious not only has a lens through which all matters will be viewed, but it also hides behind a protective veil the information that may give rise to mistaken decisions.

In other words, the unconscious mind during normal wakeful states is operating as a software program, feeding the flow of everyday life through a mosaic of interpretations written chiefly upon avoidance and attraction principles (experienced and imagined). Therefore, when the conscious mind says something such as "I can do this. I'm good enough to excel and succeed," the subconscious sends some inner-talk message along these lines: "Really, good enough for what? How about . . . ? Do you remember?"

Maybe the reason the subconscious sends the negative message is due to some fear from the past or anxiety projected through imagination. Perhaps it's due to negative input from peers, parents, or others. It's also possible that the nay-saying is due to some deep sense of unworthiness that's the result of a need to punish ourselves. It could even be the result of some deep belief that conflicts with our desires, such as the drive to become successful, and an inner belief that works along a line of logic that goes something like this: "If I want to be saved in heaven, I must sacrifice in the here-and-now. Further, the love of money is the source of all evil." There could also be a myriad of other reasons and a virtual labyrinth of entanglement among them all.

Reaching into the subconscious usually requires getting past or around the conscious sentry. One way to do so is by changing the brain-wave state. In ordinary beta consciousness, very little new information can really get in. "Very little" here is by comparison to alpha consciousness. In fact, just as an aside before going further, the methods of Superlearning and Suggestopedia clearly demonstrate the advantage of learning such schoolroom information as language, math, science, and so forth in alpha-consciousness states.[1]

Alpha Consciousness

Alpha consciousness is the state most refer to as the primary one experienced in hypnosis, which has been viewed from many perspectives and historically has held more than one definition. The agreed-upon definition of hypnosis today, however, is "a heightened state of suggestibility." This is just what the definition implies. In alpha consciousness, we're particularly prone to accept a skillfully placed suggestion. The nature of the prompt depends on who's doing the suggesting. A hypnotherapist will make healthy and positive comments, whereas a salesperson trained in the art of hypnotic selling may give personally self-serving ones.[2] The power of suggestion and the psychology of compliance are used every day in mass-marketing strategies to sell everything from illness to religion.[3]

When we're in an alpha state, whether naturally or artificially induced, our inner talk tends to slow down and become image oriented and/or guided, as opposed to constantly self-initiated (albeit often unconsciously). Freud called this "involuntary." Because we live in a modern society, we're exposed to a variety of stimuli that our forefathers never knew. Let me provide a couple of examples.

The Media

Much of the television, radio, and print-media programming of today dwells on violence, sex, and so-called taboo issues. The word is *sensationalism*. The more sensational the material, the better the reviews, the higher the earnings, the larger the audience, and so on. Rather systematically, as discussed earlier, over the past 20 to 30 years, the threshold of arousal has increased in the population in general, forcing an ever-increasing thrust into explicit areas in order to maintain the pitch of sensation.

Consequently, our inner talk, our fantasies, and our very ideation have been influenced. The resulting new tolerance for vengeance, anger, fear, violence, sexuality, and the like has tilted our society. Values have diminished to the point that there are some people who don't have a clue as to what life's about. They think that life is for living and taking, minimizing pain while maximizing pleasure. Twelve-year-old children walk into school and gun down their teachers and schoolmates. Drugs, child prostitution, gang violence, drive-by shootings, and similar issues are the chief worries of parents today. How did our society degenerate to this point? We most definitely have an idea.

Many psychologists, psychiatrists, sociologists, anthropologists, and for that matter, political scientists, have made vociferous outcries, asserting the neurotic nature of our times. They're lining up in an attempt to end the media management of arousal thresholds and value orientation. Television has probably the single largest effect on people today. It guides our purchases and provides the information we have about our world or any single issue or event in it. It merchandises everything from apparel and hairstyles to health, even wholesaling the common cold: "It's the flu season, and it's coming to your town! Everyone will get it! You can relax and baby yourself, indulge your whims, and take some time off—maybe even cement your relationships—if you have XYZ on hand."

How much sickness do you think is sold in the same way that attitudes and beliefs are sold through our media? We've discussed this earlier, but it's worth going a little deeper.

You may say, "Taylor, you're nuts. Television doesn't make anyone sick. You don't get the flu from TV!" Fair enough. Let's look a little closer. When a person is in a state of alpha consciousness, such as hypnosis, scientific literature shows us clearly that the body can be directed toward health or illness. A hypnotist can suggest a burn, place an ice cube on the arm, and a blister will almost immediately appear. As a hypnotist, I've personally witnessed phenomena that illustrate the mind's control over the body to the degree that suggesting a simple runny nose is, as Sherlock Holmes would say, "Elementary!" But to tie this suggestibility of alpha states into the problems posed by television viewing, we should also examine another area of scientific inquiry that may surprise you.

Studies have shown that the average individual will enter alpha-brain-wave states within one minute of being engaged by television.[4] If you think about it, the statistic shouldn't come as any surprise. How many times have we seen someone—or been that someone—who appeared so engrossed by a TV show that yelling was required to get the person's attention?

Okay, back to alpha consciousness and cold season—I ask you again, how much illness do you think is sold in order to create the market that buys the cure?

It should be obvious that alpha consciousness is not only natural, it can be a great time to put positive information into our bio-computing brain/mind. The essential use of alpha consciousness can also be either a matter of choice or a matter of habituation. I remember once seeing a sign in the supermarket that was selling the publication *TV Guide.* The sign underneath the current issue said, "Check Out," and a picture of a television with the initials "TV" inside it was all that accompanied the words. How many times have you heard or used the phrase "I'll watch television and check out"? Check out, vacuum the mind, and so on—these are the terms we all naturally think of when we think of TV. Turn our minds over, let go of our concerns, and let someone else program them.

Why "check out"? In alpha states of consciousness, endorphin levels increase. Endorphins are the body's natural opiate system, so this feels good—sometimes, perhaps, too good.

Brain-Wave Activity

Before we continue with our discussion of brain states, let me provide an analogy that may be helpful. If you think of brain-wave activity as the number of lines on an inch of graph paper, then you have a visual image of mental activity as we measure it with EEG instrumentation. Now, instead of thinking of the lines on paper, think in terms of a fence. The closer the lines are to each other, the smaller the fencing material, such as a tightly woven chain-link fence. The smaller the fencing, the more restrictive it is to both incoming and outgoing "stuff"—in our analogy, let's say birds. The mind is very much like this. The tighter the wire enclosure, the less information (stimuli) we can process and remember. This is why superlearning states use alpha consciousness. As the brain-wave activity slows down, the holes in our fencing material become larger and more information can get in (see Figure 15).

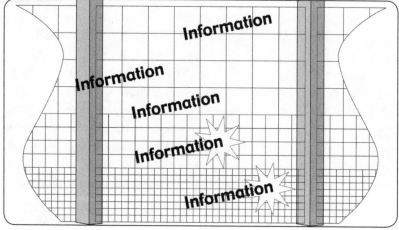

Figure 15

Altered States of Consciousness

Theta Consciousness

Theta consciousness is often associated with deep sleep and very deep levels of hypnosis or meditation. It's generally believed that the so-called superhuman feats of many spiritual masters—such as those reported to have eaten hot coals, controlled their bodily functions, and so forth—are achieved while in theta consciousness. Indeed, mystics teach that as the brain-wave patterns slow, the vibration of the body alters. In this way, many things thought to be impossible become possible. The rate of vibration may be seen as analogous to light vibrating at a rate much faster than glass, therefore it passes through the glass. A stone, however, vibrates much more slowly than glass, consequently preventing the stone from passing through without breaking the glass. Thus, there's an arguable inverse proportion to brain-wave activity and body vibration. As the brain-wave activity slows, the body vibration rate is said to increase.

Delta Consciousness

Delta consciousness is ordinarily thought of as a comatose state. For years, it was believed to be so turned in on itself that outside stimuli went totally unnoticed. However, Oliver Sacks showed the world that even in this state of consciousness, there's awareness. In his work (see his book *Awakenings*), he used massive doses of dopamine to awaken (at least for a short time) most of the patients. Stranger than fiction, these individuals reported their various records and sensitivities to the history of their treatment, the hospital protocol, their environment, and so forth.[5]

Little is really known or understood about deep delta states of consciousness; however, it's clear that they aren't devoid of awareness.

Summary

There are four brain states of consciousness: *beta, alpha, theta,* and *delta.* Most people understand that technologies, such as hypnosis, gain their effects because they induce an altered brain state (from beta to alpha) and that in this state, the subject is more suggestible. We've seen that alpha consciousness happens frequently, especially while watching television. Thus, there's much information entering our minds with the additional power gained by our defenses being down. Paying attention to this phenomenon and taking appropriate action will allow us more control over who programs our minds.

■　■■■■■

PART II

IMPLEMENTING THE HEALING: TOOLS FOR EMPOWERMENT

CHAPTER 15

Change and the Tools to Make It

"All truths are easy to understand once they are discovered; the point is to discover them."

— Galileo

What is change? The idea seems simple enough. Some consider change to be a "thing" or a commodity. For example, individuals desire more prosperity in their life, and the evidence for success is money. Okay, change in this instance is money, right? No, money is only the outer symbol that represents the shift.

The agency of change is within each person. It isn't a thing. For individuals to become more prosperous, for example, they must think in a different order of magnitude from those who are content with just getting by. At least one element in their life strategy must be altered before a change will take place.

Let's say, for purposes of illustration, that our hypothetical individual who wishes to be more prosperous was raised with the belief that the love of money is the source of all evil. A subconscious strategy may therefore sabotage his effort to achieve real fiscal success. In other words, in this instance, the ego perceives safety as avoiding evil/money.

Our hypothetical person may believe, on the other hand, that only money matters. Still, there could be subconscious strategies that get in the way. For example, assume that he seeks to build a large company, but he's afraid of public speaking. How can a large and successful company be built without its founder communicating? When will the fear (public speaking) strategy kick in and knock out the goal (large company) strategy? How will the two strategies compete?

Resistance

Competing strategies of this nature exist in nearly everyone. They often underpin what psychologists call "cognitive dissonance," the process of holding two mutually exclusive beliefs without being aware of the inherent conflict. Indeed, opposing strategies also lie beneath much of what's called *sublimation,* or acting out unacceptable fantasies in a socially acceptable way.

It's easy to see why change can be so difficult, especially since it also means giving something up. The "something" may be a counterproductive belief or a competing strategy, or it may be tangible, such as the comforting feeling that food may provide. For most people, giving up one thing means replacing it with another. A smoker wonders what will replace the cigarette—gum?

The giving up, like change itself, is only a *thing* in its outermost form. Giving up cigarettes isn't really about the cigarette but rather about the feelings associated with the use of cigarettes. These feelings may have 10, 20, 30, or more conflicting and competing strategies all rolled up into one outward behavior—in this instance, smoking.

Whenever we give something up, we must also confront the so-called unknown. This confrontation often gives rise to feelings of uncertainty. Most people are uncomfortable when they can't predict their own feelings or responses. Fear of the unknown then becomes another obstacle in the path of the person who chooses change.

Self-Responsibility

To make real changes in our lives, we must first be prepared to take responsibility for ourselves and our choices. In my years of studying the mind and assisting others in improving their lives, I've met many individuals who stated that they wished to change but then proffered numerous reasons why they were unable to implement the exercises I asked them to do.

It may surprise you to know that many people are simply addicted to the process of self-help. They spend their days searching out different tools and techniques but never give any one system enough time to take effect. Whenever something looks like it just might work, they find reasons why that system isn't for them. The more you challenge such individuals with what seems the obvious fact that they have some underlying resistance to change, the more adamant they become that they aren't at fault because they're experts at self-help—clearly the technique is at fault.

There are numerous methods for improving yourself, but first you must truly have the desire to change. I therefore created a self-responsibility questionnaire that I've found very useful in deciding how successful individuals will be at creating the change they claim to want. This questionnaire is in Appendix 2 so that you can try it out for yourself.

Deep-Mind Links

Change can produce resistance, which is the process of avoiding change. It can take many forms. True transformation is never effortless, and nothing changes until we do! This requires a willingness to endure some difficulty, a letting go, a shift in perspective with regard to blame and self-responsibility, an earnest desire to realize our potential, and a serious alteration of how we see ourselves. This last issue is where the idea of deep-mind links (DMLs) originally occurred to me.

What is a DML? For every aspect of behavior, thousands of memory traces go to some common point of origin. That common "first cause," or first principle, is a DML point. Such points serve as anchors to our belief or value system, as well to as our behavior.

When we look at an illustration on a computer screen, we're actually looking at pixels. There can be tens of thousands of them in small illustrations. What we see is the picture, not the pixels; however, when computer artists alter tiny aspects of an image, they'll most often magnify some small section by, say, 200 times until they have enlarged views of perhaps 40 or 50 pixels on the screen, which represent a tiny part of the picture. The artist then may shape or paint one pixel at a time. When the picture is restored to screen size, the changes are subtle but distinct.

DMLs are like pixels. In the deep mind rest tiny beginning points that are linked together like pixels. Close-up evaluation reveals flaws in some of our pixels, although if we back away and look at the picture, only very large (gross) flaws are visible. These larger defects are basically the disorders of interest to psychologists and psychiatrists. Diagnostic manuals for mental-health professionals provide systematic lists of gross flaws. These same volumes suggest corresponding flaws that imply likely problems in, shall we say, neighboring "pixels."

Most of us have pixels that aren't seriously enough flawed to need the help of a professional. Still, when we desire to self-actualize, to engage and manifest our highest potential, then the evaluation of deep-mind links is critical to success. Like an artist working pixel by pixel, we can begin with our own DMLs. Most of the techniques we'll examine are designed to do just this. However, very skilled artists often have effective shortcuts. For them, a spray can or paintbrush tool can be employed to make gross changes as quickly as the problems are identified.

In the material that follows, we'll look at pixel-by-pixel technology. Hopefully, you'll learn how to take the tiniest areas of your life and make them as perfect as you desire. We'll also try some spray-can and paintbrush tools.

One of my other observations about change could be stated this way: "Change behavior and you change thinking. Alter thinking and you alter behavior. Experience a positive feedback from change and you reinforce it. Shift the focus of change from the self to giving service to the world, and what follows incorporates the best of the individual and of society at large."

Teach

In his book *Love Is Letting Go of Fear,* Gerald Jampolsky makes a related observation. Jampolsky, a licensed psychiatrist in California, noticed that even terminally ill patients in unbearable pain forgot their agony and overcame other physical limitations when they went to the aid of another patient. Somehow, the act of loving, the involvement from caring, the nurturing feeling of giving of oneself to another, the focus on others instead of the self, gives life to a new *Life.* Out of the old skin rises a new individual. This new person is healed by helping others. It's reminiscent of the adage: "Teach what you want to learn."

If you wish to begin a gross overhaul of the painting called "self," begin by focusing on the needs of others—not an indulgent focus, but by teaching what you wish to learn. Share the notions of self-responsibility in loving, helpful ways. Give support to others, not pity. Help by refusing to grant permission for self-indulgence. Pierce the old ego personification by being the model you would most respect.

I once hosted a radio show in Salt Lake City called *The Good News Hour.* During one of these shows, I discussed facial expressions and how they're hardwired with the brain. For example, did you know that smiling—physically giving that big old grin—fools the mind into believing that life is great? Yes! Smile, and the brain chemistry changes. A simple expression can alleviate morose feelings almost immediately. The wired-in process can be used intentionally to alter mood states, as I mentioned earlier. On that particular day, my radio co-host, a young woman named Darlene from West Valley City, offered some advice that I'll never forget: "I guess that means fake it 'til you make it!"

Faking it 'til you make it is just what the proverbial doctor ordered when it comes to change. Remember our earlier axiom: "Change behavior and you change thought. Alter thinking and you alter behavior."

DML anchors can be moved with a broad brush when we undertake a different behavior. Self-indulgence and the ego's pettiness propel antiquated defense strategies that lie in the unconscious. This can be likened to huge blocks of corrupted pixels distorting the larger picture. Through the act of forgiveness and the engagement of caring, the old pixels disappear. The overall result is almost immediate, and then we can fine-tune the individual pixels in the picture. It's as the mystics have always said: erasing karma is entering grace. Forgiveness is the act of grace.

Somehow, in the process I've described, a mystical experience seems to be triggered. This becomes a dynamic part of the individual's life. The changed person seems to view the entire world as if it were a dream. Just as it would make no sense in a waking state to be truly upset because of something in our dreams, so in real life it makes little sense to judge or blame. Forgiveness then transcends the whole of what we generally think of as real, or the physical world. There's nothing to forgive, for the entire matter simply never occurred. Only within the dream is any power given to wrongdoing. In the eternally real, the error didn't occur.

The Four Views

Here's a story that I call "The Four Views." A wise master had four students who exceeded all others. One day the five gathered, and the master spoke to the first student: "Tell me what you see when you look into the world."

"I see savagery. The planet is raped. The world hides from the truth. Contaminating material is released everywhere. There's particulate matter in the heavens and acid rain. The rain forests are being destroyed and so is the ozone layer. There's such ignorance and self-ishness. The world needs so much correction."

The master replied, "You are right, and I shall call you *Correction,* for you by your vision have committed to a world of need."

To his second student, the master put the same query: "Tell me what you see when you look into the world."

The second student replied, "Master, I see futility. Nothing can be done to change the ways of the world, although some will repent and call for change. Still, the world is condemned by the acts of humans. The sciences teach us that too many people are being born, too much destruction has already been done, too little money is provided for

204

science to adequately assist, and there's too little concern for ethics and values. Crime escalates while families decay. Law is lost."

"You, too, are right, and I shall call you *Righteous,* for your indignation beholds a corrupt world beyond repair while your heart suffers its pain. You shall be known for your words, and your works will express the sadness of your heart."

The master turned his gaze to the third student. "And you, what do you see?"

"I see a world needing the restoration of law. I don't believe that hope is lost. I find encouragement in the words of my brothers, for they, too, recognize the need for a change. It's with confidence that I sense the willingness of humankind to change. All good government is government of the people and for the people. It's through law and government that change can be effected. The mass will follow the right action and attitude of government. The agent for change exists, and it's law and government."

"You also are right. I shall call you *Government,* for your words forge your observations and become what you teach. You'll therefore be committed to a work of law and order through government."

Finally, to the fourth student, the master put the same question: "And what do you see?"

"Master, I behold only miracles. Life is a miracle; all being is a miracle; consciousness is a miracle. I behold God in all creation. I sense the beauty of *love* in the fragrance of the flower, in the smile of a child, in the warmth of lovers, and in the glow of the stars. When I look upon the world, I'm greeted with its mysteries. It's with awe and reverence that each day unfolds its beauty. I know that all things are good and that each expresses its good in its own appropriate manner for the moment. I know that that which my brothers speak about is but illusion, for only the eternal is real. I'll give no power to thoughts of scarcity, of limitation, or of need, for all that's truly needed is here for us to behold, to recognize, and to accept. I wish only to give to the world the sight I've been given. For with these modest eyes and senses, my heart is quickened by the glory of being."

The master smiled before he spoke. "And you, my chosen student, I will call *Truth,* for your vision is of truth, and its reward is the reality it sees. You shall go unto humankind and teach from what you see, for yours is the vision of what is, and all that is possible rests in this peace. You shall be known by all people through your garments of serenity and peace."

The master, speaking to all of them, added these words: "To each of you is the blessing of your vision. As you see the world, so it reveals itself to you. You will know the world by your vision of it. To each of you will go the works of your sight. You'll experience life according to your vision."

■ ■

Not only is our reality a matter of choice but so is the power we give it. Only the eternal is incorruptible, therefore only the eternal is true. All else is inherently false by definition. To be a master, one must begin by acting like a master. To grow, we must give. The old saying "You can't receive if the cup is full" is absolutely true of the human condition. As we sow, so do we reap. The first step, then, in self-actualization is to give forgiveness and care. The old deep-mind link memories disappear; the new memories become both the process and the goal.

Tech Talk

There's almost too much talk about technology today. Still, as the information age ripens, anyone arriving late, like an imaginary Rip Van Winkle, won't just be lost but perhaps even unable to find directions. Today's language is more and more the language of the computer. The communication modalities are much less involved with aspects of behavior, such as facial expressions and body language, because so much communication is done via the highways of cyberspace, fax machines, synthetic voice greetings, and the like. We can only imagine what the communication network will be like in another two to three decades.

Technology may well be humankind's greatest achievement. It has reached a plateau still largely unimagined by most of the world's population. The abilities of science and technology today are indeed awesome. Perhaps that's why science has become a god for so many. It should be pointed out, however, that this worship has led to some of humankind's most ignoble deeds.

Science recognizes that it's a work in progress, yet many behave as though the final verdict is in. For example, what's the difference between singularity (a stable state of one thing), the Unmoved Mover of Aristotle, the God of Genesis, the Vedas, and so forth? The big-bang explanation only asks questions and renames familiar constructs. After all, how does the finite comprehend the infinite? We understand best through models, I suppose, like that of the late David Bohm. Dr. Bohm's holographic universe won a Nobel Prize—as it should have. Still, he would be the first to point out that implicate order further suggests a cosmic origin, which begs the very question it tries to explain.[1]

Before we get too far afield, let's just agree that technology is important to everyone. Today, it's a path to personal empowerment, much as ashrams, private and secret orders, and the like have been in the past. Today, technology launches out-of-body experiences, primes self-talk, generates altered states of consciousness, accelerates the healing process, and so much more. Listing it all would be a monumental task in and of itself.

Simple technologies with a great deal of power exist alongside complex ones that have little impact. Yet, like the tools of a carpenter or artist, each may have a place with any individual. We'll use the rest of this chapter to review and try on some of them.

Self-hypnosis and self-suggestion are two of the best tools available at little to no cost. They employ the power of the mind and therefore can be totally self-generated. To properly deal with these, however, we should begin with visualization.

Visualization is the process of using the mind's eye to create images, scenes, feeling, sensations, and so on. Maxwell Maltz, in his wonderful book *Psycho-Cybernetics,* informs us that the mind can't distinguish an imagined experience, if imagined in sufficient detail, from a real experience.[2] The memory stores the two as equally valid. Some of the work in neural-method modeling has shown us that imagined experiences can seem so real that they produce muscular response. Using this technique, many athletes imagine their performance —seeing it vividly in the mind's eye and feeling the tiny muscle groups respond to the mental experience—and in this way memorize the action.[3] Indeed, some work has demonstrated a real physical advantage to imagining exercise. By just imagining with vivid detail, a mental muscle workout begins to tone the physical body.[4]

We've all experienced dreams that were so real that we had to think twice to decide whether they occurred or not. Dreams of this nature are vivid, felt and sensed in every way, and emotionally strong. Innate to our human makeup is the mental wiring that has the ability to generate synthetic experiences with the full power of actual events. Our memory records the occurrence, synthetic or real, and in this way the information becomes organized as part and parcel of our total experience.

Memory

Memory is a very powerful force, playing an essential role in our self-image, expectations, fantasies, and general well-being. It makes associations for all experiences. These connections, or deep-mind links, inform us of the continuity of being. Without this continuity, existence is episodic and could well be viewed as artificial. Memory reminds us of who we are, what's expected from us, how we've chosen to see the world, what our beliefs are, where we live, what happened yesterday and the day before, and so on. Subtract memory, wake up with no recall, and each day becomes entirely different. Think about this for a moment.

When people in deep hypnosis are given amnesia for certain events, their character appears to change. When artificial events are introduced, their character is once again modified. When subjects in a deep trance are informed that they're being burned by the touch of an ice cube, a blister rises. When some multiple-personality-disordered patients switch personalities, their blood-sugar levels, eye color, or other such characteristic may change. Memory dictates the continuity that makes up our lives!

Memory is never only factual information. The mind isn't a blank slate on which all events are recorded perfectly. Indeed, each time a memory is recalled, it's also changed. Evidence shows that it's also skewed by expectation, fear, anxiety, desire, and more. In a very real sense, we rehearse the memories we wish to exist and then remember them. Sometimes this rehearsal happens in advance of an event, sometimes it's at the time of the event, and sometimes following. Moreover, it's always adjusted with each recall and in line with the investment we make. In other words, memories thought to be very important have greater investments of energy, which is usually emotional.

Emotion is a key component. Even feelings not thought to be attached to the memory assert their influence. For example, some memories are pushed down deep in the mind, so deep that we have no awareness of remembering. This can be due to the emotional tone of the event at the time of and/or following the experience. Trauma victims often recall traumatic incidents . . . until they forget them. Now that may sound rather idiotic, but the fact is that we must remember in order to forget. Some level of operation within the mind defends our well-being by suppressing the memory. It remembers to keep the recollection under wraps and therefore develops a tactical structure to defend the forgotten memory. Memories aren't erased—they're suppressed.

Each such memory has a tactical operation to keep it suppressed. Built into this are strategies to fend off inquiries. Often, these strategies are self-defeating. The subliminal mind holds these subliminal beliefs, hidden memories, and tactical strategies to ostensibly protect our self-image and well-being. Sometimes the strategies are resistance oriented, and sometimes they're attraction oriented; but from compensatory actions to self-mutilating behavior, they're always essentially diversions.

A diversion is designed to stop us from closely examining our motives, which underlie all action. Some of our motives are wired in survival-oriented ways, while others are the result of deep-mind links that camouflage or hide ulterior motives through association. Some of our motives are higher cortical ones—like that of self-actualization itself.

The use of imagery has two essential roles in our context. The first is to provide a tool for generating memories of choice—feelings of well-being, for example. The second is to get in touch with aspects of ourselves that we may otherwise be unable to reach. When we imagine information, the image draws across all links for sensory input. As such, when we recall an event, allowing ourselves to fully picture, feel, and otherwise sense, then the event will often bypass the critical mind and its defense mechanisms. Images may pop in and startle us, but linguistic approaches typically obtain bit-by-bit revelations.

One of the great healing powers of hypnosis is its uncovering ability—largely the ability to recover information in pictorial events, unfolding as on a movie screen while detaching the individual from the emotion of the event. Hypnotic regressions/recall are therefore powerful tools in the healing.

Visualization

Learning to visualize is a wonderful opportunity to access our own inner life, as well as rewrite some memory information, so let's look at how we visualize. It's surprising how many people don't see images when they close their eyes. It's also surprising how many don't believe they dream. We all dream—we must do so or lose our sanity. Remembering dreams, however, is quite different.

Since so many people report a lack of internal images, let's take it from the beginning. I strongly recommend two methods to learn how to image. The first is to take a picture of some scene, such as cooking outdoors over a fire (but this must be something you can actually relate to because of experience). Stare at the picture until the scene can be smelled and felt or becomes almost real. Using a pleasant association and a picture that reminds you of pleasant events is most productive.

Look at the scene until you feel it. If it was cold when you cooked over a fire outdoors, feel the chill. Let yourself shiver a little. Once that's accomplished, close your eyes and hold the scene in your inner eye. If at first you don't succeed, try again. Repeat the process until you have the inner image fully on the "screen"of the mind.

The second approach is to take something that already has strong tactile associations for you, such as a lemon. Hold a lemon in your hand and concentrate on it. Focus on how it feels. Think of how it tastes, and let the juices of the lemon shape your mouth. Smell it at close range. Look at its bright color, and think of the sun and its similarity in color. Allow yourself to associate any other information that comes with the lemon. Then close your eyes and see the lemon still in your hand, right in front of your face. Do this two or three times and you'll begin to open the field of inner sight necessary for visualization.

Assume that we all can image now. What do we visualize? How often? When? This process should be part and parcel of every day. By visualizing a successful, rewarding day at the outset, we're more likely to have one. Many people visualize misery in their lives without recognizing it. They dwell on fearful thoughts, think of violent reprisals and revenge, take angry actions from television and entertainment to bed with them, imagine the worst monsters, and so forth. All of these actions are visualizations. What's more, when we imagine (visualize) fighting, the world brings us a fight. Somehow the fight is never quite as we thought it would be, and when we learn this, it behooves us to imagine more peaceful events.

When we rehearse what we intend to say to someone, we're employing visualization skills. Using these skills to defend ourselves implies a need to defend. The universe is accommodating—here comes your chance to defend! When we use these skills to enhance our sense of belonging, participation in the glory of life, joy, and well-being, the Universe somehow brings exactly those opportunities. You can call this the law of attraction. The fact is that through whatever mechanism, we attract what we invest our imagery/visualizations in. Therefore, we can see that using these skills daily is something most people already do. All we're going to do is invest the energy differently.

The following two exercises have different directions. The first is for uncovering or recovering hidden information—I like to call this "power imaging." The second is for creating a matrix for realizing some event such as personal success.

Uncovering/Recovering Hidden Information

Instructions: Read the exercise and then close your eyes and follow the practice as given.

■ ■

Imagine yourself in a comfortable chair. Behind you is a slide projector with a remote control, and you're holding this control. Before you is a screen. The slide projector contains thoughts, images, feelings, and pictures that are associated together. You don't know in advance how the slides are organized. You're going to watch this slide show, although you're not even sure how many slides there are.

Now take a thought, maybe an idea of something you'd like to become, such as wealthy or popular. Or you might take a fear—but if you do so, remember that your remote control will shut off the projector anytime you wish.

Put the fear or the ambition into the context of a picture in your mind. That's the first slide. The projector will automatically associate this slide with all other relevant slides appropriate at this time, and it will organize them in a meaningful way. You may not understand it, so just trust that it's meaningful.

Put the first slide up on the screen by simply seeing it there. Spend a moment getting fully involved with the image. If there were sounds in the scene, hear them; if there were aromas, smell them; if there were other tactile clues, remember or imagine them. You can enrich this image as much as you like. You can add cheering, feel goose bumps, and so on. Whatever you sense is appropriate to bring this first slide to life—do it on the screen of your mind.

Once you've accomplished that, change the image by pushing the remote control. You can connect your thumb and forefinger to assist you with the imagery. Press your thumb slightly against your finger, and the slide changes. Close your hand tightly, and the projector shuts off.

It's permissible to wonder what slide may come next, but let it just happen. You may be surprised.

■ ■

This exercise provides a window on our desires, ambitions, and fears. It may reveal self-limiting beliefs that we no longer wish to maintain. It may produce images that we wish to desensitize. Use the next exercise to do either.

Realizing Personal Success

Instructions: Read the exercise and then close your eyes and follow the practice as given.

■ ■

Imagine yourself in a sophisticated movie studio. You're about to review the footage taken of you at a special event. You'll be able to edit this footage and make it into exactly what you wish.

The studio is fully equipped with the best audio- and video-production equipment. The screen is larger than any theater you've ever seen. It wraps around you, and when the footage begins, you'll find that it feels as if you were actually there. Unlike movie theaters, your studio is able to reproduce the events from the footage in such a way that it's almost impossible to detect the difference between the re-creation and the actual experience.

You're in a comfortable chair, and you have a thought-controlled interface with all of the equipment. When you wish to alter, edit, change, add new footage, or take whatever action you deem appropriate, you simply think about it, and the film is ready to replay just as you desire it.

When you choose your footage, keep in mind that there are virtually limitless storage devices to play or record your information. But before we continue, let me explain a little more about how to use this special studio.

Very special people have a studio just like the one you're visiting. Some of these individuals are athletes, some are businesspeople, some are scientists, and some are artists. Oh, you name the profession, and you'll find that the best in the field all have their own inner-mind studio. The reason is simple: they know they can first create their work in here. By so doing, they minimize the confusion, risk, and obstacles they might encounter in the outer world. So an athlete comes here to generate the footage that represents his or her perfect play, and a businessperson creates the film of his or her success. Some review old footage and change it. At times they change only their feelings about it, and at other points they actually alter the scenes. This is where old memories are desensitized by viewing the footage with different emotions—say, with forgiveness instead of blame, guilt, and shame. Here's where they put the wisdom of the eternal into their understanding. This is where they gain freedom from imprisoning feelings, fears, and thoughts.

You can come here with an image derived from experience, one that has held you back—a fear, an early-childhood memory, or anything that still grips you. In this studio, you can desensitize it by simply reviewing the image and editing the emotions until you have a product you feel good about. This new sequence is then stored in the memory banks and becomes the image that the mind works with. If you desire to achieve some goal, experience a new level of confidence, and so on, then create the footage here—just as you want it to be.

Now, begin to review the footage that you're going to use. Change anything that doesn't please you. Empower yourself with sensory-rich detail. Hear the crowd applauding or feel true forgiveness, whatever is appropriate. Play the footage back once you've edited it, which you can do as many times as you like. Stay with it until it's exactly perfect—just as you want it. Once you've done that, let it go. Leave the studio and wait for another day to work on something else.

If your footage requires more than one visit for you to get it just the way you wish it had been or just as you want it to be, then return as often as necessary. However, don't go on to other areas until you're satisfied with your work on each item in the order you bring it to the studio.

■ ■

Self-hypnosis should come rather easily now by just extending what you learned in your imagery sessions. Probably the best way to begin is by using what hypnotists call "the progressive-relaxation technique."

Self-Hypnosis and Progressive Relaxation

Instructions: Read the procedure and then select a quiet place where you won't be disturbed for at least 20 minutes.

You'll use an affirmation during the exercise. It's important, so write it out before beginning. Choose your words carefully and make them all positive. The affirmation itself should be as short as possible. For example, if you wish to have more confidence, you might have a statement such as *I am confident.* When you use your affirmation, feel it. Sense what it's saying in every dimension. In other words, feel the confidence fill your being as the affirmation circulates throughout you.

Set an alarm clock for 20 minutes. Let the alarm return you to normal consciousness until the time period becomes conditioned—this usually only takes three to four sessions.

■ ■

Lie down or recline in a comfortable fashion and loosen your clothing. You may choose to play soothing music or nature sounds in the background during this exercise. If you can, also try burning pleasant incense. Dim or eliminate lighting.

With your eyes closed, imagine that you're resting outdoors with a balmy sun bathing your body. You can feel its warmth touching you all over. Focus on your breathing and imagine the exchange. Your exhalations provide life-force energy for the plant world, just as your inhalations provide life-force energy for you. A certain synergy exists between you and the world—a sort of symbiotic relationship. Sense this, and imagine feeling your being extending in and out of all life with every breath.

Breathe deeply and evenly for a moment. Inhale for a count of three, hold for a count of three, exhale for a count of three, and hold for a count of three. Smile slightly as you do this, and complete it at least three times.

Imagine a bright, luminescent, pure gold light coming down from above and entering the top of your head. Feel the light begin to move down through your body, into the neck, down the back, through the legs, and right on down to the tips of your toes. And with one more deep inhalation, the light energy expands outward, radiating several feet from your body. Your entire being is aglow.

Open your mouth slightly and swallow. Let the muscles in the scalp completely relax. Think, *Relax—relax now,* and they all release. Continue the relaxation as though it were some magical potion that you just swallowed. Loosen the jaw and throat muscles, neck, shoulders, arms, back, abdomen, buttocks, thighs, calves, ankles, feet, and every single toe. To each area simply send the thought: *Relax—relax now.*

With your entire body relaxed, remind yourself that there's nothing to do. Right now is time to do nothing. Just let go and be . . . relaxed. And with a tiny effort of mind, concentrate all of your being into one of your toes. Be so wholly, totally in that toe that every minute sensation is experienced by your entire being. Do this with one toe on each foot, and then place all of your consciousness in the area of your solar plexus.

The heart region is just above this spot. Bring your consciousness between the solar plexus and the heart. From this perspective, take one single affirmation that's important to you now, and begin to see it flow back and forth between these two central points of your body. You see it and you hear it.

As soon as you see and hear it distinctly, let it begin the journey throughout your body. It disappears—but it's still there. It travels from cell to cell on a journey throughout the body, and it will be back to travel again. In fact, throughout your session from this point on, your affirmation will travel through you over and over again. As it approaches your consciousness, it may again become visible and audible. But that's of no matter; you have let it go. It announces to all of your self: *This is the way it is.*

When the alarm sounds, open your eyes slowly. Let yourself rest for about five minutes before getting back into the affairs of the day.

■ ■

The best way to condition yourself with hypnotic suggestions is repetition. Try to do this daily for a week or two. If you do, you'll find that occasional touch-up sessions can be accomplished almost anywhere and under almost any conditions. This can have many practical applications, to say nothing of the physical and mental benefits.

Self-Suggestion

Self-suggestion is the next extension of self-hypnosis. For some, this techniques works all by itself. Its power is in the repetition of a thought or phrase, the sort of repetition advised in positive-thinking books.

Repeat over and over in your mind a phrase such as the confidence affirmation from the previous exercise. Write it down on a card that you carry with you. Make a list of benefits that accompany the accomplishment, and take that with you, too.

Get out magazines and newspapers to find pictures that represent your goal. Cut them out and write your affirmation under them. Place images with your affirmation on the refrigerator, on the bathroom mirror, in your car, and anywhere else that you'll regularly encounter them. Each time you repeat the affirmation or run across it, your mind records the information. You begin to identify with the pictures. In this way, the automatic mechanism that we might call the machinery of the subconscious records and begins to script your inner talk and self-belief around your repeated exposures.

InnerTalk

Use an InnerTalk CD or other proven recording in the background to prime your self-talk with the mental language that accompanies your goal. Use this audio program when you sleep, while you're driving, with any television you might watch, and at any other time possible. You can't overdo the positive input. The affirmations prime your self-talk, getting into the deeper mind via bypassing critical awareness. One day, your inner talk will mirror your outer stated desires instead of undermining them.

As discussed earlier, the technology we've looked at has been studied by various independent researchers at leading universities, including Stanford. It has repeatedly been demonstrated to effectively change self-defeating strategies, behavioral difficulties, and even so-called physical symptomology. The affirmations range from weight loss and self-esteem to lucid dreaming and self-healing. There are even titles specific to such situations as ADHD and cancer remission. (See the resource list in the back of this book for more information.)

As I mentioned earlier, included with this book is the InnerTalk program *Serenity.* Play this CD in the background as you go about your day or even all night long while you sleep. Look at the printed affirmations (see Appendix 4) periodically, and watch how they soon become part of your self-talk.

Neurolinguistic Programming

There are a number of good books on Neurolinguistic Programming (NLP). One of my favorites is *Frogs into Princes,* by Bandler and Grinder.[5] NLP is often associated with hypnotic procedures, and one might describe it as "the friendly language." It anchors emotions and feeling, mirrors and matches to pace another person for purposes of rapport, and uses double binds and metaphors. This tool of many therapists and others is a sophisticated technology that's too complicated to treat in detail in this work, so we'll isolate only a small amount of material from NLP protocols to work with here.

A metaphor is a powerful image that affects us literally, figuratively, and emotionally and models an imagery that sinks deep in the mind. Indeed, the most powerful metaphors, in my opinion, have a mythos supporting them. They appeal to a part of human nature that's innate in everyone. Carl Jung, founder of analytical psychology, often referred to the power of myth as arising from the universal archetype.[6]

Metaphor is something we can and do use daily. Indeed, we are our metaphors. I once had a friend who used to say, "The last to starve in the jungle is a tiger!" He was a retired heavyweight fighter, and he saw himself as a tiger. What he didn't realize is that to be a tiger is to act and think like one. Tigers experience an aggressive, hostile world and are often in conflict with other tigers. My friend lived in just such an environment.

A consciously chosen positive metaphor can be a representation of what we decide to be. For full impact, it should be in story form. Each of us has a metaphor that's a collection of smaller metaphors, representing our beliefs. Sports can be a metaphor of excellence, competition, and overcoming insurmountable odds. The stories of Arthur, Camelot, and the Holy Grail; of Zeus, Aphrodite, and the entire lot of Greek mythology; and of the Garden of Eden, Job, and so on are all metaphors with tutorial images that provide models for belief and behavior. Societies everywhere are guided by such tales.

Create a metaphor that represents you. Take the time to sit down and write a story that stands for you and your beliefs, hopes, aspirations, trials, and outcomes. First write a short story showing the way you've seen your life. Then modify this narrative to be as you wish your life to be.

Create a lead character who's the way you want to be. Put this person through the trials you've experienced, and bring him out the other side as a stronger, wiser, and more human and spiritual person. Give the character a name, a look, and a manner that you admire. Describe him in enough detail for your mind to actually see the person. Hold the hero of your story/metaphor in your mind. Close your eyes and let the tale be retold from memory while you watch it on the screen of the mind. Whenever adversity approaches, think of your character. Feel his power and wisdom, and act and speak from the character. In a very real sense, you are this hero, and as you use the character to model your action in the world, you become more fully joined.

Notice how the hero in your personal metaphor walks and holds his body; look at facial expressions and evaluate gestures. Heroes stand erect, chest out and shoulders back. They have friendly, wise facial expressions, warm handshakes, and confident strides.

As soon as you've finished viewing and feeling your story, along with the role and strength of your hero character, open your eyes and go to the mirror—a full-length mirror, if possible. Stand in front of it and notice how you normally walk and stand. Then change this to stand as your hero stands, look as your hero looks, and walk as your hero walks. Feel the additional confidence you've immediately gained, and experience the change in how you respond. This is the standard you wish to represent at all times. Begin immediately making whatever adjustments necessary to portray your body as that of your hero.

There's a marvelous little book by John Diamond entitled *Your Body Doesn't Lie.* One of its themes is how your body will respond to your thoughts: with strength or weakness/fear.[7] You're training yourself. As your body responds, your mind will follow. It's impossible to feel sorry for yourself and be roaring with laughter. Like smiling, posture will influence the mind/brain, and your physical chemistry will be altered.

If appropriate, change your dress. People tend to treat you according to the manner in which you present yourself. I can put on my cowboy boots and old jeans, work outside until I'm a little dirty, run into town, and find that most people treat me differently from the way they respond when I'm in a three-piece suit. It shouldn't be this way—but it is. Clothing and appearance can be an important way to immediately alter your view of yourself, as well as the feedback you receive from others. I feel different when I'm in boots and jeans from when I'm dressed up for a lecture—even my vocabulary changes. Remember, however, that you're working on the core of your being. As you become strong, your apparel and its effect on other people become less important, although it can still be quite amusing from time to time.

In your interactions with others, try the mirror and pacing technique. Listen intently to what the person says. Look at how he uses his body, and subtly imitate it. Nod your head in agreement as he speaks. When he smiles, you smile; when he crosses his legs, cross yours. After a few minutes of imitating, begin to pace. This is done by making some slight change, like crossing the opposite leg. Watch: most often the other person will follow if you've been successful at imitating and thereby building rapport.

When you begin to speak, do so from his point of view. Take something he's said and reaffirm the statement. Then begin to build your comments and interpretations. Watch his body. If he crosses his arms and legs, be aware that he's most likely shutting you out. Slow down and regain his confidence.

The art of body talk, body language, mirroring, matching, and pacing are more than worth the time it takes to read a couple of good books on these subjects. There are lots of resources available, and therefore, if this interests you, the techniques can be more wonderful tools that assist you in building your confidence and strengthening your relationships.

M^3

M^3 is something I use to communicate the power of memory (of real and imagined experiences), mood, and modeling. Using any and all of the tools and techniques in this book, or probably any other, with the M^3 formula will enhance the results. The formula is this: create a mood that impresses the body, generating the images, thoughts, and other associations that are desirable while in this mood; model these feelings and associations in a metaphor about yourself; and then memorize them. M^3 means mood times modeling times metaphor equals memory ($M \times M \times M = M^3$). Memory is the continuity of being. The DMLs discussed earlier are M^3 events.

Spiritual Practices

There are many mind practices, as I've outlined. Some of these naturally lead toward more spiritual practices. The reason, I believe, is that the human brain is hardwired for religious experience. Indeed, there's an area in the brain that, when electrically stimulated, gives rise to a religious experience.[8] Some might argue that this is simply an evolutionary throwback, left over from a time when religion was needed by the species, and that we're outgrowing that need today. I'm not one of those people. I'm convinced that the spiritual predisposition that exists in human beings, including that which we can say as a matter of fact is anatomically present, exists for precisely the reason that the Grand Organizing Designer (GOD) placed it there.

Now that my bias is clear, let me also add this detail: the data demonstrate rather clearly that individuals who feel *connected* to some purpose, some spiritual awareness, are the very people who live the healthiest and longest lives. That isn't professing some religion; rather, it's testifying to the value of spirituality itself.

Because the spiritual is obviously important to the human condition, you may also want to look into a number of special spiritual exercises. These are designed ultimately not only to provide you with more mental control, but to reveal to you the meaning of your being. To that end, I suggest daily meditation using the yoga of breath as a beginning point. This can be as simple as concentrating on your breathing, intentionally changing erratic breathing patterns to rhythmic ones. For example, simply breathe in through your nose to the count of three or four (whichever is comfortable), hold to the same count (let's say three), exhale through your mouth to the count of three, hold to the count of three, and then inhale again through the nose to the count of three. It's amazing how the mind tends to still when you give it this simple task and how quickly heart-coherence rhythm is developed, as pointed out earlier.

Yoga itself is a wonderful spiritual and mind-body tool. The medical use of yoga is fairly widespread now on account of its overall effectiveness in keeping the body and mind fit. It isn't just about body flexibility, as some think; it's a great stress buster, as well as a marvelous way to discipline the entire person. For more information, I strongly recommend Dr. Vijayendra Pratap's books and teachings. He's the founder of the SKY Foundation, and you can take a look yourself at his Website: **www.skyfoundation.org**.

Religious practices are so many and varied that they're beyond the purview of this work. Nonetheless, a spiritual component in everything we do adds a richness and meaning that can only be experienced, not explained.

Meditation

Many wonderful books on meditation are available, but because my purpose here is to introduce the various technologies usually employed for personal growth and self-actualization, I'll present simple exercises and brief explanations. The exercises will work; employing any of the techniques will provide the tools to empower yourself. I remind you that almost every procedure discussed has had volume after volume written about it. Should you desire to use just one system, I encourage you to read as much about it as you can.

Meditation is, in fact, a system. For me, the principal difference between using meditation techniques and hypnotic procedures is in the destiny or goal, not the brain-wave activity or the method through which an altered state is achieved. Indeed, a good hypnotist will have studied many meditation methods and may employ some to induce hypnosis. Still, where the general aim of hypnosis is therapeutic, the goal of meditation is contact with the Most Holy One, Universal Spirit, Higher Power, or whatever other term you're comfortable with. Meditation seeks to touch the quintessential core of being—our own and that of all things.

There are methods to use the body in meditation, such as eurythmics and physical yogas. There are techniques of the mind, such as Jnana yoga (yoga of the intellect) and Transcendental Meditation, and feeling meditations from the heart and solar plexus. Some invoke the use of mantras, and some begin with visual displays such as mandalas.

There are meditation systems built on nature, such as those used by the Lakota Sioux (the Native American tribe), and on and on. Nevertheless, there are some common denominators, and our exercise will draw, as we have already, on an eclectic application of the universal theme. We're going to still the mind. "Be still and know," it's written in almost all traditions. We shall seek to be still.

Be Still

Instructions: Read the following exercise and then follow it.

■ ■

Choose a comfortable, quiet place where you can recline or lie down. Light pleasant-smelling incense and two white candles. Place the candles so that you see both of them when you're sitting down, then turn off or dim all other lighting. Play some gentle music or a nature sound track very softly in the background. Take an object that you consider to be spiritual—for instance, a book such as the Bible, *A Course in Miracles,* a volume from the Upanishads, or whatever is appropriate for you. Place it in your lap after loosening your clothing. Set your alarm clock for 30 to 40 minutes for this exercise.

Begin by staring into the candles. Watch the flames flicker and dance, and think of the dance of life. Imagine life force as a flame. Think of the fire as in your heart center, an infinite flame. Concentrate on the flames. Close your eyes and see them still burning. Open your eyes and watch them again, close your eyes and see the flames, then open your eyes and watch once more. Use approximately one-minute intervals between opening and closing your eyes. Do this three times. Then keep your eyes closed and hold the flames on the screen of your mind.

Concentrate on the flames on the screen. If thoughts enter that distract you, bring them to the flames. Let them dance in the fire, but you stay in front of it. It may help to think of the thoughts as passersby, persons walking along a trail behind the flames. You aren't a puppy dog. You don't follow any and all sets of legs. You just let them

Change and the Tools to Make It

pass while you remain in front of the flames. You might even begin to anticipate what other new thought (set of legs) could pass by. You'll notice that as you anticipate them, the thoughts cease. Flames, only flames, in your thoughts. Only flames on the screen of your mind. The fire of life. The life-force energy. Flames—and as you hold them, you see them grow stronger and brighter. They may begin to fill your mind with so much light that the entire screen of the mind glows white.

Be still—only the flames. Let your being merge with the flames. Let your mind become the mind of the fire. Be the fire. Expand the fire. Let the flames thrust upward and rise with them. There's no limit to how high they rise. Ride the flames up and up and up. As they rise, they join. One flame, one strong bright flame. It reaches so high that it joins a ball of fire. You see the brilliance of the ball approaching. Glorious brilliance the likes of which you've never before seen. Golden brilliance, prisms of golden brilliance forming a globe like a royal aura as you approach.

You move ever closer to the one orb of fire, brilliant golden white fire. The blues and reds of your flame leap to the orb. As you enter the aura, the fires become indistinguishable. It's one glorious globe, an orb of golden white fire. You're one in the fire. All of the glistening aspects you beheld as you approached are individual aspects of the one orb, as you are now within the golden white glory of one beingness.

Feel the peace. Feel the warmth. Feel the strength. Feel the universal love. Immerse yourself in feeling, and hold the glory of the light in thought. Be—just be here now. Be—just be here totally now.

■ ■

After you've returned from this exercise, think of the two flames that first became one and then joined many, perhaps billions, in becoming one, also. The two lights represent the union and separation of physical and spiritual reality. Their strength is great when they become one. They're both the flames of your physical presence on this planet now and of your eternal life force. The *One* Life Force Energy that is all. Each time you use this exercise, you'll feel more in harmony with the One Life Force, experience deeper and deeper insights, have a stronger presence of being, and in so many other ways gain from the stillness—the knowingness. If there's only one exercise you ever use from this material, I encourage you to let it be this one.

Automatic Writing

This is a powerful exercise. You're going to dialogue between yourself and some other aspect of you. To do this, just relax and let what comes come.

First, get a writing instrument and paper. Take your pen or pencil and prepare to write a dialogue. On the first line, write "First person" and put a colon after it. Skip down a couple of lines and write "Second person," followed by a colon.

Your dialogue is between first person (you), and second person (higher consciousness). You may find that second person takes on a different identity at some point. Many have reported communicating with angels, guides, and masters. The point of this exercise isn't with whom you communicate but the communication itself. It matters not whether the second person is real, imagined, an alter ego, a master from the past, or anyone in particular. This exercise will assist you in your growth and understanding, as well as put you more in touch with you.

On the first line, after "First person:" write a question. Think for a moment and imagine that an all-wise response will follow. If it helps, see yourself asking the question of someone you admire, love, and trust. Pick a person who would never betray you, someone who only loves you and who knows the answers to all that you might ask. Formulate your question with this sincerity, and make simple. Try to avoid compound questions. Look to ask something important to you, but don't roll every possible issue up into one query.

Take a moment to think about it—one important, straightforward question. It doesn't have to be answerable in an oversimplified yes or no format. Write down your question, and then relax. Let the answer just come, and record it. Don't be critical. Don't question it, and try not to anticipate where it's going. Simply write it as the thoughts come in. Who knows where it will lead? Just take it down as a secretary would.

If the answer leads you to another question, write it down, following the first person/second person format. Even if you think you're making it all up, let the questions and answers come, and do the exercise.

■ ■

Continue to work with this exercise over the course of at least a week. Remember to just trust what comes and let it happen. I've found that much of my life's work has been given me through this tool. Very often when I've sat down to write, something has started that's simply not coming from ego-conscious me. I believe that my best work and most creative insights have been given to me in much this manner.

Regression

Whether or not a person believes in prior lives, past life karma, and dharma, there can be great value to a regression exercise. To a pragmatist, whether the information revealed is actually from a prior life or not is academic. What *does* matter is the quality and importance of the data itself. So for some, regression can be looked upon as the ability to access deeper parts of the self due to the displacement of responsibility: *This isn't me—this is from another life.* For others, it's all so real, so verifiable, that it's evidence of previous lives. Still others may look upon the procedure as having some connection to the collective unconscious. So, perhaps the information is memory—but not a personal memory per se.

Again, does it matter? I think not, at least from the perspective of using the tool to gain a greater understanding of oneself. For what it's worth, the phenomena I've witnessed and experienced predispose me to believe in prior lives. But then, I also believe that each and every one of us has an innate spiritual intelligence that's in some varied stage of awakening. Indeed, for me, most insights, intuitions, and so-called serendipity in science could be called "anomalous memory"— that is, something remembered without context. We know that the information is correct, but we lack the accompanying knowledge that we typically expect: where we learned this, who told us, and so forth. The remembering process seems to intensify as the awakening process increases.

Let's try an exercise so that you can judge for yourself. Some claim the existence of a record where everything we've ever done or been is written. A library, if you will, that contains our records, as well as those of all souls. In the East, karma and dharma shape our current lives. The former is the law of consequence, and the latter is the path by which we rectify things. So a karma-laden consequence of performing a cruel act in a prior life may be that we're on the receiving end of such a deed in the current life. The dharma sets up the people and circumstances to fulfill our karmic debt. We have karmic credits as well as debits, and we may also use dharma to set up a life in which we employ our credits to assist our growth or the improvement of all beings—but then, in a very real sense, as one person grows, so do we all.

Before beginning the exercise, let's look at some ways you can use your experience to heighten your spiritual awareness. As I said, I like to think of this as the awakening of innate spiritual intelligence. As it awakens, our spiritual IQ, or Spiritual Quotient (SQ), grows. In fact, my experience has taught me repeatedly that as SQ increases, so does the quality of life. People simply live longer and healthier lives.

I find it interesting that certain other predictable things are associated with increased SQ. In fact, I believe that so-called insights, such as those reported by the geniuses of history, are actually anomalous memories. Einstein remembers, as an example, that space is curved. He has no framework for the memory—but he's certain without proof. He's also prepared by the study of a lifetime and therefore applies what he's learned to demonstrate or prove what he already knows. This is an anomalous memory.

I suspect that as you progress, other areas of your life will present you with flashes of insight. Are they memories? One way to evaluate the information you obtain during these regression exercises is to consider it carefully. To do so, you'll have to be aware of certain aspects that most people don't pay attention to.

Begin by getting a piece of paper and a writing instrument. Divide the paper into two columns. The left column will have the questions, and after the exercise you'll fill in the right column to the extent that you can. Here are the questions:

1. What style was the furniture? What woods and fabrics was it made of? Describe it in detail. Draw any ornate carving.

2. What finish was on the wall of buildings—inside and out? How was it applied?

3. What type of clothing did you see? Describe the fabric colors, styles, and so forth.

4. What smells did you encounter?

5. What did the landscape look like?

6. What other outstanding items, dates, or other information did you witness?

Upon your return to normal consciousness, your first priority is to answer the questions. It should be obvious that they may hold some validation information for you. In other words, should you wonder whether or not you just made up the experience—not that this really matters except in an academic sense—you then can begin to systematically check your experience.

Past-Life Regression

Close your eyes and assume a comfortable and relaxed mental state. Breathe deeply as you've learned to do in past exercises. Let everything go and turn your mind inward, for your journey begins from the center of your being. Concentrate all of your mental awareness on the solar plexus.

You see before you a porthole such as those in large, luxury ocean-going vessels. This one is bigger than usual. In a moment, you'll open it like a window and exit. Know that you'll travel up and out into what first appears to be outer space and then beyond, deep into a region familiar, yet not remembered. It will feel comfortable and safe. Higher and higher you'll travel until you reach a forgotten library. The building will be white with large, ornate columns. Sculptures covered in gold leaf will appear on the columns. You'll enter the library, find the librarian, and ask for the book of seals on your life.

Vividly see your journey. As soon as you sense balance, you're at the center of your being and ready to begin. At this moment, open the portal and exit. Travel ever higher and higher—out into space— upward and upward. It takes a few moments at the speed of thought— higher and higher. See the library in the distance, like a building aglow on an island in space. Notice it approaching. You're safe and calm. You're certain of finding something most important to you now. You might be a little anxious—*What will it be?* Let that thought go and arrive at the library.

Walk up the steps and enter the building. This is the most spacious structure you've ever imagined, and it's full of volume after volume of beautifully crafted and bound books. Each is a true work of art. Ask the librarian for the book on your life and the page that describes the last day of your last lifetime. Accompany the librarian and accept the volume, but don't look at the page. Rather, place your hand on it and begin to sense and feel the lifetime.

Like a motion picture, a scene will open in front of your mind's eye; it's from the last day of your last lifetime. Do nothing—just let it happen. Count to three, using the still, silent voice within, and know that on three you'll be there . . . in the last day of your immediate past lifetime. You'll be present without emotion, judgment, pain, or other hardship. You'll see it as though detached, as if you were watching a movie of other people. Count to three and be there now.

Take a moment and look around. Take note: How did you succeed in this lifetime? What did you learn? Go to the very moment that you passed from the physical world. What did you leave and what did you take?

Take a moment more and see your loved ones. Do you recognize any of them from your present life? As with the proverbial drowning person, appearing before you are all the important events—the story of your entire life passing before you in an instant. What did you do? Did you accomplish what you came for? Did you set up any patterns to learn from in the next lifetime? Let the images, like film clips, just come in and through. Simply witness the scenes. You aren't here for any other reason at this time. Let the scenarios unfold before you.

Take a moment more before coming back.

It's time to return. Do this with a backward count from five to one. At one, your eyes will open; you'll be fresh and alert, feeling very good and remembering all that you saw. You'll recall it without judgment.

Begin with number five: you're beginning to come back now . . . don't try to stay . . . coming back. Number four: coming back . . . calm and comfortable. You're coming back with direct lessons for your lifetime in the here-and-now. Number three: back . . . almost all the way. Number two: coming all the way back now. Number one: you're back . . . here-and-now.

Open your eyes and turn your attention to the sheet of paper you prepared before your journey. Take whatever time is necessary to answer the questions, and write any other comments that are important to you.

How do you feel? Think about that. This evening when you go to bed, think again of what you saw. You can use this same exercise to return to any lifetime—just begin by going to the library. Keep a diary of these visits, and look for patterns, which teach you what you wish to learn. The pattern will illustrate the lesson by coming back to the same repeated issue or question. You might be surprised by how many times you can have the same pattern before you recognize it.

Dream Diaries

Dreams are a powerful form of communication with a number of theories to explain them. It's certain that dreams vent unresolved conflict, consolidate memories, and serve in yet another tutorial fashion to reveal and teach. Many individuals either don't believe that they dream or forget their dreams. Still, the imagery can be haunting, affecting attitudes and emotions, even when the dream isn't recalled.

The best way to get a handle on the subject is to begin a dream diary. Record your dreams each morning. To begin, choose only very graphic and powerful ones for interpretation. Let me share a useful interpretation method that can translate their otherwise ambiguous language.

Take one of your dreams and create a story. Choose the central character as the hero or villain, and write a short description of the plot. Create a list of the images that appeared. If you dreamed of a monster, list it as, say, a dragon or whatever you saw. Alongside each word in your list, provide another word, symbol, or definition. For example, for the word *dragon* I might write *fearful, frightening, dangerous,* or *evil.* Rename each image with a feeling. Once you've completed this, rewrite the dream using words from your list. So, if I dreamed that a dragon chased me, I might write something like: "Fear chased me."

Using this simple technique can take the most vague meanings and make them crystal clear. Also remember after the final writing that the characters in the dream are almost always some aspect of yourself. If you dream of a black knight battling a white knight, you're seeing an inner struggle between what most might just call good and evil.

Lucid Dreaming

Life is described by mystics as a dream within a dream, and lucid dreams are very close to sensing what that might be like. Simply stated, you're dreaming, and in your dream, you're aware of it. This provides a marvelous opportunity to engineer outcomes. You can learn to have lucid dreams via a number of means, including a remarkable lucid-dream machine made by the real expert in this field, Dr. Steven LaBerge.[9]

Let's take a look at a couple of simple ways that you may trigger and train lucid dreaming. Post a "sentry" in your mind. You might say that this is an imaginary being—it's a part of your mind that will watch over your sleep and dreams. When you go to bed at night, instruct the sentry to awaken you when a dream comes in. The watchman is to nudge your consciousness just enough for you to become aware that you're dreaming. This is a simple process, but don't underestimate it.

When the sentry calls you, don't attempt to awaken. Simply acknowledge the alert and begin monitoring the dream. If it takes a turn that you don't like, change it. Enter the dream and alter the action. Replay it just as you did in the studio exercises earlier. Make the change, then let it continue to unfold. Shift it again if necessary and appropriate.

Another simple method is to use a pillow petition. Instruct your higher self to monitor for dreams, and say what you wish to dream about. You may choose to see something hidden, to obtain an answer, to create a feeling, and so forth. Write down your desire and instructions, then place the written note under your pillow. Put a glass of water beside your bed. Include in your instructions the requirement to be fully awakened if you fail to acknowledge the dream when it begins. Also request to remember the dream the next morning.

When awakened in the middle of the night, drink half the glass of water. Say to yourself: *I prime the waters of consciousness with half of my awakened abilities to have and remember the dream now.* Go back to sleep. You'll have the dream.

Vibrating the Body

Subtle effects resulting from environment, thoughts, and other factors alter physical vibrations in the body, which are analogous to the tuner on a radio. Where your body vibrates is the frequency of thought that you're tuned to. Sometimes this thought is from a collective within the body and sometimes from without. Most often, it's both.

The color of clothing we wear affects vibration, as does the food we eat, what we smoke and drink, the types of garments we wear and how restrictive they are, the colors of a room, the lighting, the sense of space, and so on. A number of books and several published studies on these effects are available. Certain psychics tend to see these vibrations in the form of auras. Kirlian photography, also known as electrophotography, has been used to diagnose and prognosticate disease based upon photos taken of the aura, which is also called "bioplasma" or "corona discharge."[10]

Following is an exercise that changed my life.

Go Meatless

Edgar Cayce, considered by some to be one of America's most documented psychics, asserted that the vibrations taken into the body influenced the mind. He insisted that opening up higher awareness, so-called psychic abilities, could be best done by eliminating meat from the diet. The Edgar Cayce Foundation designed a study to evaluate this, and I had the good fortune to participate.

Cayce believed that the fear and other negative emotions in an animal were transmitted via vibration rate to the human when the animal was consumed. These lower vibrations decreased the resonance of the human condition. If an animal had been treated in an undignified manner, deprived of freedom, butchered savagely, or otherwise given no respect, then the fear, anger, and group of terror emotions would influence human development.

All you must do to test this hypothesis is stop eating meat for 30 days. If the theory is as true for you as it was for me, the results will be obvious. A side benefit is that this change tends to increase psychic abilities.

Love Yourself

"Love thyself" is an ancient admonition that's as true today as at any point in history. For many of us, it can be difficult to truly love ourselves. We may feel shame or guilt, or we may look upon our bodies or parts of our bodies with disdain. Louise Hay has a marvelous book called *You Can Heal Your Life* that everyone should read. In a few convincing words, she shows us that we should love even our illnesses or diseases.[11] Now, that's not to say we enjoy getting them. No! It simply means that *love* is a healing force second to none. In order to become true to ourselves, we must accept what we are. There's no growth in self-deceit or denial, for this is akin to building a house on a sandy foundation.

Goals

The power of setting goals is so well known that many think it's old-fashioned. It's not! Goals are essential to success. There are thousands of books and CDs on the subject, so we'll limit our discussion to some straightforward steps.

To use any techniques in this area, you must first identify a clear goal. It must be attainable, realistic—perhaps very ambitious, but still within the realm of possibility—and something you truly desire! Let me emphasize this last notion with a story.

It seems that a bright young man once sought out a master in the East. When he found the master, he demanded that the master teach him the mysteries and truths of the universe. The master looked at the young man and walked away.

The young man was insulted. He was successful, bright, educated, and used to being treated with more dignity. For years, the young man ridiculed the master as being a master of only nonsense.

One day, however, the young man again felt the urge to seek the teachings of the master, whose fame had only increased since their first meeting. This time, when the young man approached the master, he asked him sincerely to become a student. The master looked upon him for some time and said, "When you are ready." With no more words than this, the master walked away.

The young man thought about the words of the master for several months. Then one day he returned. He found the master washing his clothes by a stream. Once again, he approached. "Master," he declared, "I truly wish to learn the secrets of the universe. I wish to be your student."

The master took the young man behind the head with a strong grip and submerged his head in the water. After a moment, he raised the young man's head and looked into his eyes. "Tell me, what did you want most while your head was under water?"

The young man answered, "Air. Why, air, of course."

The master smiled. "When you desire knowledge as much as you desired air—then you are ready."

This story has been criticized of late in some of Eckhart Tolle's work.[12] However, my point in using the tale is to draw attention to the importance of focus.

The first step is to crystallize your thinking and formulate the goal—with *desire!* The next step is to identify clear steps to the goal. These should be landmarks that attest to your achievement and commitment. Write down the steps and timelines. When will they be reached or achieved?

This goal sheet then is like a ladder with the ultimate desire on the top rung. You'll get there one step at a time. Each rung is a step that you'll work to achieve on some realistic schedule. Even if you're not on time, you won't be discouraged because you've fired up your goal with desire!

Become a Professional

Ask two or three professionals how much time they spend on continuing education, journal reading, and generally maintaining their level of expertise. They'll all tell you on average at least an hour a day.

Professionals know that information is constantly changing, that new techniques, discoveries, and research are constantly fine-tuning their knowledge. Most licensing requirements insist on continuing education to ensure quality that could otherwise be nonexistent.

Act as a professional care provider for yourself! Allocate time each day for yourself. Upgrade your knowledge bank, practice self-care and self-actualization training, pursue personal growth, or just plain old relax. Set time aside for you! Make an appointment with yourself, if necessary, recording the time in your daily log and keeping your commitment. Whether you use this time for daily meditation or reading, for a quiet walk in nature or enjoying the humor and company of others, treat yourself every day to time with and for you.

Happenstance opportunities won't provide the systematic framework necessary for personal empowerment. To have the tools and fail to use them due to a lack of time is analogous to cutting dead wood in a forest with a stone because you didn't have time to bring your chainsaw.

Invest in yourself just as any professional does. Attend workshops and seminars, read books, listen to CDs, watch related videos, and so on. In the modern world, you're bombarded daily with so much garbage and negativity that spending an hour each day on positive self-training is essential. And from time to time, indulge yourself. Spoil yourself. You deserve it!

Attend to Your Self-Talk

Guard your inner talk. Watch what you say and think. As you've already seen, this is most important! Avoid those old sayings such as "I caught a cold." What do you mean you "caught" a cold? You chased it down and tackled it? Remember that what you say—you claim! And you'll claim your thoughts soon enough if you don't cancel them.

Prime your thoughts with information that produces feelings of warmth and genuine well-being. I try to play InnerTalk CDs all day in the background and all night while I sleep. Protect your thoughts from nonsense and rubbish! Choose audio programs that are in line with your personal goals.

Use Affirmations

There are a number of recorded affirmation programs on the market. One series that I like is called *Self-Talk*. The author, Shad Helmstetter, has done an excellent job building statements that are audibly repeated over and over again. The idea is simple: you listen to the positive, self-affirming statements and mentally repeat them. Over a number of repetitions the material truly gains a foothold in your mind.[13] Affirmation recordings, such as those offered by Hay House and others, including the *Self-Talk* series, can be most beneficial.

With that said, if you find your self-talk "talking back," negating the positive statements with doubt and so forth, get your InnerTalk program from this book and wash away the doubt from the inside out.

Dowsing Emotions

Dowsing is the practice that practitioners say permits them to detect hidden or buried water, metals, gemstones, or other such objects without the use of scientific apparatus. Would you be surprised to know that there are parts of the United States where more wells are sunk due to dowsing than science and engineering? It's true. I live in an area in Washington, for example, where each of my eight neighbors placed a well according to a location given by a dowser. This is legitimate. Indeed, it was one of the best ways our military had to find booby traps in Vietnam.

You can dowse your emotions. Muscle testing uses body strength responses to discover information that's somehow known in the mind. This is great if you have two people or sophisticated instrumentation to uncover emotional blocks. The wonderful thing about dowsing, however, is that it doesn't require another person.[14]

There are a number of different dowsing tools and many good books that teach the art. I'd defer to that material if you wish to pursue the subject, but here you'll learn one simple, revealing practice. Take a word, a thought, the name of a person, or any other issue you feel may be related to emotional disturbances of some kind, and write it down on a small piece of paper. Fold the paper so that you have a small, flat sheet; then prepare five other identical pieces that have nothing written on them. (The blank pieces of paper are just to stop you from influencing the outcome.)

Lay the sheets of paper out in a circle as shown in Figure 16.

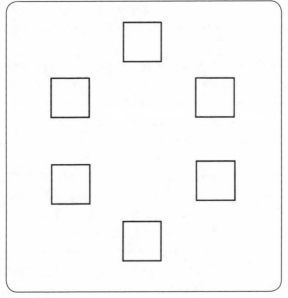

Figure 16

Balance a spoon on your forefinger with the bowl in the direction of your other three fingers, which should be folded back. In a smooth motion, begin to pass the spoon above each piece of paper. Think only: *Is there an issue with [whatever you wrote down] that I haven't resolved?* Continue a slow smooth motion over the paper for ten complete passes. If there's no response from the spoon, you can be relatively comfortable that there's no lingering problem. If there *is* a response, then it may behoove you to take a look at resolving whatever conflict remains.

This is a technique that helps us stay honest with ourselves. It has a particular advantage when we notice something, or someone else points something out to us, that we may have denied or ignored. Try it. Don't be fooled by its simplicity.

Entrainment

This technology differs a bit from what we've most recently reviewed. A number of entrainment tools are available to slow down brain-wave activity. They range from light and sound machines to computerized brain-wave synchronizers. Some options are very expensive. Because of that, we'll look at affordable methods to induce an altered state of consciousness through the mechanical means known generally as "entrainment."

A number of CD companies offer audio recordings that will entrain the mind. This is an inexpensive method to accomplish our means mechanically. If you've done the exercises included in this chapter, you've already experienced an altered state. Still, if you wish to induce such a condition for very specific purposes, such as out-of-body experiences, a CD is the fastest means.

These audio programs combine some sophisticated frequency formats to produce different effects. Employing technologies such as frequency-following response, canceling beats, binaural beats, and sometimes even rates from radionics literature, the better CDs generate a matrix pattern that elicits specific responses from the brain. The Monroe Institute is a leader in this field, and I personally recommend their material. Progressive Awareness produces an entire line of entrainment programs for different purposes and usage parameters. Obviously, since I made these, I also recommend them.

Leading-Edge Technologies

Our overview of some of the best options for personal improvement is finished—but not complete! Many other technologies are available and emerging in the field of human development. For example, there are extra low frequency programs (ELF) units that control electromagnetic environments, cortical electrostimulation (CES) machines that influence brain chemistry and have been reported to substantially improve IQ, and a host of others.[15] In fact, I have worked with one of the leading experts on CES, Dr. Charles McCusker, and this is a tool you'll hear much more about in the future.

To discuss all of the equipment available for mental training would take a book in itself and is beyond the scope of this work. However, with that said, there are a couple of items that I'll introduce you to because they're among my favorites.

Years ago, I had the opportunity to work with Pat Flanagan's Neurophone. I reported an initial finding with it in my book, *Subliminal Learning*.[16] The device has been demonstrated to electronically induce languaged messages through skin contact and was originally invented to enable the hearing impaired to enjoy sound, such as Bach's fugues.

Although taken off the market by the U.S. National Security Agency, an associate of mine in Canada obtained one for me. An educational psychologist friend and I immediately began experimenting with different levels of communication via the device, as compared to similar levels without it. The Neurophone has an output control that, when raised, will cause electronic signals to be *heard* inside the brain as though the sound was generated from outside the ear. When lowered, it will pulse the same signal but without sufficient intensity to be consciously perceived.

Pat Flanagan's rights were eventually returned to him and the Neurophone is now available. The drawback is its monaural output. Since the technology I patented requires a stereo output, I went looking for a similar device with that capability and found it in the Echofone. I've personally logged many hours on the Echofone and have found it to be a marvelous device that both appears to work like the Neurophone in every way and enhances the audio with its stereophonic ability. You can read more about the Echofone by using the search box on my site: **www.innertalk.com**.

If you enjoy biofeedback and computer games, the Wild Divine is perfect. This software program is affordable and fun to use. The interface is more than just a chart measuring skin conductance and so forth, although you probably do want the chart mode when you get the software. The program is designed as a magical journey where you move objects and accomplish certain feats by managing your bio response. A quick search of the Web will help you find this product, or you can once again go to my Website and read much more: **www .innertalk.com**.

241

If you're interested in real mind control, biofeedback plus, there's a program that consists of hardware (radio transmitters) and software that I really like. This isn't an inexpensive investment like the earlier ones I covered. It runs into the thousands of dollars, but it's at the leading edge of mind-training products. The item is known simply as IBVA. IBVA Technologies, Inc. allows real-time brain-wave activity to control digital videos, music, home-automation systems, and more. Its two-party interface makes it possible to even do mind battles of sorts with a live opponent. You can read more about the IBVA system here: **www.ibva.com**.

As I indicated earlier, there are many machines and software programs designed to plug the mind into a special state. One of the most interesting may well be the adaptations that have been done with the Persinger helmet discussed in the first half of this book. Some have called this device "the God helmet" because it purportedly induces religious experience.

I recently learned that an adaptation of the product could be purchased, and I placed my order. The one I ordered is called the Shakti helmet. I spoke with Todd Murphy, owner of the company offering the new device. He told me in the phone call that he didn't believe that there was a God center in the brain, but rather a God process. I can't personally speak to its effectiveness at this time since my helmet hasn't arrived yet. I decided to include the information simply because I find it very intriguing.

Let me make you aware of this caveat as well: according to Richard Dawkins, author of *The God Delusion*, the helmet doesn't work unless you already believe in God. I'll let you decide how much credence you wish to place in the Dawkins statement. Take a look for yourself by searching the Internet or visiting the site I ordered from: **www.spiritualbrain.com**.

Finally, I do believe that the nontechnical tools discussed earlier in this chapter are the best for the beginner and nonprofessional alike. It isn't necessary to spend hundreds or thousands of dollars to begin the journey into becoming all that is your birthright. Again, for the nonprofessional, the technologies I've discussed are both the most available and the easiest to work with. All are affordable and will yield tremendous advantage. I hope you enjoy!

Summary

Many different techniques can be used to program your own mind and to *undo* the programming that has been done by others. The techniques range from visualization to automatic writing, and most of these don't require any special equipment. A number of exercises were given that will assist you in accessing your own mind power. A number of technological means were also suggested. The key is to try the different techniques, find out which methods you prefer, and then work with them regularly. Remember, keep your expectations reasonable.

CHAPTER 16

Guarding Against Overstimulation

*"Intellectual virtue in the main owes its
birth and growth to teaching . . . while moral
virtue comes about as a result of habit."*

— Aristotle

This chapter takes on the issue of morality and respect. I hesitated to include it, for I have no desire to lecture anyone on values. In the end, despite its brevity, I couldn't omit it. The issue is altogether too important, especially for the future of our younger generations.

Look around you today. Observe the discourse in the news, and listen to how young people talk to their parents. Give the telephone solicitor a moment or two before saying "No thanks," and hear the response. Pay attention to other drivers and the levels of friendliness and courtesy they exhibit. When you make these observations, you may ask the same question that I do: "Where has the civility gone?"

I admit that picking up the telephone to some solicitor who starts right off with something along the lines of "Hello, Eldon—this is Eldon, right?" annoys me. It does so for multiple reasons, including the fact that my phone number is on the "Do Not Call" list. There was a time that the caller would have greeted me as Mr. Taylor and been polite as a part of the sales pitch. What happened to this courtesy?

Everywhere except in Congress (and even there in hostile circumstances) and maybe with your doctor, it's a first-name game. "Hi, Bambi, I'm calling from Congressman Cole's office" or "Hi, Tom, I'm calling from Dr. Smith's office" are the only examples of formality or genuine politeness that we see and even then it generally only goes in one direction. All languages provide ways to greet someone or ask a question that are informal and other ways that are formal. As a foreigner visiting another country—for example, Mexico—you're advised always to use the formal option.

Why does this matter? The future of this country, and arguably much of the world, is in the hands of our young people, who are constantly bombarded with stimuli that fail to teach ethics, morality, or the general rules of etiquette. Instead of civility, they're shown how to virtually kill, maim, and rape in the name of gaming. Children today expect everything, and they expect it to be easy or think that they're being deprived. Altogether too many young people take life for granted. The result of this and much more stimuli than we can cover here is that there's an ever-increasing and alarming incidence of child violence. Children shoot each other, they beat each other and videotape it, they kill and then turn the weapons on themselves.

It wasn't so long ago that children were allowed to take their guns to school and shoot them during a marksmanship class. Can you imagine that today? It wasn't long ago that an R-rated film contained less violence and sex or nudity than today's PG-rated films. And I've said before, our population is being systematically desensitized to what used to be totally unacceptable.

Humans need stimulation. Each of us has a threshold that a stimulus must pass in order for us to be excited by it. As the stimulus is presented over and over again, its signal strength weakens with respect to our arousal. Over time, it takes stronger and stronger stimuli to satisfy the requirements involved in producing arousal. Thus, sex becomes more explicit, as does violence. In the end, we erode the decency of the human condition.

History bears witness to the future of moral decadence and culturally relevant values that allow anyone to do almost anything in the name of their value system. Our society faces many challenges, and this is one of them!

For most of us, the best way to deal with this constant bombardment of stimuli is to turn it off. Do so for our children as well as ourselves. I would even go so far as to suggest a return to the more formal ways of past generations, for this formality does instill a certain order that's helpful in cultivating respect, which is what we need more of—respect for ourselves and others, respect for all life.

In an earlier chapter, I addressed what it means to be human. Perhaps this is just so much redundant tripe to some. For me—and I sincerely hope for you, too—this is the starting point for reweaving a strong, healthy societal fabric. All of the technologies and methods outlined in this book have no value if they're only used for personal gain. However, when individual power grows while fostering family strength, which prospers while promoting better neighborhoods and so forth, then the world can truly change for the better, one person at a time. One act followed by another builds a new habit.

Summary

It's very easy to consider the changes occurring in society to be just a sign of the times. However, if you pay attention to what's going on, you still have the ability to choose whether these shifts are beneficial to you or not. By being constantly aware of the bombardment of stimulation we're all subjected to, it's possible to find ways to reduce it and therefore return to habits that are much healthier for ourselves, our families, and our relationships.

CHAPTER 17

The 50-Day Plan

"Everything you see has its roots in the unseen world.
The forms may change, yet the essence remains the same.
Every wonderful sight will vanish; every sweet word will fade,
But do not be disheartened,
The source they come from is eternal, growing,
branching out, giving new life and new joy.
Why do you weep?
The source is within you and this whole
world is springing up from it."

— Jalal ad-Din ar-Rumi

What would you do if you only had 50 days to live? What do you think about the possibility of having a death wish that you aren't aware of? Is it possible to unconsciously create a timeline to exit life or to have a preset schedule for exiting and be able to alter it? Do you think an animal could give its life for you and thereby let you live?

Some years ago I had a wonderful dog named Duke. Not long after I moved into a new home, Duke was shot. It was a belly wound, and he slowly expired over a seven-hour period. I think that I know who shot him. I approached the person with a great deal of anger and pain, and he denied the incident. My many years of interrogation and investigation experience exposed his contradictions in such a blatant, immediate manner that it required all my courage not to do something I'd regret. I walked away full of anger. I knew that I should forgive, but it simply wouldn't come. My thoughts seemed to be possessed by the nastiest, most vengeful fantasies possible. They were the only thing that mitigated the pain.

A couple of days passed, and my dear friend Yolanda visited from Mexico. She's a very gifted individual. I hold her in high regard and respect her insights. She looked at me and said, "Eldon, your dog died so his master would not have to die. He did you a favor, and so did the man who shot him. When I was young, I, too, lost my dog. He came to me, however, and informed me that pets very often die to save their masters. This is an especially high act for an animal and honors the animal."

I admit that this thought felt good—but it also seemed absurd. A few days later, my own "50 days" were announced (more on that later). I spoke to very few people about Yolanda's story or my so-called 50 days. Then one day a friend brought me a book and urged me to read it. It was *The Choice* by Og Mandino, a writer whose words I have cherished. In this book, the author tells the story of a man too busy for his family. He stops one day and makes a complete career change in order to be with his children and enjoy his wife. He becomes a self-help writer and then learns of his impending death. Ultimately, he turns everything over to God and lets go. The character's words are some of the most powerful I've ever read. His appreciation for each and every day is matched only by his inhalation of the value of life.[1]

After I read the book, my oldest daughter, Angela, phoned. Her son, John David, was eight weeks old at the time. Angela said, "Dad, I have something strange to share with you. I'd like your opinion. My cat died a couple of days ago, and then I had this dream. In the dream, my cat came to me and told me that she'd died so that John David could live. She was somehow all cats but just one cat. She went on to inform me that everything was okay with her but that it was time for me to wake up because John David had stopped breathing.

I awoke immediately, and John David wasn't breathing. I gave him mouth-to-mouth resuscitation, and he's okay. Is this bizarre?"

What do you think? Is it bizarre? I certainly can't separate the three situations with a mundane label such as "coincidence."

When it comes right down to it, everything ordinary can be explained as just that—ordinary. There's no special anything. This definition fits comfortably with the explanations of life that argue for humanity being only a product of evolution with no creator, no future, no life after death, no anything other than the physical stuff of here-and-now. When it comes right down to it, only the experience of that which defies explanation gives us the hope that life is more than mere mortal stuff. It's the experience that prompts us to recognize the higher meaning in all matters—the good in all—the *awe* that sometimes can become an *Aha!*

My Choice

A short time later after Angela's phone call, I was awakened from my sleep by three messengers. Standing a few feet off the ground near the end of my bed, they simply said to me: "You have 50 days left. What would you like?"

I knew that I could have fame, fortune, or any other thing I could imagine, but I decided to spend my 50 days doing my work and being with my family. I found my choice as surprising as the event itself. The decision brought me much peace, however, and for the next 30 days I gave little thought to any downside and focused instead on the caliber of each day. I tried to write and tie up some loose ends, but I also found it equally important to have quality time with my family. The winter snow became absolutely no inconvenience, rather an awe-inspiring act of nature. The cold only meant that the fireplaces could be enjoyed. Dreams, ambitions, plans, fears, and whatnot dimmed unless they were important in the next 50 days. Next year was simply of no importance.

I felt no panic, only a certainty that insisted the deadline was real, if only in metaphor. I knew that I must treat the days as though they were the last ones of this lifetime. Then there came a time when I paused. *Why did I accept the notion of only 50 days? Where's the fight in me—the will?*

During the next few days, I systematically generated a mind map of all the reasons I had to live and any conflict that might be solved should I not. Surprisingly, I discovered that within me was a deep struggle that ostensibly appeared as though it could only be resolved by stepping out of this plane. Now *that's* a battle. It's too personal to relate here, but what it came down to was a true catch-22.

So I sat down with the person involved in the conflict and discussed it openly. Somehow, there was instant relief in just getting it out. There was no resolution between us, just honesty. As it turned out, the other person was also in turmoil. We simply agreed to allow each other to have our own solutions and to do so with dignity and respect. I let the whole thing go and turned it over with blessings.

What I Learned

Letting go is another real lesson that comes out of this 50-day plan. When you live as though your days are truly limited—too short for "I'll do it tomorrow" or for the so-called bulletproof mentality that so many go through life with—you must let go. Death holds this release as a requisite. You relinquish plans, dreams, ambitions, people, things, and more. Much of this is painful, and some is a surprising relief. Notice both. Where there's pain, there's great joy and hope. Where there's relief—well, perhaps you should let go of those things with or without a 50-day plan.

During the process, I discovered several things about myself. First, I tended to procrastinate on long-term projects, saving them for the last minute. I realized that when there were only 50 days to complete everything I had in progress. Second, I had no clear priorities in my work. My philosophy was to take care of the urgent matters and get around to the rest when I could.

My third discovery had to do with fun. Often, I'd put off taking time to just have fun. I could find time to do little things, but little time to do *fun!* My personality somehow attributed time off as being wasted or something that would happen when I had more time. Now that's a genuine circular argument that makes no sense whatsoever.

My fourth lesson was the value of relationships. I'd also tended to procrastinate returning phone calls, sending that special note, or simply taking the time to make something special for my son Roy, who was two years old at that time.

I'd gotten somewhat into the rut that's commonly called "same old, same old." Well, all of a sudden there was new excitement in my life. I made plans to do things I'd never done. I undertook new projects with zeal. I remembered all the joys of living. I once again became excited, connected, and emotionally awed by the beauty of all things.

It was very clear during the dream of the messengers that I wanted more than anything else to have time with Roy. I longed just to hold him and play with him—to watch him and imagine his life unfolding. The morning after the dream, I was equally clear that I didn't wish to telegraph any alarm.

Cherish the Moment

Within a few days of the dream, one of my older sons came to live with me. He was having trouble in school, and his mother was convinced that if something didn't change, he was headed for certain disaster. He taught me the next lesson. The only thing that's sad about life is wasting it while you have it. Living as though you only have 50 days remaining tends to impress upon you the value of each day, the glory of every sunrise, the warmth of each smile, the joy in laughter, the love that supports instead of smothers, and much more. It also tends to automatically prioritize some things.

I believe that the dream was a tutorial metaphor. It prompted much creativity and even another child. I wanted to write something that was motivating and not tied up chiefly with science. I basically knew what I wanted to communicate but hadn't taken the time to do. I also had a pet project that I'd put off, the development of an album designed to make many esoteric teachings available in simple, straightforward exercises. So immediately I committed to myself to finish both. (This album is called *Mystical Mind* and many people have told me how powerful this collection is.)

Of course, I also gave some thought to such things as my will. I was totally unprepared in this area. Yet, I must also admit that very little energy was spent on matters of this nature.

Clear priorities emerged, a new enthusiasm sprang forth, and fatigue was almost unknown. Boredom was unacceptable, as were poor relationships and harsh words. Yet I also found the power within me to be very strong. I didn't become passive and hopeless. Those matters I'd always tended to dislike, I continued to dislike—and perhaps I had even less patience. I don't honestly know if this was counter-productive or revealing or both. What I *did* learn is that false nobility is ignoble; false feelings are lies. If life has taught me anything, it's that we must be genuine.

I wrote a book titled *BE,* and I made certain it was completed during my 50 days. Cover designs, page layouts, and so forth—ready for press. This book is all about being. How do we just *be?* Each of us is unique. Each of us has our strengths and our Achilles' heel. Life is about first accepting who we are. Knowing when to try to fix something about ourselves and when that something is simply who we are—that can be an interesting trial. But it's very clear to me that we must be true to ourselves! More than anything else, my 50-day plan revealed just who I was and what was important. What I learned surprised me.

We all deal with many struggles and conflicts. Indeed, that's the process underlying much of our growth. A 50-day limit tends to reveal the tensions and their relative importance in no uncertain terms. Some may be less important, others may be conflicts that we've always lived with, and still others may be present patterns that beg for resolution and have been ignored. The outer world is generally a reflection of the inner. When confusion exists within, it will also be present in the so-called out there. The 50-day plan shows us confusion in a hurry. Again, however, for this to really work, we must approach the plan as though the 50 days really are final.

I've learned many other things about myself and the people around me. I'm sure that I'll learn more before my time is over. I have a very strong belief in life, and it's grown much stronger and more appreciative. You must believe in life more than death! I'm certain of that. My guides and teachers have given me many opportunities and experiences. As I said, I see the 50 days now as a metaphor. From what I've already learned, I'd recommend this exercise to one and all.

Decide to live the next 50 days as though they were your last. Make your decisions based on that timeline. I guarantee that if you really do so, it will change your life! Remember, though, you'll live to do the 50 days again and again—such fun! Thank you, thank you, thank you!

Summary

It's easy to get caught up in our lives, get upset over numerous events, and basically forget who we are. The 50-day plan is a marvelous exercise to get us to focus on those things that really are important to us. For most of us, the lessons from this process will be life changing.

CHAPTER 18

The Seven Fundamentals

"The significant problems we face cannot be solved at the same level of thinking we were in when we created them."

— Albert Einstein

Now I'd like to look at something I've called "The Seven Fundamentals of the Master Secret," or the keys to living a truly successful life. These are seven principles that can and will release so much power from within, and are so obvious that you may become as bemused by them as I have over the years. These principles were given to me in what I describe as an "automatic-writing session." Perhaps they came from my subconscious, perhaps from the collective unconscious, perhaps from—well, you decide.

The Seven Fundamentals

What's success? Have you ever wondered why it is that for some, everything works, and for others, nothing works? Why is it that two people can have essentially the same opportunities, but one is happy

and the other miserable? Is it not true, therefore, that happiness con-
stitutes the true meaning of success?

Success is happiness! Truly successful people are content, and
when you're cheerful and whole in yourself, all good things follow.
Where, then, do happiness and wholeness come from? How does a
person who experiences frustrations in life become complete? Can
personal wholeness provide happiness; improve self-esteem; and lead
to riches, fame, peace, balance, and harmony? Can relationships with
family, friends, and associates improve because one person assumes
the responsibility to be personally unified, takes the initiative to exude
joy and happiness, and seizes the opportunity to empower his or her
own life by using the secret of the ages? The answers to all these questions lie in the seven fundamentals of the master secret.

Fundamental 1: You

First, look at the absolutely awesome and incredible *you!* This isn't
the you of self-doubt, the one that fears rejection or failure and questions your abilities, but the real you! Those other voices aren't you.
They're synthetic *"yous"* built upon limited and false notions of who
you are and what you may become.

For most of us, those erroneous ideas originate as we mature. In
our early attempts to achieve acceptance, we often abandon our real
selves. The desire to be loved is so strong that many of us give up care
or respect for ourselves to obtain security. That trade-off never works,
because what we're insecure about in the first place exists within us.

Happiness is a state of mind. The kingdom is within. The real you
is a higher you, a greater power that resides within you or is available
to you whenever you ask or seek. The fact is that it's your birthright
to manifest the glory of the incredible you. You absolutely have the
power and ability to experience all the bounties and many miracles
in your life—for you yourself are a miracle, and all that you are or can
ever be is a gift!

So the first fundamental is you. The power resides within you,
and no one else can do it for you. Your thoughts are reflections of

your expectations. What has been sown in your subconscious mind is what you reap. Doubt produces failure, fear yields anger, and belief in limitation is the greatest of all self-fulfilling prophecies.

Fundamental 2: Thoughts Are Things

The thoughts we have reveal the beliefs we have about ourselves. Listen to how you talk to yourself. Is the language from the inside reflecting optimism, or is it filled with negative and self-limiting ideas?

What we expect is what we get. Science refers to this phenomenon as the Pygmalion effect. It's a fact: if we expect the worst, we get it. And some of us must love it, because we keep on getting it! Oh, we may complain about it, we may yell and scream when it happens, but what do most of us do about it? We speak and act as though there's absolutely nothing we can do about it. After all, isn't life full of everyday events that produce reasonable responses? Isn't it normal to become angry when we're cut off in rush-hour traffic? Isn't it normal to become fearful when the boss speaks harshly? Isn't it reasonable to be frustrated by a child's lack of respect or self-responsibility? Doesn't everyone become stuck or just fed up?

Such reactions may be normal, but are they appropriate or conducive to happiness? Has anger ever produced a peaceful sense of harmony within you? Has it ever solved a problem or led to anything other than more anger, guilt, and feelings of being out of control? Such reactions may be normal, but another word for *normal* is *average,* which can be defined as the best of the worst and the worst of the best. Neither end of this definition is the highest expression of who you really are.

You are your thoughts. You manifest your subconscious beliefs in everything you experience. Do you believe that you deserve happiness, wholeness, and success? You must truly know at every level of your being that all good things are yours in order for them to ever appear. You create your own realities. Events aren't pivotal points in your life; *you* are the pivotal point in your life. When your thoughts are in agreement with your desires, what you dream of will magically materialize.

Fundamental 3: Forgive and Let Go

This idea may be a bit startling at first, but think about it for a minute. Do you consider yourself a victim of your circumstances? Or are you willing to assume responsibility for who you are? There are two ways to be tied up in the world. One is to be literally, physically restrained by someone else, and the other is to tie yourself figuratively, by refusing to let go of beliefs that limit your expression of the whole and complete being you are. In other words, as long as you displace responsibility by blaming someone or something for who and what you are, you eliminate your power to be anything other than partial and incomplete.

All behavior is the result of choice. Sometimes our decisions are made at an unconscious or subconscious level. For example, we opt to avoid conflict by repressing our true feelings. Later, our emotions become so strong that we can no longer suppress them, and some small incident triggers an overkill response. That's a reactive model— we've lost control. When we assume responsibility for every aspect of our lives, we get in touch with our deepest fears and feelings. The power we gain over our former reactive behavior provides us with the ability to respond appropriately to all stimuli. That's a proactive model—we're always in control.

It's been said that the highest act of consciousness is inhibition— the restraint of animal stimulus-response conditioning. When we accept responsibility for our every thought and action, we empower ourselves by performing this highest act of consciousness, but that means we no longer have anyone to blame.

In fact, as long as we blame, we effectively eliminate our ability to grow; to be in control; or to experience peace, balance, and harmony. The power to grow resides in forgiveness. Letting go will set us free. Forgiving everyone, including ourselves, provides the opportunity to become more than we have been, which in many cases is but a mere shadow of our real selves. And the irony of all this is that most of us know that we're much more than we've acted out in our lives!

Fundamental 4: Love

The most powerful force in the world is love. It cancels fear, which is the only obstacle to overcome so that all of our experiences can take on new dimensions of meaning and joy. This isn't the romantic bond, but the unconditional love we give our children. We're all children in some relative stage of development, learning how to live in joy and happiness. When we truly understand this, it becomes easy to forgive others for acts that are selfish and self-centered—and to forgive ourselves, as well. "Above all else, respect thyself," said Pythagoras. To care for others, we must first cherish ourselves. We can't pour from an empty container.

Contemporary studies of behavioral dysfunctions ranging from learning difficulties to criminal activity indicate one common denominator: low self-esteem. This grows out of fear of rejection—by a loved one, an employer, a stranger, anyone who might laugh at our efforts, or who would misunderstand or disapprove. On the other hand, high self-esteem grows out of self-acceptance, which is self-love. We can't care for anyone unless we care for ourselves.

Fundamental 5: Acceptance Is Mastery

Loving unconditionally suggests accepting others as they are. Furthermore, it means accepting yourself as a whole and complete being on the journey of learning we call life.

Acceptance, love, and forgiveness are as necessarily interrelated as each side of a triangle is to the whole shape. Acceptance is the natural process we knew as children. When light faded into night, each of us knew that this was just the way it worked, and we learned to live accordingly. As we grew older, we began to control our world by means of electricity. Some things can and even should be manipulated for our benefit—turning the dark into a bright space by flipping a light switch may be one of them. But there are other elements in our environment over which we have absolutely no control, nor should we. We can't control other people and make them into what we want them to be, yet that's how many of us have spent our lives.

The best way we can influence our environment is in our presence of being. When we accept other people for who and what they are, we've taken the first step toward accepting ourselves and contributing to the improvement of any condition or situation. Jiddu Krishnamurti stated that "you are the world." When we reflect peace and joy from an inner level of being, it's mirrored back to us. When we judge, condemn, hate, lust, and so on, our environment shows us these qualities. The world is a mirror, for its principal function is to provide us the opportunity to learn.

What we resist, we often become. What we like least in another is almost always a reflection of something in ourselves. When we love and accept ourselves, we do the same for others. Each individual who comes into our lives is a teacher; each has something to contribute to our learning. We, in turn, have something to add to others' experience. From this perspective, our every transaction transcends the limitations of manipulation.

The fifth fundamental has been called the Golden Rule: Treat others as though they were you and according to the best "you"—and the rest just happens. What goes out is what you get back. Just as the biblical story of the prodigal son teaches us that God has already accepted and forgiven us, so this fundamental suggests that for many of us, the least of our brothers and sisters has been ourselves! Accepting and loving ourselves provides the ability to accept and love others, just as caring for others provides the ability to care for ourselves.

Fundamental 6: Interdependence

Martin Luther King once said, "I can never be what I ought to be until you are what you ought to be, and you can never be what you ought to be until I am what I ought to be." He went on to say that the mutually related network of reality is the fabric of the human condition.[1]

The sixth fundamental, then, is the principle that each of us is an aspect of the whole. We each invite respect or disrespect according to what we give others. Down through the ages, this concept has been given many labels, including the popular one of "karma." In law, it's called "reciprocity." What we sow is indeed what we reap.

Interdependence means individually assuming responsibility for any condition that's contrary to the quality of humanness in its highest form and then acting to produce, out of the condition or situation, balance and harmony for all. That's not to say that we take up causes and shove them down someone else's throat. It means that we can work in harmony through example and right action to produce an environment that's loving and nurturing for all.

Many people operate in a codependent manner. Their method of assuming responsibility is to manipulate others by placing blame, finding fault, or assuming a contractual posture that goes like this: "If I do this, will you . . . ," "If you loved me, you'd . . . ," "Don't you feel sorry that I feel . . . ," "You need me to . . . ," and so on. Codependence is manipulating another person to provide you with security, sensation, and power. If someone else can't live or function without you, then your self-worth has been validated—and vice versa. Such a person is a victim, both of his or her surroundings and of other people. The need to control another is a classic symptom of codependency, which grows out of insecurity. All insecurities are externally oriented. The codependent sees stimuli through the lens of expectation, which is a contract that goes like this: "I'll behave this way, if you behave that way." The fear of unfulfilled expectations gives rise to internal conflict.

Happiness is a state of being. It exists moment to moment in the eternal now. If it doesn't exist, conflict takes its place—even if the struggle is only the difference between what we think we should be experiencing and we really are experiencing. In other words, when we have what we desire, we experience joy. Furthermore, when something is unconditional, as opposed to contractual, then we experience only joy.

Insecurity fuels fear, which is a very creative force. What we dread most is therefore often what we create as our experience. Instead of accepting what is, we project what might be or lament what might have been. We're responsible only for ourselves individually. We must be whole before any event in our lives will exist. Therefore, true inter-dependence assumes the role of fixing the self.

Fundamental 7: Do It Now

The seventh fundamental is the culmination of all that preceded it. This is a world of action, not procrastination. For anything to change, you must do something. Nothing happens until you make it happen! Only you can do it for you.

If this were a world of theory, then none of us would be here. Nothing in this plane stands still or waits. No action is inaction, and all inaction is action. The form and the function are the same. Live with the awareness that God's presence exists in all!

Summary

Many individuals have told me how deeply the seven funda-mentals have affected them. Use this philosophy to guide you in all your interactions, and you'll find your life much brighter and be fully empowered to become the person you were meant to be.

■　■ ■ ━■■

CHAPTER 19

Practical Metaphysics

*"All matter originates and exists only by virtue of a force. . . .
We must assume behind this force the existence of a conscious
and intelligent Mind. This Mind is the matrix of all matter."*

— Max Planck

We live in a time when more and more people are feeling an urgent need to find the spiritual component in their lives. Ironically, it's also an era when families have deteriorated, juvenile gangs speed through residential neighborhoods and fire automatic weapons at innocent people, schoolteachers are rapidly becoming candidates for wearing flak jackets, and entertainment packages sell well only if they're full of graphic violence and sensational sexual scenes. It's almost as if two competing forces were flying at each other head on—the magnitude of which surpasses every other epoch in modern history. This juxtaposition in values has generated large rips in the fabric of society.

For many, science and technology are God, life is but a thrill, values are antiquated religious notions, and religions are Dark Age instruments to be discarded in the light of modernity. So while more and more people seem to be addressing the importance of the spiritual, many are also moving further away from spiritual values.

265

Science is no exception to this pattern. Many of the brightest minds in the field are finding God in their work. Indeed, one of the true visionaries of our biological sciences has dedicated more than 20 years to finding a cure for AIDS based upon words that were given to her in the midst of a presentation. You might dismiss this notion unless you know that the scientist is Dr. Candace Pert, author of *Molecules of Emotion*, or unless you reflect for a moment on Einstein's own description of the inner vision that led to proving space/time curvature.

An ever-growing body of scientific knowledge continues to demonstrate the mind as a causal factor. Some of the most prestigious organizations in the scientific community have openly turned mystical—legitimizing the study of consciousness, parapsychology, and ancient spiritual traditions. It's commonplace to hear a scientific paper delivered with examples and quotations from spiritual systems.

At the other extreme are scientists whose agenda openly calls for debunking any and all suggestions of higher consciousness, super consciousness, the paranormal, God, and all other areas that could suggest that the human being is something more than a terminal animal in a temporal world with selfish genes.

So while I may find Albert Einstein's statement "I want to know God's thoughts . . . all else is details" compelling, others find the notion of God to be a "sugar-coated neurotic crutch," to quote Sigmund Freud. In such a context, a chapter dedicated to practical metaphysics may be greeted by some with disdain. Regardless of our individual spiritual inclination, however, if we define metaphysics in this application to be "the approach taken in life that provides for the fulfillment of a self-actualizing individual, engaged in the joy of life and moved by the Spirit of awe," then what follows should neither offend nor mystify anyone.

Practical

I've deliberately used the word *practical* in this approach to metaphysics to avoid entanglements in theology. This approach is one of common sense: does it work? The ideas that follow have been tested, and they work! Most of them are simple day-to-day reminders of the glory of living. As such, they add an element or perspective that empowers everyone who employs them. They not only make living more exciting but they actually alter body chemistry, strengthen the immune system, and improve health and well-being in general.

Gratitude

Begin each day with gratitude in your heart. When I first open my eyes each morning, I silently speak these words: *Thank you, thank you, thank you!* This little shift in my morning mental state changed the old negatives of "Thank God it's Friday," "Life sucks and then you die," or "Damn, I have to get out of bed" into positive expectations and appreciation for the day. Faithfully doing this simple exercise will bring beauty and peace to life's most disturbing situations. Why? Because for the most part, the trials that upset us aren't as important as we make them out to be. That realization leads to another simple practice.

And So What?

"And so what?" is perhaps the single most valuable therapeutic tool I've ever worked with. Using it goes something like this: I have a concern about something. Perhaps I'm anxious about my business, thinking that something will happen to ruin me. The worry lodges in my mind, and I can't dismiss it. It just keeps coming back, no matter what, so I simply stop and ask: "And so what?" What's the worst that can happen? The immediate response is usually not the end of it. Say that the answer that comes is something like this:

"Well, then what will you do? Sell shoes for a living?"

Again I put the question: "And so what?"

The answer may be: "Is that what you want? To let everybody down?"

Again I answer, "And so what?"

By now the thoughts may get nasty. "You can end up in a bankruptcy, that's what. How would you like that?"

"And so what?"

"Then you'd be starting all over without anything."

"And so what?"

"Doesn't it bother you that you can be so flippant?"

"And so what?"

"Well, what if there's an emergency and you don't have the money? You're on the street, in the cold. You and your family. Now how do you feel?"

"Then we'll pitch in together and begin again. And so what?"

"And what if you end up poor and destitute?"

"If I do, so what?"

With every question, the shift in attitude tends to bring both resolution and a sense of priorities about the worry. "And so what?" places the situation in an entirely different perspective. Indeed, often the anxiety becomes unimportant, and the solution is obvious.

The power of this process rests in the realization that worry will accomplish nothing. It only makes things worse. Beyond worry is hope, which ultimately always comes down to a spiritual awareness. What will be, will be. We're not in charge, and we only fool ourselves if we think that we are. All we can do is the best we can do. "And so what?" puts a laugh into the so-called problem.

Problems Are Opportunities

Every problem we encounter holds within it an opportunity. Realizing this is an important step in self-actualization. Troublesome issues exist for a variety of reasons, and each one we encounter challenges us to grow. Our typical problems are always ego oriented. They arise from disappointment. "I expect this or that," "My expectation has burst," "It's not fair," "Why is it always such a struggle?" and on and on.

When we meet the world with an expectation, we've chosen to believe that we can predict and therefore, at least to some degree, control the world we live in. Where there's evidence for mind as a causal factor, there are many minds creating or contributing to the cause. Not all minds are what we might call enlightened. Our response to stimuli in the world is all that we're ever in charge of. Where we choose to invest our mental energy and moods is where we'll come from when problems arise. It's a rather circular argument to add that perhaps they'll come up because of where we invest our energy and belief. Still, as with most truths, when you find paradox, you're very close to seeing through the conflict. This circularity is one of those paradoxes.

An attitude that expects good in all things greets problems with something like this: "I can't wait to see what good comes from this!"

Good in All

Here's a statement that will get the attention of the skeptic: a self-actualized person expects good in all. There are no judgments to be made; discernment simply indicates whether we desire more or not. Judgment and discernment are not the same thing.

"Good" isn't a judgment. Expecting it is a statement about our own attitude and sense of self-responsibility. If everything comes to us for some reason, then there must be good in it somewhere. In the alternative, expecting bad is a self-fulfilling prophecy that will most certainly yield an unpleasant harvest.

Practical or pragmatic approaches to the world consider the alternatives. If expecting bad produces a tendency to find bad, then changing that expectation is only pure and simple common sense. We need no psychobabble or cosmic fluff to choose the positive alternative.

There's No Such Thing as Coincidence

Several new scientific theories assert the role of consciousness and its interplay in connecting mind to universe. Summed up, these theories essentially assert that mind is a causal factor! The implications of this theory have scientists in many disciplines reeling with the possible ramifications. Some believe that we're on the brink of an entirely new scientific paradigm. It will include the mind as an agent in all observations, experimentations, outcomes, the fabric of the universe, the nature of subjective events, and so forth.

Perhaps one of the most provocative of these new theories can shed some light on this point. There's a general view of mind as a force in the universe. We find this view particularly prevalent in such areas as parapsychological research. When a random number generator, for example, seems to respond to the mind, it's easy to view that result as a power of the mind. Ergo, force!

However, another theory asserts something called Decision Augmentation Theory (DAT). According to DAT, nature is unchanged by the action of the mind. It states that the mind has simply participated in some larger "mind field" or interacted somehow with the generator in our example, and this interaction/participation, albeit unconscious, has primed our decision process.[1]

Whatever the ultimate outcome of the current mind/effect debates, it's certain that the mind is both a force and a field participating with other like fields, perhaps "the field" or zero point, as McTaggart suggests.[2] We must recognize that everything we experience has somehow been attracted to us for some reason. Each of us has a role in what we'll experience; we aren't casual passengers on a sea of mindless fate. Since our journey transcends the strictly temporal stuff we call "reality," then underlying what we perceive is something even more real, although unseen—the implicate becoming explicate.

Coincidence is something that happens in a so-called purely chance, random way. While it might be convenient sometimes to think of life this way, it's simply untrue. There is no such thing as coincidence!

Meeting everything that comes to us with the expectation of good while recognizing that there's no such thing as coincidence lets us see the world through an entirely different lens. The practical side of this provides for excitement and growth while minimizing conflict and pain. We meet each day with excitement: What will the universe bring to me today? What will I learn? We greet everyone we meet with a different expectation, knowing that each of them is there for some reason. The synchronicity of the world reveals a purpose, relationship, harmony, universal kinship, and love, and we know peace and balance as a result.

Awe

It's not possible to say too much about awe. When we're children, the world is full of awe. Everything is absolutely *awesome!* This is reverence. In its absence is a cold, false pride that insists there's nothing to be in awe of, for we know how everything works, where it came from, and how to use it.

As we grew, we learned the names of things and tended to accept that we knew what they were. We understand what electricity is because we can name it and use it. We know all about the creation of the universe because we know about the big bang. But do we? While electricity is a part of nearly everyone's life, it's still not understood by science. As pointed out earlier, the big bang is just another way of saying: "In the beginning there was One. The One divided itself and became the many."

Knowing the name of something isn't the same as knowing the something. When it comes to the latter, very little is understood. Hardly anything in the world doesn't deserve of awe. For this wonder to be known, however, we must be willing to become innocent, unknowing persons. We must be willing to sacrifice our arrogance to overcome our ignorance.

Involvement

Study after study has demonstrated the healing value of involvement. Indeed, when we examine the characteristics of our ever-increasing centenarian population (persons 100 years old and older), we find that involvement is a common denominator. These people are truly wrapped up in their communities or a cause, and all sense a deep spiritual connection. In fact, that's most often an underpinning for their participation in other work.

Involvement is both self-fulfilling and therapeutic. And anything that tends to be self-fulfilling becomes somewhat self-identifying. Involvement is connectedness, which instructs us to become responsible for everything in our lives. Nothing is unconscious when we're linked to others; every act affects something or someone. We experience thoughtful concern for the well-being of others, the planet, and all life.

We can strengthen our sense of connectedness by working with groups or individuals. We can also build this bond by spending time in nature, which has always been humankind's best teacher and most patient mentor. The art of being human seems so complex until we view the art of being a grasshopper, frog, squirrel, or deer. Grasshoppers don't pretend to be frogs or squirrels. They're simply grasshoppers —they *be* grasshoppers.

People, on the other hand, often forget what being human is. "I want to be me!" means what? Nature is the master teacher that illustrates through all life forms what it is to just *be*. No games, no pretense, no personas, no artificial nonsense, and no prestige status is respected by nature. Learning to *be* is an important aspect of self-actualization and brings both definition and meaning to involvement.

Cancel, Cancel, Cancel!

I happen to enjoy football. Invariably, at some time during a game, a commercial comes on that says something along these lines: "Experts agree—this will be the worst year ever for flu. You'll get sick! Take our instant remedy and pamper yourself." I don't always have the remote control handy enough to change the station and stop this nonsense before it's in my brain. What I do in these instances is simply assert with enough emotion for a listener to think I'm angry: "Cancel, cancel, cancel!"

This powerful technique helps the mind remember that you're aware of such psychogenic initiatives and will have no part of them. It's also a useful tool for canceling self-defeating thoughts. Indeed, as you grow in awareness, it becomes more and more important to monitor your inner talk. Monitor, reinforce or rescript, and cancel nonsense. It's this simple: if your mind believes that you'll get sick, then you *will* get sick! If your mind believes that you're undeserving, you'll be found undeserving. When your belief in death becomes stronger than your belief in life, you'll die.

Up Until Now

Every day, I hear someone say something such as "I can't understand that" or "I know what I should do, but I'm always anxious." When people speak this way to themselves or to another, they're claiming the situation. Whenever you're tempted to say something that suggests a situation or condition you don't wish to keep, simply add the magic words *up until now.*

Watch what happens when we take one of our examples and add our phrase: "I know what I should do, but I'm always anxious—up until now." A whole new space is created to assist us in remembering that what we say and what we think is what we claim.

There's no law of limitation. There *is* a law that essentially states: "What you believe to be true will be true; what you expect is what you'll get; how you talk to yourself is how you'll see yourself and where you'll find yourself!"

Languaging

We've all "caught a cold," and this "languaging" has been pointed out earlier. We've all also said things such as "That's awfully good." What does *awful* have to do with *good?* The words we use and think frame a context, even if we aren't totally conscious of what we're saying. We've seen how context can preclude intelligent awareness—remember the three-feet-by-seven-feet wood door mentioned earlier?

Becoming consciously aware of your languaging can change the patterns of your thinking. If you truly wish to think outside of the proverbial box, then you'll find this simple step to be very powerful.

Summary

Incorporate these simple exercises with whatever other activity works for you (hopefully many of those previously discussed in this book), and your life will become as fulfilling as your highest dreams.

■ ■ ■ ■■ ■

CHAPTER 20

The Maximum Self

*"The person who risks nothing, does nothing, has
nothing, is nothing, and becomes nothing. He may
avoid suffering and sorrow, but he simply cannot learn
and feel and change and grow and love and live."*

— Leo F. Buscaglia

We started this book comparing our minds with the journey a stream takes, flowing from high up in the mountains, clear and sparkling, down into the darkest and dirtiest of inner cities. Now our metaphorical water has concluded its journey. It's in a place where its natural purities can be cultivated, and the contaminants can be removed. The mind can be filled anew with thoughts that generate peace, balance, and harmony—within and without.

I sincerely hope that you aren't one of those hoax holdouts at this point. It has been my intent, perhaps sometimes at the expense of being too specific, to provide sufficient evidence that this whole "bully them with ridicule and laughter" nonsense has lost its power. By doing so, I believe that you and others can better defend against the kind of mental intrusions that are truly dangerous and self-sabotaging.

I believe that, as psychologist and researcher Martin Seligman puts it, we all have a "maximum self" that's far greater than most of us accept. With all the negative programming everywhere, perhaps it's clearer why it may seem difficult to accept a far greater potential. Many have been duped into a special type of learned helplessness, one that, as Edward Bernays might insist, means that they deserve to be herded, for they're simply unable to participate intelligently. As for you—hopefully your eyes are now wide open, and your destiny is in your hands.

My friend Stephen James Joyce tells a marvelous story in his book *Teaching an Anthill to Fetch.*[1] He describes a sea squirt, a peculiar creature that, not long after being born, seeks a permanent place to attach itself. Once it finds that place and settles in, it devours its own brain. It's as if the creature needs the brain only to get comfortable. Many human beings are more similar to the sea squirt than we might think at first glance. Perhaps the reason so much manipulation is present in our society is that we simply don't want to know. Like sea squirts, we just want to be comfortable.

I've also shared with you a few examples of how persuasion technologies can work for the benefit of humankind. In other works, particularly *Choices and Illusions,* I've spent much more time on the bright side of persuasion tools. In this book, by contrast, it was my conscious choice to make the more sinister side of these powerful methods known to all who make the effort to become informed. I do apologize for what at times must have seemed horribly distasteful, but that's precisely what tells the real tale.

With this in mind, using the simple tools set out in this book will change your life for the better—and that's my promise to you!

■ ■ ■ ■■■

EPILOGUE

The Deep End

"Equipped with his five senses, man explores the universe around him and calls the adventure Science."

— Edwin Powell Hubble

I've always intuitively sensed that mind was a causal factor in the universe. Somehow—and I don't think as the result of coincidence—my readings have always vacillated between physics and the spiritual/mystical/metaphysical. I've always had some proclivity for mathematics, and I knew geometry before I studied it. Now that may sound ridiculous, but it's true. When I walked into geometry class for the first time and picked up the textbook, the material was so familiar that skimming it reminded me of what I already somehow knew. I always found that interesting, but only recently has it had some meaning relative to what I do.

Geometry, for me, has always been a divine science. That is, I've expected that geometry would ultimately be the math that revealed both the beauty and the secrets of the universe. Recently, I read some of the last 30 years of Einstein's work—it was geometry. He approached the unified field theory from that perspective. This was quite different thinking for a man who placed imaginary clocks around the world to pictorially envision and communicate his theory of relativity.

I was struck by his work, and a sort of general-systems gestalt occurred with me. (Notice that I say *with* me—not *to* me.) I went to bed one evening with all of this math/geometry stuff, string theory, quantum theory, and general relativity spinning in my head. I awoke at 4 A.M. and began a mind map.

Mind Mapping

For me, mind mapping has been a practical tool like those we've already examined. I tend to extract from different systems the most usable construct for myself. You've probably already noticed that. Consequently, following this pattern, let's look at the form of mind mapping I used (but for the real expert's view, see *How to Mind Map,* by Tony Buzan[1]).

Begin by taking a question or issue and focusing on it as though it was the nucleus of everything important, at least for a moment. Draw a small circle in the center of a blank piece of paper (the larger the paper, the better). Then allow some free association. Think first of matters associated with your issue. For every association, draw a line from the center circle (issue) to the association, as shown in Figure 17.

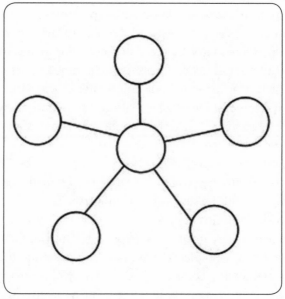

Figure 17

If your association item begins to provoke ideas further associated with it, put those ideas around the first association, and so on, as shown in Figure 18.

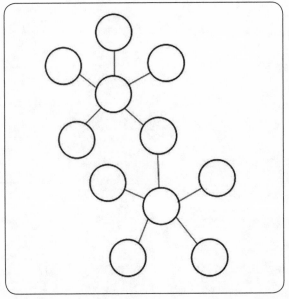

Figure 18

As you can see, you're building what I think of as orbits among items, primary associations, and secondary associations. This orbiting pattern helps both to relate and remember the information, as well as "get it out of the head," so to speak, in the first place.

When you've completed your initial mind map, connect arrow pathways that bring clusters of secondary information directly to primary issues, if appropriate. For example, take a look at one of my mind maps (Figure 19) resulting from my night's turning of the unified field theory.

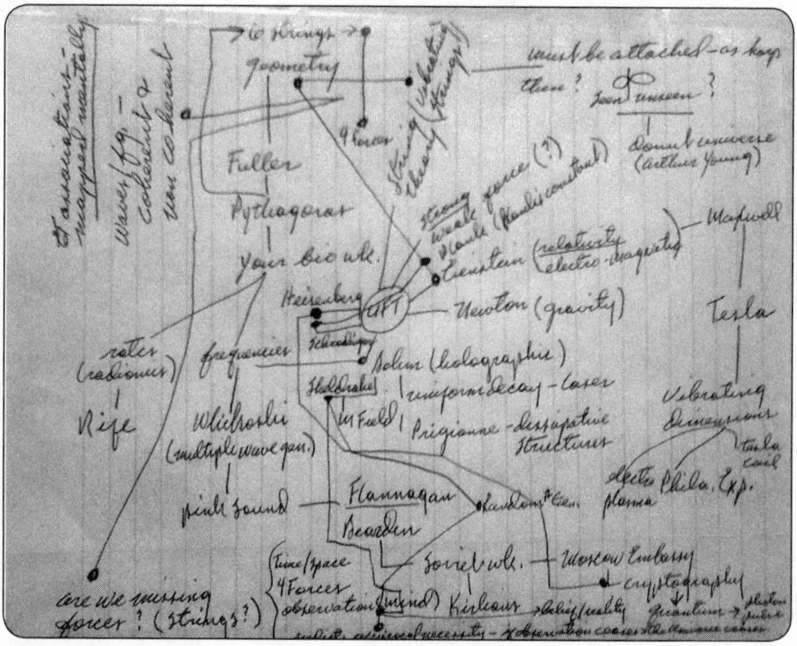

Figure 19

Now that you can see how to mind map, we're going off the deep end—or perhaps I should correct myself: I'm going off the deep end. You see, I theorized that the mind was a causal force in attempting to cement a unified field theory. What follows is only my ramblings. I'm not a physicist, so please bear with me. This is more of an exercise in following ideas and what they might spawn than anything else. I do believe that ideas are gifts and shouldn't be ignored. And with that introduction, here we go.

Quantum Physics

In very simple terms, the quantum deals with strong and weak forces at a subatomic level, relativity deals with space/time, gravity bends light but tends to be difficult to explain at both a macroscopic and subatomic level, and string theory asserts that everything in the universe is vibration and therefore is the grand unifying theory of

physics. In other words, gravity, light (the electromagnetic continuum), and strong and weak quantum forces are the essential powers
of the universe, which can be seen as vibrations analogous to, say,
emissions from the strings of a harp.

Both intuitively and from the perspective of all that I've read or
learned, string theory, the universe as vibration or frequency, must be
at least close to how things work. Still, a known force is overlooked.
I'm not certain whether this force should be seen as the musician with
the harp strings or as a consequence of the harp's vibration, but I
sense that it's both.

The force lacking in all of the equations and/or explanations is
that of the mind. We have more than enough evidence from random
number generators, psi experiments, work with M-fields[2] and simple
common sense to intuitively acknowledge the mind as a force in the
universe. Some assert that Heisenberg's uncertainty principle insists
on both the observer and the observed as fundamentally necessary
to each other. Indeed, there are many such elegant and eloquent
accounts by leading physicists of the mind's role in reality. Some even
postulate a sort of mind field or zero point energy field.

Please remember that the reason I ventured here is to propose a
hypothesis that developed from an idea about the unified field theory. If you'll be so kind as to bear with me, the physics per se aren't
important—it's the process I followed getting here that matters and is
why I've included this Epilogue to the book.

Mind as a Causal Factor

An old philosopher's conundrum asks, "If a tree falls in the forest, and no one is there to hear it fall, does it make a sound?" The
answer is always relative to the perspective from which the question
is approached. However, if the relationship of the observed to the
observer is fundamentally necessary, then there's no tree to fall.

Thus I ventured out with the mind—individual and collective—as
a causal factor/force. The mind holds the final key to understanding
and uniting a unified field theory. The so-called weak force is often the

strongest; it's the most difficult to measure or quantify. Mathematics is based on logical necessity—reliability. We can deduce the value of pi by simply measuring the radius and circumference of a number of circles. The relationship becomes mathematically obvious. It's a constant or has a constant value: pi = 3.14.

It's possible that the mind is a constant, but it's more likely that if at all possible, it will be represented by an equation that uses a constant. Perhaps, like the relationship of a straight line to a curved one, we'll find a constant that expresses itself within the equation but requires the equation for the variables of the mind (number of minds, energy of mind [focus], and so forth). I suspect the latter to be true. Indeed, I imagine that an evaluation of the effects of the mind may be worked backward, deduced as pi was, by taking some of the data from better experiments that demonstrate the influence of the mind.

For me, a hypothesis was spawned from my mind map. The axioms underlying the hypothesis are those readily recognized by science with one slight addition: physics is related to mind as body is to physics. Therefore, my hypothesis asserts that mind is a necessary reciprocal force in nature.

My work has already shown me that mind modulates body, and body will resonate to frequency. Cells have a vibratory signature. The immune system itself is a signal system identified by its vibratory signature. Everything in the universe resonates, including the mind. The energy that the mind emits is more than small electrical emissions measured by an EEG instrument. Its transceiver-like qualities suggest a kinship with some aspect of the electromagnetic continuum, such as radio waves. Maxwell's equations suggest aspects of the electromagnetic continuum not yet directly observed. Indeed, they insist on this unknown side of it. And yet, the mind is more than an aspect of the electromagnetic. The mind and life force itself are intimately threaded in the seen and unseen.

Then I had another idea and started working on it immediately. I sat right down and wrote a proposal. The reason for this Epilogue is how one idea spawns another if it isn't ignored. It's not always the first idea that we follow through on.

Hypothesis

The second idea suggested a hypothesis that humankind has an innate spiritual intelligence and, further, that its development or awakening is both of urgent social consequence and of immediate individual-health benefit.

I proposed to initially test this hypothesis in areas where prior research using clinically developed cognitive-behavioral interventions, delivered via audio subliminal programs, have resulted in findings of treatment efficacy. As you know, I've created InnerTalk audio programs that have been studied in both clinical and double-blind designs. Further, I've created InnerTalk programs that have been studied in other areas relative to human health and happiness, from time management to relationships.

It's been my experience that affirmations that appeal to a higher sense of being—a supreme purpose to creation, the beauty and miraculous nature of life itself—have produced the most remarkable outcomes. I therefore proposed a series of studies repeating that initial research. However, in the upcoming trials, an emphasis on awakening the innate spiritual intelligence of the subjects would replace the clinical dialogues (affirmations) employed in the past.

A History of Spiritual Quest

In written and oral history, there's no such thing as a society that thrived by being agnostic or atheistic. Indeed, history bears witness to the unending quest to find God and to live a spiritually rewarding life. Nothing is more obvious about the past than the impact of religious belief on direction and destiny. It's true that perhaps more human beings have suffered and died in the name of religion than for any other reason in history. Still, it's equally true that the human spirit appears to be driven by some innate spiritual awareness, need, or meaning.

This human tendency led me to believe that a necessary element in the individual-wellness equation, as well as the fabric of society at large, depends upon a variable that science has chosen to ignore for the past 300 years. Flying in the face of science's obvious avoidance of religious investigation have been the words of our greatest thinkers. Isaac Newton stated: "My metaphysical writings are more important than my science," and Hans Kepler said it all in these words: "I think God's thoughts."

We live in a world that largely seems to be occupied by alternative healing, anomalous physical effects, parapsychological findings, spiritual how-to books, and the like. This is a time when science is beginning to discover an interface between hard physical matter and the mind, an influence of consciousness on the outcome of experimentation, whether with machines such as random number generators or models of healing such as group-meditation activities. The ancient writings and practices of shamans and gurus are fair research for funded projects.

We live in a time when humans must make a difference or perhaps cease to know the world as it is. This is an era of forward-thinking hypotheses such as the Gaia principle, morphogenetic-field theories, and advances of consciousness at a distance. It's an exciting time full of opportunity to contribute to the growth and understanding of one harmonious world. I therefore set out to investigate what has been called the innate spiritual intelligence within.

The tale of spiritual healing is older than the history available to us. The idea of humanity's connectedness with a mind that's the creative force of all life is just as old. The belief that the kingdom is within us is common to the fountainheads of all extant religions. The sacred scripts of old from all cultures hold the notion that life is a journey through which the immortal soul passes. Most traditions also state that within the human condition is a memory of who and what we all are, a divine being created by and of God.

In the world of science, it's often easy to dismiss these ideas as old and outgrown. We tend to use new definitions but often say nothing new. It's trendy today to speak of the emotional quotient (EQ) as well as IQ. The latter is a derivative of a mathematical interpretation of the human condition in one small area—intelligence. Regardless of the controversy that from time to time challenges IQ testing and interpretation, IQ evaluation will always have certain predictive values and therefore is assured a place in the future. The newer idea of EQ appears to have some of the same predictive power and will therefore most certainly win a place among psychometrics technicians.

I contend that SQ, the spiritual quotient I mentioned earlier in this book, will have the same robust predictive value. To that end, one of the objectives of the current study's proposal is to develop just such an instrument. At a minimum, it should be correlated to family and health issues. Where some effort has already been taken to distinguish a so-called profile of the psychically inclined, no correlation beyond the relative comparison of psychological stability between inclined and not so inclined has been made.

In consultation with a broad spectrum of spiritual teachers, I developed a list of eternal life affirmations (ELAs). If my contention is valid, these affirmations will work like a so-called magic bullet. Therefore, the same set of affirmations could be employed in every domain of study. Each domain will be set apart from the others by incorporating no more than ten subject-related affirmations (SRAs). These SRAs are believed to have only the power of association to the ELAs (eternal life affirmations). In other words, when the problem of a moment is viewed from the scheme of eternal being, the problem not only diminishes but might cease altogether.

Aims

There are three immediate aims of the proposed research. The first is to test the hypothesis: "Is there an innate spiritual intelligence?" Is this intelligence demonstrable via the same cognitive-behavioral-modification intervention technique formerly employed with clinical affirmations? The second aim is to measure innate spiritual intelligence (ISI) on a pre- and post-test basis. Theoretically, as this intelligence awakens (is remembered), the life-healing benefits should become more obvious. The more subjective nature of awakening ISI should be measurable via a self-appraisal evaluation instrument. It's expected that a high correlation between instrument scores and objective outcomes from the various studies will emerge. Third, I recognized a certain bias that asserts a value to awakening ISI, both for the individual and society at large. I believe that ISI is nondenominational. I hold that the result of modest memory priming will be much stronger in yield than in stimuli intensity. In other words, priming inner talk with shadowed (masked) messages will yield a more complete life change than priming inner talk with clinical information, no matter how personally relevant or beneficial.

I understand the possibility of interpreting data as arising from spiritual self-interest as Freud's "sugar-coated crutch" and therefore the possibility of someone asserting that the most robust of findings don't necessarily represent a demonstration of ISI. Where this is possible, it's so only if ISI and self-interest have a common link. This was suspected.

Further, I believe that studies will reveal innate spiritual intelligence to be dynamic. That is, as it's awakened, the spiritual quotient will increase. In fact, I believe that the inherent spiritual tendency of the great scientists has been a product of their own awakening. Often, this is experienced as anomalous memory. Information, often thought of as *inspiration* or *serendipity* in science, is indeed—at least in part—the result of remembering information without having a context to frame the memory. Therefore, it's as if the information is known, but the how or why is unknown. I refer to this as "anomalous memory." Additionally, a high spiritual quotient should be predictive of a positive correlation with a high emotional quotient and at least abstract reasoning ability on intelligence-quotient instruments.

Overall, awakening innate spiritual intelligence will result in increasing spiritual quotient and will have predictive values with regard to creativity, abstract-reasoning ability, health, wellness, longevity, and emotional stability. (See Appendix 3 for the ISI affirmations and self-questionnaire.)

Results

The proposed study was never carried out. When I first presented the hypothesis, it met with quite a bit of resistance. Maybe the time just wasn't right. However, if you'd like to run this experiment on yourself, you can download the program by going to **www.eldontaylor .com/mindprogramming.html** and clicking on "Free SQ MP3." You can use the questionnaire in Appendix 3 as both the pre- and post-test measurement. I'd love to hear your outcome.

Summary

This Epilogue has explained how one idea can lead to others and suggests that we don't always follow through on the first idea. Furthermore, ideas are a gift and shouldn't be ignored, even if they seem to involve areas completely out of reach. By following the first idea, other ideas are spawned, and sooner or later one of the new notions is within our reach. It's been said that new success is only one idea away.

To me, perhaps the most exciting aspect of science is the emerging legitimacy being given to research into this stuff called "mind." For now, I hope you've enjoyed this work, obtained some tools of value, learned about yourself, and found some interest in other intriguing issues.

Thank you.

Research Results for InnerTalk®

**A Study of the Effects of Subliminal Communication
on Inmates at the Utah State Prison**
Taylor, E.; McCusker, C.; and Liston, L. (1985–1986)
Utah, USA

The aim of this double-blind study, conducted within the Utah State Prison system, was to evaluate a self-esteem audio subliminal program with inmates assigned to the Youth Offenders unit (first-time offenders under the age of 25). This study employed the MMPI with the Fowler lens developed for incarcerated environments for both pre- and post-testing. It also used the Thurstone Temperament Schedule as a sampling instrument on a pre-, mid-, and post-test basis. The experimenters administered the MMPI via a computer terminal for each subject. The Thurstone was administered by one of the experimenters who was blind to which group the participants had been assigned. Following the pre-test procedure, 38 subjects were randomly placed in one of three groups (experimental—14; placebo—13; and control—11). For 20 days, the subjects in the experimental group received and played the subliminal program containing verbal messages designed to increase self-esteem and lower the adaptation toward dominant and aggressive behavior. Also for 20 days, the placebo group played the same sound track recording without subliminal content. The control group had no exposure to the sound track.

A comparison of the experimental and control groups demonstrated a significant decrease in dominance scale scores while the reflective and stability scale scores increased in the experimental group (desired effects). The dominance scale scores increased while the reflective scales decreased in the control group. In the experimental group these results would be predicted by the focus of the subliminally embedded messages. The opposite effect, which was found in the placebo group, may be explained by the fact that the subjects listened to a recording without the message and felt no change. They therefore possibly experienced frustration. It should be noted that this was a pilot study with limitations, especially as regards time of implementation and sample size. It's also noteworthy that the Utah State Prison employs subliminal audio programs as a regular part of their rehabilitation procedures due to the findings of this study and the continued observations of the counseling staff.

Subliminal Relaxation: Myth or Method
Galbraith, P., and Barton, B. (1990)
Weber State University, Utah, USA

This study was carried out to ascertain whether subliminal audio programs are effective as relaxation tools and, if they are, how lasting is the effect. It was hypothesized that the subliminal messages would cause a lower anxiety score on both the physiological and subjective measures and that these effects could be maintained for at least 24 hours. The true purpose of the experiment was disguised from the subjects to reduce the bias that might accompany the demand characteristics. The experimenters were kept blind by not knowing the content of the subliminal and placebo programs until all the subjects were run.

Three biological measures of anxiety were used:

1. Middle and index finger's galvanic skin response
2. Peripheral skin temperature recorded at the wrist
3. The digital extensor muscle potential

To obtain pre- and post-test measures of the subjective level of anxiety, the State Trait Anxiety Inventory was used.

Although the biofeedback measures for the experiment didn't uphold the original hypothesis for the experiment, the State Trait Anxiety Inventory did show a significant decrease due to the subjects' exposure to the subliminal recording.

Free of Depression **Subliminal Tape Study**
James Joseph Reid (1990)
Colorado State University, Colorado, USA

The purpose of this study was to test the effectiveness of the subliminal audiotape *Free of Depression* with 28 subjects who were experiencing situational depression and were in therapy. The subjects were measured on several variables (level of depression, faith in subliminal tapes, progress, and involvement in therapy) at the beginning and at the end of the 30-day period of listening to the tape.

The study's conclusion indicated no meaningful findings for subjects who used the program fewer than 17 hours. However, all subjects who used the program during the 60-day study for more than 17 hours demonstrated marked differences on the Beck Depression Inventory (an average score lowering of 10 points). This study suggests not only the efficacy of subliminal usage as an adjunct to therapy but also a dosage relevancy.

The Effect of Subliminal Auditory Stimuli in a Surgical Setting Involving Anesthetic Requirements
Eldon Taylor (1990)
St. John's University, USA

This study explored the effect of subliminal auditory stimuli in lowering anesthetic requirements in surgery. It was carried out by Eldon Taylor and the surgical team of Robert Youngblood, a Salt Lake City plastic surgeon, and involved 720 patients. An audio subliminal program was designed specifically to lower stress levels before, during, and after surgery. Half the group, or 360 patients, were the control group. The other half of the group, or 360 patients, listened to the subliminal program for three relevant hours. All subjects were advised that a "positive message" subliminal would be played pre-operatively, intra-operatively, and post-operatively. The programs were used an average of three relevant hours by the patients. Results indicate that verbal messages presented subliminally did lower anesthetic requirements during surgery by 32 percent, building upon and replicating the work of Hess (1981).[1] This study suggests that subliminal auditory messages could be employed successfully as an ancillary aid in medical interventions.

Suggestion and Perceptual Instability: Auditory Subliminal Influences
Kruse, P., Stadler, M., and Kobs, M. (1991)
University of Bremen, Germany

This study examined the theory of intrusion effects on cognitive processes as a mechanistic element involved in preconscious processing (subliminal perception). The study was conducted in the German language using the Whole Brain® InnerTalk technology by Eldon Taylor. The effects were measured using thematic apperception testing means.

The findings strongly demonstrated the effect on the experimental group.

Application of Subliminal Therapy to Overweight Subjects
Rainier B. Pelka (1991)
Armed Forces University, Munich, Germany

The aim of this study was to test on overweight subjects the effect of a subliminal audio program designed to aid weight loss. The technology used was the Whole Brain InnerTalk technology created by Eldon Taylor. The subliminal messages were recorded in German.

Thirty-four female subjects were used, aged between 24 and 49 years. Approximately 25 percent of the subjects were under medical treatment specifically for their weight problem. During the experiment, the subjects made no changes to their normal diets or to the amount of exercise undertaken. There was an average weight loss of 6.4 kg after an average tape usage of nine weeks. The subjects also reported feeling slim, vital, and fit. After the experiment, most of the subjects reported making greater efforts to eat a more nutritious diet.

The results obtained were in agreement with the previous work of Lloyd Silverman and Robert Beck and were deemed so promising that a follow-up study was recommended.

The Influence of Aerobic Exercise and Relaxation Training on Coping with Test-Taking Anxiety
Plante, T. G.; Doan, B. T.; DiGregorio, M. P.; and Manuel, G. M. (1993)
Stanford University, CA, USA and Santa Clara University, CA, USA

This study sought to examine and compare the impact of brief aerobic exercise and relaxation training with the Whole Brain InnerTalk subliminal audio program *I Excel in Exams* and *Breathing,* by New Harbinger Publications.

The 52 subjects in the study were randomly assigned to one of three conditions: aerobic exercise, relaxation training, or control (magazine reading). The statistical data indicated significance supporting the hypothesis that Whole Brain InnerTalk subliminal technology could be an effective tool in lowering test anxiety.

The Effect of Subliminally Presented Reinforcing Stimuli on Factual Material
Diana Ashley (1993)
University of Southern California, CA, USA

The purpose of this study was to determine the effects of supportive factual subliminal messages (using the MIP) on recall of facts. There were 62 subjects, 25 in the experimental group and 37 in the control group. The experimental group was shown a video that had been programmed with textual subliminal messages that supported the supraliminal information. The control group was shown a video with the same supraliminal presentation but with no subliminal messages. The findings showed a significant increase in learning among students in the experimental group.

The Effect of a Whole-Brain Subliminal Program on Children Diagnosed with Attention Deficit Hyperactive Disorder
Kim Roche (1993)
Colorado State University, CO, USA

A Whole Brain InnerTalk subliminal program was created specifically for children with attention deficit hyperactive disorder. In a double-blind experiment to test the effect of this program, the findings indicated a significantly positive effect.

Longitudinal Study: Cancer Remission
Eldon Taylor (1988–91, reported in 1992–1993)
Progressive Awareness Research, WA, USA

A cancer-remission subliminal audiotape was designed and made available to cancer patients through consent and concurrent care of physician. A follow-up with subjects who had received the tape was conducted by mail.

Initial findings, generalized, consist of the following observations: The average patient outlived original prognosis in excess of 12 months (extremes were three years and 6 months). Ratings by physicians indicated positive correlations between the subliminal and patients' attitude toward their disease. Attitudes of the physicians are suggestive of patient outcome, according to early correlations between mortality rates and physician attitude. Of the patients who used the program, 43 percent went into remission.

The questionnaire developed for this study was designed to evaluate four categories:

1. Patient attitude (pre- and post-tape)
2. Quality of life experienced by patient
3. Remission/survivability
4. Physician attitude

Clinical Studies
Julian Isaacs (1991)
The Other 90%, CA, USA

Experimenter Julian Isaacs and team investigated the influence of subliminal audio programs created by Eldon Taylor for this study, which involved seven different themes:

1. Procrastination
2. Time management
3. Self-confidence
4. Anxiety
5. Positive relationships
6. Assertiveness
7. Self-esteem

It was concluded after three studies that the programs were definitely of significant efficacy in their expected directions.

Self-Responsibility Quiz

	Never	Sometimes	Usually
1. Do you believe that you're a lucky person?			
2. Do you worry about what others think of you?			
3. Do you fantasize about hurting someone?			
4. Do you like violent movies?			
5. Is it easy to accept others' mistakes?			
6. Do you dwell on negative experiences?			
7. Do you look forward to a very long life?			
8. Do you make enemies?			
9. Do you blame anyone for your circumstances?			
10. Do you like your work?	-		
11. Do you look forward to life?			

	Never	Sometimes	Usually
12. Do you fear death?			
13. Do you take good care of yourself?			
14. Do you like your body?			
15. Do you consider yourself fortunate?			
16. Do you blame yourself?			
17. Do you blame others?			
18. Do you pity people?			
19. Do you feel sorry for them?			
20. Does the weather upset you?			
21. Do you get angry?			
22. Do you yell at others?			
23. Does risk frighten you?			
24. Do delays frustrate you?			
25. Does health worry you?			
26. Does living excite you?			
27. Do you wish you could get even with someone?			
28. Has someone stopped you from good things?			
29. Do you deserve more?			
30. Do you begrudge others?			
31. Are you jealous?			
32. Are you deserving?			
33. Does your work anger you?			
34. Do others aggravate you?			
35. Do you like yourself?			
36. Does pain usually frighten you?			
37. Does illness scare you?			
38. Are you happy?			
39. Do you get along with others?			

	Never	Sometimes	Usually
40. Does losing upset you?			
41. Do you wish you were different?			
42. Is life good to you?			
43. Do you make friends easily?			
44. Is it important to be right?			
45. Do you lie to others?			
46. Do you exaggerate your experiences?			
47. Do you love easily?			
48. Do you like learning?			
49. Do you enjoy new experiences?			
50. Do you look forward to new adventures?			

Special Instruction/Disclaimer

Take this test just for fun. It hasn't been tested for its validity. As such, the evaluation of this instrument isn't based on rigorous scientific methods, and the results should therefore be seen as entertaining more than informative or educational.

Scoring Instructions

A. Add up the total S answers. Multiply by 1 point and subtract from 100.

B. Count U's for questions: 3, 4, 6, 8, 9, 12, 16–25, 27, 28, 30, 31, 33, 34, 36, 37, 40–42, 44–46. Multiply by 2 points and subtract from the answer for A.

C. Count N's for questions: 1, 2, 5, 7, 10, 11, 13, 14, 15, 26, 29, 32, 35, 38, 39, 43, 47–50. Multiply by 2 points and subtract from the answer for B.

Responsibility-Scale Evaluation Table

— **80 points or higher:** This subject is in charge of his/her life and usually won't experience seasonal illness or other psychologically aggravated diseases. A score of 80 or more should also be evaluated for denial. Life circumstances, health, and pain thresholds will reveal whether a score of 80 or more indicates self-responsibility/control or other mechanisms, including dishonest answers.

— **70 to 80:** This subject normally is in control, is capable of high pain thresholds, finds life invigorating, is optimistic, and generally loves living.

— **60 to 70:** Normally this subject tends toward self-actualizing goals. He/she is probably working on personal growth and/or growing through trauma or catastrophe. Subject's outlook on life tends toward self-guidance, but individual isn't ready to accept the idea that he/she is indeed the fabric of responses to life's stimuli.

— **50 to 60:** This subject wishes to believe he/she can change circumstances but is unwilling to give up the traditional victim role.

— **49 and lower:** For this subject, the world acts on him/her and the individual can only respond. Subject will have mechanistic views of life, health, and so forth. This person is a victim in a hostile environment.

Innate Spiritual
Intelligence Affirmations

I am vital energy.
I am connected to the Mind of God.
We are all One.
From the One we all are.
I am a creation of God.
God's perfection is who I am.
The All-Wise, knowing intelligence flows through me.
I am awakened.
I remember.
I am enlightened.
My consciousness expands.
My being is unlimited and eternal.
My awareness is open and receptive.
I am in harmony with all life.
Joy and Love are my being.
I am a creation of Love.
I am a gift of Love.
All that I can be is a gift.
I see God in all people and all creation.
I am unconditional love.
I radiate unconditional love to all.

I unconditionally love and accept myself.
I am worthy.
I am patient and understanding.
I accept my holy being.
I do unto others as I would have others do unto me.
I am secure and free.
I live in the now.
I release the past.
Every day in every way I improve—better, better, and better.
I live in the kingdom within.
I feel the power within.
I am responsible for my life.
I am truthful.
My being is eternal truth.
I am honest.
I am humble and courageous.
I am sensitive to others.
I have empathy for all.
I am a lucid dreamer.
My dreams communicate with me.
I remember my dreams.
I respect myself.
I respect all others.
I live in the now.
Every day my joy increases.
I have a powerful imagination.
I visualize easily.
I use my imagination to power visualization.
I have the power to create.
I create joy, happiness, health, and Love.
My manifestations are realized quickly.
Change is growth.
I accept change.
I find awe in all.
All inspires me.
Creativity is natural.

My talents and abilities increase every day.
I can do anything.
I am a genius.
I am a master of focus and concentration.
I am a healing agent.
I trust myself.
I trust my impressions.
I see holiness in all.
Love heals all.
I am unconditional Love.
I am that I am.
My body is strong and powerful.
My mind is keen and alert.
My immune system operates perfectly.
My body functions optimally.
Health and wellness are mine.
I am radiant health and vitality.
I am safe.
I am comfortable.
I am secure.
I am fulfilled.
My being prospers.
I am abundant.
I accept peace.
I know the peace that passeth understanding.
My being is at peace.
Peace, harmony, and balance are mine.
Thank you, thank you, thank you, and so it is!

Suggested Emotional Quotient Evaluation

Answer the following questions according to how you normally feel. There's no right answer. Please respond as honestly as possible. Rate your usual feelings according to always, sometimes, seldom, and never.

	Always	Sometimes	Seldom	Never
I sense a plan to my life.				
I feel protected.				
I've had a spiritual experience.				
I believe in guides or angels.				
I believe life is a miracle.				
I've had psychic experiences.				
My dreams have guided me.				
I'm comfortable with God.				
I see humankind as inherently unworthy.				
I usually feel guilty.				
Guilt is natural.				
I have those I blame.				
Anger is sometimes justified.				
I have many friends.				
I trust my friends.				
I'm a trusting person.				
I like myself.				
I believe the world has a purpose.				
Spirituality is important to me.				
I believe mankind is eternal.				
I believe all life is sacred.				
I believe there's a Devil.				
I don't believe in ghosts.				
I don't believe in the supernatural.				
I feel punished by God.				
I long to believe in a God but don't.				
I consider myself an atheist.				
I like to hunt.				
I like to fish.				
I enjoy the outdoors.				

Innate Spiritual Intelligence Affirmations

	Always	Sometimes	Seldom	Never
It hurts me when I see an animal hurt.				
I feel pain when another suffers.				
I feel connected to all life.				
I don't believe in animal rights.				
Animals are for humankind to rule.				
The planet is for humankind to use.				
I like to help others.				
I often intervene when I can help.				
I expect to succeed.				
I'm lucky.				
I'm afraid of illness.				
I'm sick two or more times a year.				
I expect to get a cold every year.				
I like my work.				
I enjoy the people I work with.				
I'm a confident person.				
People like me.				
People respect me.				
I enjoy animals.				
I like children.				
I like to laugh.				
My sleep is peaceful.				
Shame can be healthy.				
I look forward to each new day.				
I'm engaged with life.				
A spiritual life is important.				
My spiritual life is fulfilling.				
Spiritual stuff is nonsense.				
Science has obliterated religion.				
Science and religion will never agree.				

	Always	Sometimes	Seldom	Never
Thinking people give up superstitions.				
Religion is a superstition.				
I believe in me.				
I take the most from life.				
I believe life is for giving.				
I believe love is what life's about.				
I believe life is about fun.				
I believe suffering is unfair.				
I think humankind has gone to the dogs.				
Life sucks and then you die.				
I'm happy with my life.				
I find life full of awe.				
I think people are untrustworthy.				
I believe you must protect yourself.				
I worry about crime.				
I find the state of the world hopeless.				
I feel hopeless.				
I respect other's beliefs.				
I think everyone should believe as I do.				
Fear is a creative force.				

The actual test, together with scoring instructions, is available upon request. Please go to: **www.eldontaylor.com/mindprogram ming.html**.

The preceding is a new instrument. Although it's believed to have both validity and reliability elements structured within it, the evaluation is still only experimental. The data from the proposed studies will ultimately give rise to the relative success (predictability) of the instrument.

Serenity Affirmations

Please note that this list contains positive words and phrases, as well as conventional affirmations.

I am relaxed.
I am safe.
I am calm.
I remain calm and composed.
Love is what I am.
I am a gift.
I am grateful for the gift.
I am blessed.
I accept the Divine plan.
The Universe is purposeful.
I am serene.
I acknowledge the good in all.
I am nonjudgmental.
I am caring and sharing.
I am loving.
I am compassionate.
I am detached from worldly woes.
I recognize the illusion.

Only the eternal is real.
I invest myself in the eternal.
I am infinite wisdom.
I am infinite composure.
I am serene and calm.
I am good.
I am in the hands of God.
I trust.
I am nonresistant.
I am noncombative.
I am accepting.
I allow.
My spirit guides me.
The expanse of spirit is like a clear sky.
Undisturbed.
Peaceful.
Tranquil.
At ease with myself.
At ease with the world around me.
Grateful.
Happy.
Joyful.
It's all so good.
Everything is so okay.
Thank you.
Thank you.
Thank you.
I forgive myself.
I forgive all others.
I am forgiven.

Brainwashing on Trial in America

(Reprinted by permission from *Thinking without Thinking* by Eldon Taylor)

It's 1994, a decade after Orwell's year. We still have America, land of the free and home of the brave. There is no "Big Brother."

Americans relax comfortably. They enjoy their technology. Television, video players, radios, and other entertainment systems babble together. Favorite music plays in the background. Magazines rest on sofas and tables. Informative articles and advertisements tell all of us of the latest and best in everything one can imagine.

Less than a hundred years ago all of this normal stuff would have appeared miraculous! Where else but America could you expect to find all of this so freely available? Multiple televisions and radios, portable computers, games that simulate reality and interact with children, slick glossy magazines delivered to the door, free television stations with incredible variety, satellite and cable transmissions with ridiculous variety—only in America. America, land of plenty—land of the free and home of the brave.

Liberty and justice for all. We know and cherish that ideal. We know we must guard it. We know dreams can become nightmares. So let us recall a day from 1985.

Two teenage boys had difficulty adjusting to life. Ray had just split up with his girlfriend. James had just lost his job. Neither of them were blameless. Both of them were confused. With most young people, the approach to adulthood provides struggles. It should.

Two days before Christmas, Ray gave James a gift of music. The music had particular significance. James had once collected the music of this particular artist. He found the music violated his Christian beliefs. He threw them all away.

That was a few years ago. James no longer pursued any religious affiliation. He had turned away from religion. Many people do at some point in their lives.

On December 23rd, James received the album. The boys decided to play the album while they drank beer. The words and music of one particular song held their interest. They played it repeatedly. The lyrics in several songs encouraged suicide with such rhymes as: "Leave this life with all its sin; it's not fit for living in."

Picture these two young men: attractive; on the slight side—skinny, according to more than one description; unskilled; not doing well in school; anticipating a life of difficulty and with delusions of grandeur driven by frustration, pretending to be mercenaries, or imagining themselves as heroes.

Mid-afternoon, the lyrics going around in their heads included, "Why do you have to die to be a hero?" The two looked at each other as though acting in some movie. The hero says, "Let's do it" just before mayhem begins. One of the boys said, "Do it!" The two began chanting "Do it." One of them grabbed a shotgun. They went out the bedroom window to the church playground. Ray placed a shotgun under his jaw. James chanted "Do it!" Ray fired the gun. The blast stunned James. Ray was dead.

James lifted the gun, wet with blood. He said later that he trembled. He felt afraid. He could be blamed for Ray's death. He wondered why they had chanted "do it." He placed the gun under his own jaw. He pulled the trigger.

James had failed to brace the shotgun. As he pulled the trigger the gun lurched forward. The blast shot off the front of his face. It did not kill him. It left him severely wounded and disfigured. He lived for nearly three years.

You have the graphic pictures in your mind. Two young men have shot themselves, inflicted death and injury from their own hands—or was it from their own hands? Can we explain such senseless tragic irrevocable acts? Could we prevent them?

Try to imagine yourself and a friend suddenly deciding to jump up and commit suicide together! People who commit suicide take a long time to reach their decision to commit the final act. They go over and over the idea in their minds. Even if they do not intentionally speak of suicide, it becomes part of their conversation. They plan it. They wonder what will happen after their death. Police always expect to find a note. Mutual suicides rarely occur. On these rare occasions, police expect to find a manifesto. Can you find another case of an impulse double suicide? Surely a tragedy so incomprehensible and odd demands useful explanation and effective response.

Obviously, we can do nothing for the dead. Therefore, we will discuss this as a general case. Naming individuals and groups involved, at this point, would imply that they had behaved differently and more culpably than others. Even when true, that could distract from the purpose which I hope you will share with me. Again, I do not seek to blame. I seek understandings that we can all use in our lives.

Perhaps you know some of the history of physics. Maybe you have done some physics experiments in school. Then you know the difficulties of discovering, let alone isolating, proving and measuring cause and effect in physics. All the more so in psychology.

The recording the boys enjoyed so much had been "cooked." Unknown to them, it included statements which a listener could not normally consciously hear. Could this have had some effect? Bizarre and unlikely behavior tends to have bizarre and unlikely causes.

You have probably seen people come near to physically attacking each other without ever noticing that their tones of voice, and not any words, triggered their emotions. Ample research demonstrates that we can respond to what psychologists term "subliminal perception." We can respond to events without consciously noticing and remembering them. We need to. Imagine having to consciously perceive and respond to all the information of balance and pressure and muscular contractions and relaxations and visceral sensations necessary to stand up, let alone walk! Boxers know that they have to react before they know why—or it's too late. You may know of some of the clinical studies in which people in various conditions have reacted to stimuli without consciously knowing that the pictures, print, sounds, or words existed.

The sound track the boys listened to included viscerally offensive nonsense like "Sing my evil spirit, f— the lord . . ." and the very simple command, "Do it!" The command was spoken forwards. The "satanic" messages were backwards. The boys had no conscious awareness of the subliminal content. They just chanted, "Do it!" Then they did.

Three years pass. James has died. In a courtroom in the boys' hometown, an attorney stands before a judge. He pleads for his client. He insists that his client, the multinational media corporation that released the music album, and that owns the largest broadcasting systems in the world for both radio and television, has the constitutional right to put whatever they wish in the form of subliminal information, on any broadcast or other means of communication, because that is a right granted by the first amendment: Freedom of Speech.

The judge proposes a hypothetical case. Suppose Media Giant uses subliminal messages to sell us a politician. He asks the attorney whether they believe the First Amendment protects this type of conduct. The attorney affirms that it is indeed their right—but they would never do it. Why not? They could.

Weeks turn into months. The trial goes on. The media report the proceedings as a ludicrous waste of taxpayers' money. The experts for the families of the deceased young men suffer ridicule. The media present them in the worst light.

Media Giant fails to produce the original 24-track music master for analysis. They say they can't find it. A former Scotland Yard detective is hired to search high and low for the master. He tells the court under oath that he was not allowed to look in the vaults.

Employees and others call it very strange that the Media Giant could not find this master, which made them millions of dollars, and which they need to produce the album.

Media Giant, through able and expensive attorneys, argues that no subliminal messages exist. The judge listens to the messages, as rendered audible. Media Giant explains this as a "coincidence of sound." Members of the band that recorded the music have admitted to putting subliminal messages on recordings. They now deny putting any on this one.

Media Giant's attorneys put on their witnesses. They assert "everything can be quantified" and "there is no evidence that a subliminal message could cause anyone to do anything." These witnesses receive good press.

Just before the trial, one spokesperson against subliminals, a psychologist, became more prominent. You become an expert if you come from out of town. He certainly qualified as an expert. He came from Canada. He had written an article a few years earlier telling America to ignore subliminal "stuff" in songs, advertising, and the like, because it didn't work. He wrote that subliminals wouldn't motivate anyone to do anything. He then became a witness for Media Giant.

Earlier in the trial the "subliminal messages" had to be proven to exist. Witnesses for Media Giant have conducted scientific studies proving the failure of subliminal messages to influence their subjects. This requires a new definition of "subliminal." According to the new definition, if any means of analysis whatsoever can detect the presence of information, then that is "supraliminal" information—not "subliminal"—and therefore protected as free speech. Information qualifies as subliminal only if no means whatsoever can detect it. You can't get more subliminal than that! So you have to agree.

At the conclusion of the trial, the judge learned that the Media Giant had, at great expense, manipulated the media before and during the trial. It released continuous press packages through a publicity and public relations firm. Such firms and such packages have a simple purpose: to control public opinions. The judge warned the Media Giant on the morning of his verdict that, "The court will be investigating this action, since some of the material given in press releases is totally improper and could constitute slander." He then fined the Media Giant $40,000 for impeding the discovery process and not bringing forward the original music track master.

Nonetheless, the judge stated that, in the wrongful death action that had been brought, the attorneys for the deceased young men failed to prove that the subliminal command was intentionally recorded on the album. Further, the judge concluded, these two young men were at risk and would probably have committed suicide without the subliminal messages.

The trial ended. The media repeated reporting the absolute waste of taxpayers' money spent on such a foolish issue. Newspapers and magazines around the world received media packages scoffing at the entire concept of subliminal perception. Large-dollar advertisers sent slanted packages to the press, and placed advertising if the copy was accepted for print. Experts for the Media Giant began speaking out. They argued that subliminal information-processing did not exist except as a subject for laughter, and that it depended on the foolish idea of a smart subconscious mind able to receive and process this subliminal information.

Finally a report appeared, allegedly a U.S. Army study, debunking subliminal information-processing along with a host of other popular notions such as hypnosis, meditation and the like. In short, according to this report, anything that has to do with the so-called power of the subconscious mind made categorical nonsense.

When contacted, the Army said they had no prior knowledge of the study. The press did not report that the reporting agency (National Research Council) was under investigation for improper use of tax dollars and had returned monies to the government that had been used inappropriately by staff. Further, the press also ignored that these same people turned out a previous report that many scientists criticized as a flagrant and false representation of the data. The press did not link any of this to the reporting agency in context.

The so-called scientific report allegedly generated for the Army came from an organization with its own agenda. In fact, we discover that those who adamantly oppose the idea that subliminal messages could have been a contributing causal factor in the death of our two young men were all connected through public presentations and/ or papers to the Committee for the Scientific Investigation of Claims of the Paranormal (CSICOP) and one of its founders. This "founder" also founded an atheistic publishing company. One of the members of CSICOP once stated through one of its chapters: "I want people who are willing to get dirty. . . . What we will do is employ a very thorough, proven technique for getting the point across to people who have no demonstrated facility to reason." Who do they mean?

Some people do reason poorly. A founding member of CSICOP once said, "Religion is the paranoia of optimists."

Most people reason poorly about something. Sometimes some people deliberately reason poorly. Sometimes it's hard to tell the difference. You need only refer to some of the reasoning cited earlier.

Many people need to learn to think. We can teach logic. Some have used "lack-logic" as a means to manipulate.

> After scrutiny, we found several interconnected organizations that have the same founders or executive committee members. These organizations all attack beliefs that suggest anything more to who and what we are than what we have objective conscious awareness of knowing. They attack meditation, para-psychology, holistic health, spiritual values, ideas of a subconscious or superconscious mind and so forth. They have used ridicule as their principal tactic: "A horse-laugh is worth ten thousand syllogisms."

What do you think of this? Would you like to be subjected to propaganda in this manner? Would you like your children to live in this environment? Before you decide, let's continue with the story.

> Another psychologist, called as a witness for the Media Giant, reported that three double-blind studies, each a replication of the other, clearly showed that subliminal effects are due only to expectation or placebo impetus. Of the three studies he cited, two were part of a doctoral dissertation by a marketing student. This study examined the effects of audiotape labels on expectations. The design of the study did not aim to measure the effect of the audiotapes themselves. The design of the three studies did not replicate each other.
>
> The student did not intend to study subliminal messages. The study aimed to measure the effect of labels on expectation. This study used some commercial subliminal tapes made by companies who may not have known what they were doing. These studies did not examine anything scientific with regard to a controlled message or a controlled subliminal technology.
>
> Academic journals heated with the controversy. The case awaited appeal. New reports came out that subliminal messages were nonsense. These reports continued to hit the news stands in popular magazines. Many scientific articles demonstrated the opposite.
>
> Earlier our informed Canadian expert, who wrote that America had nothing to worry about as subliminal communication did not

work, filed a complaint with the ethics committee of the American Psychological Association (APA). In the complaint he alleged that one of their members, a licensed psychologist, claimed that subliminals worked to aid and assist people with behavioral changes and that he had used this technology. The APA ethics committee unanimously rejected the complaint. Our informed expert went on a campaign with a major liquor company, which has been accused of using subliminal information in its advertising. Together they told America, "Don't worry. It doesn't work, and we'd never do that."

This all actually happened.

Perhaps you have begun to imagine a deliberate conspiracy to keep America in the dark about the power of subliminal communication. We need no conspiracy to explain any of this. For now, put yourself in their positions.

Suppose you made yourself rich as a rock musician, or that you worked your way to an executive post in a huge corporation—would you like to think that one of your products had contributed to a double suicide? Wouldn't you rather believe anything else? Suppose you had built yourself a university career and a reputation as an authority in your field; wouldn't you want the fame and adulation and money available outside academia? Wouldn't you want to say and write what would bring you all that? Wouldn't you feel better and like yourself better if you could make yourself believe it?

Orwell made a mistake. *1984* described elaborate technologies and torture that rulers used to make people deceive not merely others, but themselves. We require nothing elaborate. We do it daily. We do it to ourselves.

Please remind yourself that we must refer to a real and specific incident to illustrate general principles. The particular corporations and professionals mentioned here have proven no more callous and irresponsible than similar corporations and professionals. You must protect yourself from imagining otherwise.

Does any hard evidence suggest any power in subliminal messages? Obviously, this became a major issue at the Reno, Nevada, trial where the families of Raymond Belknap and James Vance filed a wrongful death action against CBS and the rock group Judas Priest. As one of the witnesses, I was asked if any direct corollary research had ever demonstrated that subliminal stimuli could elicit action as serious as that taken by young Vance and Belknap.

Questions can require complex answers. This critical question contains the implicit idea that some researcher has taken troubled young people, given them some beer, exposed them to suicidal arguments that embraced childish notions of courage and romance, added emotionally compelling and confusing nonsense, and then added subliminal commands urging action. No such research has ever been done. Thank God! Not since World War II has such a heinous research design been recorded in science. No human subjects committee would allow such a study.

At the time of the trial I explained that this type of study would have been irresponsible. I also referred to research with subliminal stimuli in conjunction with alcohol and in conjunction with depression. Many positive outcomes demonstrated subliminal information could alleviate human suffering. Perhaps people have only done that research because it could lead to profits. Very little research has been done to prove the opposite.

I could discuss all this more eloquently and argue it more persuasively than I did in the deposition. I will let you see what I actually said.

The first question I was asked was how I had come to my conclusions regarding whether or not the subliminal messages contributed to the double shooting. I answered:

> Well, I looked at all of the information and essentially said, based on my knowledge, these two boys could have been provoked to a violent action against themselves or against society at large at a given point in time. In order to determine whether or not the subliminal content was a cause in the suicide, I had to satisfy in my mind that something occurred out of the ordinary that could have precipitated this.
>
> There were a lot of dynamics going on with these young men, so I looked to see if there was a point in the given day when there would be indications that neither of these young men would have been thinking about suicide, actively thinking about suicide. I believe for Raymond Belknap that was when he got his haircut, and for

James Vance it was his description under hypnosis of a shower he had taken. Therefore, at about 1:00 P.M. for Raymond and 2:00 P.M. or so for James, I don't believe that there was anything at that point in time that indicated these two young men had planned to commit suicide on the 23rd of December.

Something had to occur that was different. My understanding is that, although they smoked marijuana and they used some alcohol, it was low-grade marijuana and it was not enough alcohol to be out of the ordinary for their pattern of events.

Precipitating factors that I took into consideration were the alleged argument that occurred with Vance's parents, the loss of the paycheck, and the fact that it was the 23rd of December. Christmas is a major Christian event and regardless of your beliefs you're still nevertheless aware that it is a Christian event and it is a moral event. It was the proximity to Christmas and the fact that the Stained Class album was given as a Christmas present. Remember, this album had previously been thrown away because of a conflict that existed, at least in James's mind, between his axiological perspective, religiously speaking, and his attitude toward his interpretation of the Judas Priest group.

I systematically reviewed the scientific literature regarding subliminal studies in light of the character of these young men as I had determined it from the materials sent me. I evaluated or initially looked for studies that had been done where the presentation of subliminal stimuli and depression were associated.

In a study done by Henley in 1975, it was determined that presentation of subliminal stimuli had an effect on decision making, and that we analyzed and integrated information when it was presented in a metacontrast method or in a subliminal method.[1]

In a study that was done by Kostandov in 1980, it was determined that there was a role on the choice of reaction as a result of subliminal influences, that subliminal stimuli had a determining role on the choice of our reactions or in decision making.[2]

I evaluated the fact that Vance had suffered the loss of his father, not through death, as I understand, but through abandonment. I drew inferences that I believe are valid inferences and looked for specific studies having to do with the loss of a primary caretaker and the presentation of subliminal stimuli.

I found a study done by Jill Miller at New York University that essentially said that subliminal aggressive stimuli, when presented to survivors who had lost a parent, causes hypomania defenses to break down and increases depression.[3]

I looked to see the influence of prior suicidal threats or attempts and studies that would have been relevant directly or indirectly, and I found a study by Rutstein, performed in 1973. The study essentially demonstrated that there was increased depression in suicidal subjects following aggressive subliminal stimuli.[4]

I then looked to combine these aggression tendencies and depression in any particular studies. I found a study by De Martino of New York University. In this study, De Martino presented the messages "Kill" and "Tell" and determined that the effects of subliminal stimuli were carried by individuals who identified themselves in the self-rating index to be aggressors.[5]

I found another study done by Silverman where aggressive stimuli were shown to alter pathology—manifest pathology, actually—and essentially Silverman argued that congruent drives gave rise to the degree of manifested pathology.[6]

I looked for direct behavioral connection studies, studies that would report a direct effect on behavior. I found a study of Dr. Lee's, which was written up in 1983. The study was done on agoraphobics.[7] I drew upon some of my own work at this point, including a study that was conducted at Weber State University, one of my undergraduate schools. The study used the state trait anxiety index to see how subliminal messages effected behaviors related to stress.[8]

I then looked at religious conflict as it seemed relevant to hypomania defenses. We ordinarily look at that in the traditional psychoanalytic sense as a conflict between ego and superego, superego being the area where we have taboos, our moral values, and ego being the mediator where our drives are coming from, the id. I looked at the back-masking study that was done by Leclerc—that is, of course, presenting language backwards. Leclerc's study was done at the University of Montreal, Quebec.[9]

Leclerc's study showed us that indeed information that was presented back-masked—sometimes that is called metacontrast where audio subliminal is concerned, but that is not a strict, appropriate use of the word *metacontrast*—was acted upon, was perceived.

I looked and found a study by Henley in 1975, the study I mentioned earlier where once again music was presented to one ear with subliminal words, to the other ear backwards, back-masked, and had significant subliminal effect.[10]

I added to that my experience in a number of anecdotal reports ranging from individuals who have worked with programs we created for specific health care interventions to programs that have been employed in settings I would never have thought of. For example, an educational psychologist friend of mine took to his niece, who was in the hospital in Salt Lake City in a coma, a subliminal tape on healing and played it in an auto reverse player. When she came out of the coma, the nurses and the physicians themselves basically said that the first words out of her mouth were what we call affirmations that existed on the tape.

I was advised by Mr. McKenna in one of his last phone calls to me that an educational psychologist had been deposed that knew James Vance and that she had indicated that James had told her that they chanted "Do it."

We have in this literature the association of music and words, the aggressive drive, aggressive behavior, and then the chanting, and in context I thereby came to the conclusion that the subliminal messages on the Stained Class album were a factor in the double shooting.

The attorney for CBS and Judas Priest (Q) asked:

Q: Are you able to say how much of a factor?

A: I don't believe anybody on this earth is qualified to do that.

Q: Which is to say the answer to the question is no, not you and not anybody else; right?

A: The nature of the situation—I appreciate what you're trying to get me to say, Ms. Fulstone.

Q: I'm just trying to get an answer to the question.

A: The nature of the situation, I don't think lends itself to a yes or no. I don't believe that we can fractionate all the elements that came together on that day to say one was more important than another. The man that is contemplating suicide standing on the edge of a building, ledge of a building, and somebody says, "You're no good; do it," is that a factor? We're inclined to believe so. How much of a factor, how do you fractionate those factors? I can't give you an answer, is what I'm saying, short of an explanation. I wish I could.

Q: Again the question I asked you was, Could you say how much of a factor and that is the question I want answered here. You're shaking your head no. Is that the answer?

A: Are you asking me for percentages?

Q: I'm asking you if you can say how much of a factor, in your opinion, the subliminal messages were in this double shooting?

A: In my own mind, by my best belief, as I understand all the information that I have in front of me, without those messages, without that chanting, without the association to the lyrics "This world is not worth living in," et cetera, I don't believe these young men would have killed themselves on that given day.

Q: I'm going back to my question again and limit yourself specifically—you have said in your opinion the subliminal messages on the Stained Class album were a factor in the double shooting.

A: Yes.

Q: My question is, Can you say how much of a factor?

A: I think I have answered that. I'm not certain now what it is you're asking honestly.

Q: You combined it with the actual lyrics, the chanting and, you know, whatever facts you may think you have. I'm trying to get you to tell me, either you can isolate the subliminal messages as a factor and tell me how much of a factor they were, or you can tell me that you can't do that which is what I understood you to say initially.

A: I don't believe I can tell you how much of a factor it was.

Q: Is it your opinion that the suicide and attempted suicide of Ray Belknap and James Vance would not have occurred but for the subliminal messages?

A: On that given day, yes.

Q: When you say that, are you separating out the subliminal messages from the other factors that you have described?

A: I don't believe that is possible, Ms. Fulstone.

Q: Okay. How is it that you can say the suicide and attempted suicide would not have occurred but for the subliminal message?

A: I believe that everything coming together on that day combined with the presentation of an album that in itself was significant to Mr. Vance and to Mr. Belknap. It was Belknap's friendship offer to Mr. Vance. It was something Mr. Vance had discarded because of a conflict in his Christian view of the world. That album contained lyrics that they chanted "Do it" to, the lyrics of which I believe suggest to some that life is not worth living and that combined in a gestalt to produce the act of total alienation from life and basic despair.

Q: This is all essentially speculation, is it not?

A: I would ask you to define speculation, I guess, Ms. Fulstone. If you mean speculation like I'm speculating on an unknown situation without extrapolating from known, I would say no. If you mean speculation from I'm making inferences, I'm extrapolating, I'm doing my level best to bring all the information together that I have learned in a lifetime through various means to make a judgment, then I would say yes.

Q: Are you saying, then, that just as in your opinion the suicide would not have occurred but for the subliminal content, that it likewise would not have occurred but for the alcohol and the drug use on that day?

A: No, I'm not saying that. The answer is no.

Q: Are you saying that the suicide and attempted suicide would not have occurred but for the confrontation with Vance's parents?

A: I would consider that the confrontation with Vance's parents could be a contributor. I wouldn't say that you could isolate that. To me the significant factors of this given day once again were the confrontation, the loss of the paycheck, the proximity to Christmas, the despair of the young men that seems to have been provoked, at least in part, by all of these things coming together while simultaneously being presented with the Stained Class album in its lyrical content as well as its subliminal content, and all the other meanings it had for the Vance boy.

I believe that the fact that they chose the back of a churchyard to commit the crime with that same proximity with these other conflicts is more than coincidental.

The fact that the Vance boy apparently is quoted as saying he saw fire fly from the back of Belknap's head, when indeed that didn't happen, would indicate that his perception is somewhat skewed, and I believe that it's more than coincidental that the album cover would be essentially presenting what it is that Vance says he saw.

There comes a point, I believe, that we can take all these elements, add them together, and coincidence doesn't explain them.

ACKNOWLEDGMENTS

"Behind every good man is a good woman." "The road to success is filled with women pushing their husbands along." "Behind every good man is an even greater woman." These sayings all describe my life with my wife. My wife—how inappropriate to put *my* in front of *wife,* as if it were some ownership thing akin to my house, my book, my checking account! Our language sometimes seems so inept at expressing what we really feel.

To the lovely person who calls herself my wife, I must express my deepest gratitude. This book simply wouldn't have been without her tireless support. If this book serves its purpose to inform you about how your power can be taken and how you can take it back, it's due to her relentless persistence and gregarious encouragement.

Thank you, Ravinder. You have my love, respect, appreciation, and the acknowledgment you so deserve!

I must also thank my wonderful editor, Suzanne Brady. For more than 20 years, she has been both my faithful friend and talented editor. If you like my work at all, then credit must go to Suzanne, for she takes my scribbles and polishes them in ways that only she can do.

Thank you, Suzanne!

I would also like to thank the incredible team at Hay House: Jessica Kelley, who repeatedly tweaked and structured the manuscript; Jill Kramer, who is one of the most efficient people I've ever worked with; Charles McStravick, for the great cover design; all the other team members who work behind the scenes; and of course, Louise Hay and Reid Tracy for their incredible achievements.

Thank you, Hay House.

In Honorarium of Roy and Lois Bey,
without whom this work would not be.

Figure 20

ENDNOTES

Preface

1. Overbye, D. 2007. "Free Will: Now You Have It, Now You Don't." *New York Times,* Jan. 2.

2. Ibid.

Chapter 1

1. Kant, I. 1965. *Immanuel Kant's Critique of Pure Reason.* New York: St. Martin's Press.

2. Boone, J. A. 1939. *Letters to Strongheart.* Upper Saddle River, N.J.: Prentice Hall.

Chapter 2

1. Baars, B. 1997. *In the Theater of Consciousness: The Workspace of the Mind.* Oxford U.K.: Oxford University Press.

2. Libet, B., et al. 1967. "Unconscious Process and the Evoked Potential." *Science,* 158, page 1597.

3. Soon, C. S.; Brass, M.; Heinze, H. & Haynes, J. 2008. "Unconscious determinants of free decisions in the human brain." *Nature Neuroscience,* 11, 543–545. As cited by: Hotz, R. 2008. Get Out of Your Own Way. *Wall Street Journal,* June 27, A9. **http://online.wsj.com/public/article_print/SB121450609076407973.html**.

4. Bernays, E. 2005. *Propaganda.* Brooklyn, New York: Ig Publishing.

5. Ament, P. 2006. "Fascinating Facts About Joseph Swan: Inventor of the Light Bulb in 1879." **http://www.ideafinder.com/history/inventors/swan.htm**.

6. Bullock, A. 2004. *The Secret Sales Pitch.* San Jose, Calif.: Norwich Publishers.

7. Ibid.

8. Ibid.

9. Bernays, E. 2005. *Propaganda.* Brooklyn, New York: Ig Publishing.

10. Pratkanis, A. and Aronson, E. 2001. *Age of Propaganda.* New York: W. H. Freeman.

11. Orwell, G. 1992. *1984.* New York: Everyman's Library.

12. Obrec, L. 1999. Marketing, Motive and Dr. Freud. *Detroiter Magazine.* Dec. 1999.

13. Ibid.

14. Packard, V. 1957. *The Hidden Persuaders.* New York: Pocket Book.

15. Pratkanis, A. and Aronson, E. 2001. *Age of Propaganda.* New York: W. H. Freeman.

16. Hansen, G. P. 1992. "CSICOP and the Skeptics: An Overview." *The Journal of the American Society for Psychical Research,* Vol. 86.

17. Bornstein, R. F. and Pittman, T. S., Eds. 1992. *Perception Without Awareness: Cognitive, Clinical, and Social Perspectives.* New York: Guilford Press.

18. Warrick, J. Dir. 2008. *Programming The Nation.* Ignite Productions.

Chapter 3

1. Cialdini, R. B. 1992. *Influence: Science and Practice.* New York: Harper Collins.
2. Ibid.
3. Ibid.
4. Ibid.
5. Ibid.
6. Ibid.
7. Feinberg, R. A. 1990. "The Social Nature of the Classical Conditioning Phenomena in People." *Psychological Reports,* 67, 331–334.
8. Bornstein, R. F.; Leone, D. R.; and Galley, D. J. 1987. "The Generalizability of Subliminal Mere Exposure Effects." *Journal of Personality and Social Psychology,* 53, 1070–1079.
9. Aleccia, J. 2008. "Without Ads, Restless Legs May Take a Hike." *MSNBC.* May 14, 2008. **www.msnbc.msn.com/id/24603237**.
10. Milgram, S. 1963. "Behavioral Study of Obedience." *Journal of Abnormal and Social Psychology,* 67, 371–378.
11. Cialdini, R. B. 1992. *Influence: Science and Practice.* New York: Harper Collins.
12. Ibid.
13. Ibid.
14. Frankl, V. 1963. *Man's Search for Meaning.* New York: Pocket Books.
15. Cialdini, R. B. 1992. *Influence: Science and Practice.* New York: Harper Collins.

Chapter 4

1. Donohue, S. 2008. "Corrie Coup for Slater PR." *Manchester Evening News.* May 27.
2. Bullock, A. 2004. *The Secret Sales Pitch.* San Jose, Calif.: Norwich Publishers.
3. Key, W. B. 1992. *Subliminal Ad-Ventures In Erotic Art.* Brandon, Vt.: Brandon Books.

Chapter 5

1. Langer, E. J. 1990. *Mindfulness.* New York: Perseus Books Group.
2. Taylor, E. 2007. *Choices and Illusions.* Carlsbad, Calif.: Hay House.
3. Gergen, D. 1996. "Harvard's 'Talented Tenth.'" *U.S. News and World Report.* March 10.
4. Carpenter, S. 2008. "Buried Prejudice." *Scientific American Mind,* May 2008, 33–39.
5. Correll, J.; Park, B.; Judd, C. M. & Wittenbrink, B., 2002. "The Police Officer's Dilemma." **http://home.uchicago.edu/~jcorrell/TPOD.html**.
6. Jackson, H. 2004. "Research of the Effects of Television." **www.labouroflove .org/tv-toys-&-technology/television/research-on-the-effects-of-television**.

Endnotes

7. Lippmann, W. 1997. *Public Opinion.* New York: Free Press.

8. Ibid.

Chapter 6

1. Romains, J. 1960. "CIA Study on Brainwashing." **http://www.fdrs.org/brainwashing_america.html.**

2. Keith, J. 1997. *Mind Control, World Control.* Kempton, Ill.: Adventures Unlimited Press.

3. Ibid.

4. Ibid.

5. Ibid.

6. BBC. 2003. "God on the Brain." **http://www.bbc.co.uk/science/horizon/2003/godonbrain.shtml.**

7. Jones, T. F. 2000. "Mass Psychogenic Illness: Role of the Individual Physician." *American Family Physician.* Dec. 15.

8. Alexander, M. 2001. "Thirty Years Later, Stanford Prison Experiment Lives On." *Stanford Report,* August 22.

9. Amitrani, A. and Di Marzio, R. 2001. "Blind, or just don't want to see?" *Cult and Society,* Vol. 1, No. 1, 2001.

10. Keith, J. 1997. *Mind Control, World Control.* Kempton, Ill.: Adventures Unlimited Press.

11. Ibid.

12. Ibid.

13. Ibid.

14. Ibid.

15. Ibid.

16. Chaitkin, A. 1994. "From Eugenics to Assassination." *British Psychiatry.* Oct. 7.

17. Wanttoknow.info. 2008. "Mind Control Cover-up: The Secrets of Mind Control." **www.wanttoknow.info/mindcontrol.**

18. Ronson, J. 2004. *The Men That Stare at Goats.* New York: Simon and Schuster.

19. Keith, J. 1997. *Mind Control, World Control.* Kempton, Ill.: Adventures Unlimited Press.

20. Wikipedia. *Project MKUltra.* **www.en.wikipedia.org/wiki/Mkultra.**

21. Norton, P. J. 2008. "Bush and the CIA." Freedom of Thought, Public Journal. Mar. 12. **http://journals.aol.com/pomansings/freedom-of-thought/entries/2008/03/12/clinton-george-h.w.-bush-and-the-cia/1032.**

22. Select Committee on Intelligence. 1977. *Project MKULTRA, The CIA's Program of Research in Behavioral Modification.* Joint Hearing, U.S. Senate. Wash.: Government Printing Office.

23. Drosnin, M. 1994. "Mind Control in Waco? The FBI, the Russians and David Koresh." *The Village Voice,* 39, page 18.

24. Ibid.

25. Wikipedia. *Skull and Bones.* **http://en.wikipedia.org/wiki/Skull_and_Bones.**

26. Begich, N. and Manning, J. 2002. *Angels Don't Play This HAARP.* Anchorage, Alaska: Earthpulse Press.

27. Wikipedia. *High Frequency Active Auroral Research Program.* **http://
en.wikipedia.org/wiki/High_Frequency_Active_Auroral_Research_Program.**

28. Begich, N. and Manning, J. 2002. *Angels Don't Play This HAARP.* Anchorage,
Alaska: Earthpulse Press.

29. Keith, J. 1997. *Mind Control, World Control.* Kempton, Ill.: Adventures Unlimited Press.

30. Smith, J. E. 1998. *HAARP: The Ultimate Weapon of Conspiracy.* Kempton, Ill.:
Adventures Unlimited Press.

31. Unknown. 1976. The Microwave Furor. *Time Magazine,* March 22, 1976.
http://www.time.com/time/magazine/article/0,9171,911755,00.html.

32. Begich, N. and Manning, J. 2002. *Angels Don't Play This HAARP.* Anchorage,
Alaska: Earthpulse Press.

33. Ibid.

34. Adachi, K. 2006. "Mind Control: The Ultimate Terror." *Educate Yourself: The
Freedom of Knowledge, The Power of Thought.* **http://educate-yourself.org/mc/.**

35. Krawczyk, G. 1993. "Mind Control and the New World Order." *Nexus Magazine.* February/March.

36. Keith, J. 1997. *Mind Control, World Control.* Kempton, Ill.: Adventures Unlimited Press.

37. Weinberger, S. 2008. "Army Yanks 'Voice-To-Skull Devices' Site." *Wired Blog
Network.* **http://blog.wired.com/defense/2008/05/army-removes-pa.html**

38. Weinberger, S. 2007. "The Other MEDUSA: A Microwave Sound Weapon."
Wired Blog Network. **http://blog.wired.com/defense/2007/08/the-other-medus.
html.**

39. Hambling, D. 2008. "Microwave ray gun controls crowds with noise." *New-
Scientist.com* news service. **http://technology.newscientist.com/article/dn14250-
microwave-ray-gun-controls-crowds-with-noise.html.**

Chapter 7

1. Dunham, W. R. 1984. *The Science of Vital Force.* Boston, Mass.: Damrell and
Upham.

2. Taylor, E. 2007. "Subliminal Information Theory Revisited: Casting Light on a
Controversy." *Annals: The Journal of the American Psychotherapy Association,* Fall 2007,
pages 29–33.

3. Taylor, E. 2007. *Choices and Illusions.* Carlsbad, Calif.: Hay House.

4. Choi, C. 2007. "Subliminal Messages Fuel Anxiety." *Live Science.* **http://www
.livescience.com/health/070802_micro_expressions.html.**

5. Motluk, A. 2006. "Subliminal Advertising May Work After All." *New Scientist,*
2549, 16.

6. CBC News. 2007. "Ontario removes video slot machines flashing winning
images." *CBCNEWS.CA,* Feb. 26. **http://www.cbc.ca/canada/story/2007/02/25/
video-lottery.html.**

7. Nauert, R. 2007. "The Influence of Subliminal Messages." *Psych Central News.*
**http://psychcentral.com/news/2007/12/27/the-influence-of-subliminal-
messages/1712.html.**

Endnotes

8. Claburn, T. 2008. "Apple's Logo Makes You More Creative Than IBM's." *InformationWeek,* March 19. **http://www.informationweek.com/news/internet/showArticle.jhtml?articleID=206904786.**

9. Lee, J. 2008. "Ten investigated on split-second ads." *The Sidney Morning Herald,* Feb. 21.

10. BBC News. 2007. "Subliminal images impact on brain." March 9. **http://news.bbc.co.uk/2/hi/health/6427951.stm.**

11. Spiering, M.; Everaerd, W.; Karsdrop, P.; and Both, S. 2006. "Nonconscious Process of Sexual Information: A Generalization to Women." *The Journal of Sex Research,* 43.

12. Ibid.

13. Shrinkage Control Technologies. 2007. "Does Subliminal Programming Work?" March 20. **http://www.shrinkagecontrol.net/work.asp?page=work.**

14. Bullock, A. 2004. *The Secret Sales Pitch.* San Jose, Calif.: Norwich Publishers.

15. Ibid.

16. Perkins, S. 2003. "Dirty Rats: Campaign ad may have swayed voters subliminally." *Science News,* 163/8, pages 116–117.

17. Key, W. B. 1992. *Subliminal Ad-Ventures In Erotic Art.* Brandon, Vt.: Brandon Books.

18. Romano, A. 2008. "Expertient: The Political Psychology of Race and Gender." *Newsweek,* Mar. 12. **http://blog.newsweek.com/blogs/stumper/archive/2008/03/12/expertinent-the-political-psychology-of-race-and-gender.aspx.**

19. Weinberger, S. 2008 "The Weird Russian Mind-Control Research Behind a DHS Contract." *Wired,* Sept. 20. **http://www.wired.com/politics/security/news/2007/09/mind_reading?currentPage=all.**

20. Ibid

21. Stark, T. I. 2007. "Do Subliminal Audio Tapes Work?" *Real Magick.* **www.realmagick.com/articles/50/550.html.**

22. Pratkanis, A. and Aronson, E. 2001. *Age of Propaganda.* New York: W. H. Freeman.

23. Epley, N. 1999. "What Every Skeptic Should Know about Subliminal Persuasion." *Skeptical Inquirer,* Sept.–Oct.

Chapter 8

1. Whitehead, J. E. (1991) "Vance, J., Vance, E.J.R., Vance, P., Robertson, A., -vs-Judas Priest, CBS et al." *Case No. 86–5844 and 86–3939. Dept. No. 1. Judicial District Court of the State of Nevada in and for the County of Washoe.*

2. U.S. House of Representatives. 1984. *Subliminal Communication Technology: Committee on Science and Technology.* Honolulu, Hi.: University Press of the Pacific.

3. Whitehead, J. E. (1991) "Vance, J., Vance, E.J.R., Vance, P., Robertson, A., -vs-Judas Priest, CBS et al." *Case No. 86–5844 and 86–3939. Dept. No. 1. Judicial District Court of the State of Nevada in and for the County of Washoe.*

4. U.S. House of Representatives. 1984. *Subliminal Communication Technology: Committee on Science and Technology.* Honolulu, Hi.: University Press of the Pacific.

5. Ibid.

6. Ibid.

7. Ibid.

8. Ibid.

9. Ibid.

Chapter 9

1. Roche, K. 1993. "The Effects of Auditory Subliminal Messages on the Behavior of Attention Deficit Disordered Children." University of Phoenix, AZ.

2. Plante, T. G., Doan, B. T., DiGregorio, M. P. & Manuel, G. M. 1993. "The Influence of Aerobic Exercise and Relaxation Training on Coping With Test-Taking Anxiety." Children's Health Council/Stanford University, CA.

3. Ashley, D. 1993. "The Effect of Subliminally-Presented Reinforcing Stimuli on Factual Material." University of Southern California, CA.

4. Isaacs, J. 1991. Unpublished report. "The Other 90%," CA.

5. Pelka, R. 1991. "Application of Subliminal Therapy to Over Weight Subjects." Armed Forces University Munich, Germany.

6. Kruse, P. et. al. 1991. "Suggestion and Perceptual Instability: Auditory Subliminal Influences." Bremen University, Germany.

7. Galbraith, P. & Barton, B. 1990. "Subliminal Relaxation: Myth or Method." Weber State University, UT.

8. Reid, J. 1990. "*Free of Depression* Subliminal Tape Study." Colorado State University, CO.

9. Taylor, E.; McCusker, C. & Liston, L. 1986. "A Study of the Effects of Subliminal Communication on Inmates at the Utah State Prison." *Subliminal Communication.* Medical Lake, WA: R. K. Books.

10. Taylor, E. 1990. "The Effect of Subliminal Auditory Stimuli in a Surgical Setting Involving Anesthetic Requirements." Progressive Awareness Research, WA.

11. Taylor, E. 1992. "Longitudinal Study: Cancer Remission." Progressive Awareness Research, WA.

12. Moore, T. 1990. On live radio.

13. Urban, M. 1992. "Auditory Subliminal Stimulation: A Re-Examination." *Journal of Perceptual and Motor Skills,* 74:515–541.

14. Pribram, K. 1982. *Holographic Paradigms and Other Paradoxes.* Ed. by Ken Wilbur. Boulder, Colo.: New Science Library.

15. Kruse, P. et. al. 1991. "Suggestion and Perceptual Instability: Auditory Subliminal Influences." Bremen University, Germany.

16. Taylor, E. 1990. "The MIP Paradigm." Unpublished paper.

17. Smith, G. & Danielsson, A. 1979. "Anxiety and Defensive Strategies in Childhood and Adolescence." *Psychology Issues,* 12 (Monograph 3). International University Press.

18. Pribram, K. 1982. *Holographic Paradigms and Other Paradoxes.* Ed. by Ken Wilbur. Boulder, Colo.: New Science Library.

19. Ibid.

20. Ibid.

21. Skinner, B. F. 1930. "On the Inheritance of Maze Behavior." *Journal of General Psychology,* 5, 427–458.

22. Taylor, E. 1988. *Subliminal Learning: An Eclectic Approach.* Medical Lake, Wash.: R. K. Books.

23. McTaggart, L. 2002. *The Field: The Quest for the Secret Force of the Universe.* New York: Harper Collins.

24. Sperry, R. W. 1969. "A Modified Concept of Consciousness." *Psychological Review,* 76: 532–36.

25. Zaidel, E. 1985. *The Dual Brain.* New York: Guilford Press.

26. Ibid.

27. Blumstein S. & Cooper, W. 1974. Hemispheric Processing of Intonation Contours. *Cortex,* 10, 146–158.

28. Ross, E. 1981. "The Aprosodias: Functional-Anatomic Organisation of the Affective Components of Language in the Rich Hemisphere." *Archives of Neurology,* 38, 561–569.

29. Ornstein, R. 1970. *The Psychology of Consciousness.* Orlando, Fla.: Harcourt Brace Jovanovich.

30. Ibid.

31. Ferguson, M. 1991. "Auditory Laterality—the Dominance of One Ear or the Other—Is a Key Factor in Childhood Dyslexia." *New Sense Bulletin,* 16 (9):7.

32. Ibid.

33. Springer, S.P. and Deutsch, G. 1981. *Left Brain Right Brain.* New York: Freeman and Co.

34. Ibid.

35. Ibid.

36. Ibid.

37. Ibid.

38. Ibid.

39. Ibid.

40. Oates, D. 1991. *Reverse Speech.* Minneapolis, Minn.: Knowledge Systems, Inc.

41. Ibid.

42. Ibid.

43. Taylor, E. 1991. *Thinking Without Thinking.* Medical Lake, Wash.: R. K. Books.

44. Kappas, J. 1985. *Professional Hypnotism Manual: Introducing Physical and Emotional Suggestibility and Sexuality.* Van Nuys, Calif.: Panorama Publishing Co.

45. Oates, D. 1991. *Reverse Speech.* Minneapolis, Minn.: Knowledge Systems Inc.

46. Moore, T. 1992. "Subliminal Perception: Facts and Fallacies." *Skeptical Inquirer,* 16:273-81.

47. Wonder, J. & Donovan, P. 1984. *Whole Brain Thinking.* New York: First Ballantine Books.

48. Dixon, N. 1981. *Preconscious Processing.* New York: John Wiley and Sons.

49. Galbraith, P. and Barton, B. 1990. "Subliminal Relaxation: Myth or Method." Weber State University, Utah.

50. Reid, J. 1990. *"Free of Depression, Subliminal Tape Study."* Colorado State University, Colorado.

51. Taylor E. 1990. "The Effect of Subliminal Auditory Stimuli in a Surgical Setting Involving Anesthetic Requirements." Medical Lake, Wash.: Progressive Awareness Research.

52. Kruse, P. et. al. 1991. "Suggestion And Perceptual Instability: Auditory Sub-liminal Influences." Bremen University, Germany.

53. Pelka, R. 1991. "Application of Subliminal Therapy to Over Weight Subjects." Armed Forces University, Munich, Germany.

54. Plante, T. G., Doan, B. T., DiGregorio, M. P. & Manuel, G. M. 1993. "The Influence of Aerobic Exercise and Relaxation Training on Coping With Test-Taking Anxiety." Children's Health Council/Stanford University, California.

55. Roche, K. 1993. "The Effects of Auditory Subliminal Messages on the Behav-ior of Attention Deficit Disordered Children." University of Phoenix, Arizona.

Chapter 10

1. Taylor, E. 1991. *Thinking Without Thinking.* Medical Lake, Wash.: R. K. Books.

Chapter 11

1. Godel, K. 1992. *On Formally Undecidable Propositions of Principia Mathematica and Related Systems.* Mineola, NY.: Dover Publications.

2. Hawking, S. 1988. *A Brief History of Time: From the Big Bang to Black Holes.* New York: Bantam.

Chapter 12

1. Nelson, J. 1987. *The Perfect Machine: TV in the Nuclear Age.* Ontario, Canada: Dec Book Distribution.

Chapter 13

1. Hagelin, J. S.; Rainforth, M. V.; Orme-Johnson, D. W.; Cavanaugh, K. L.; Alexander, C. N.; Shatkin, S. F.; Davies, J. L.; Hughes, A. O.; Ross, E. 1999. "Effects of Group Practice of the Transcendental Meditation Program on Preventing Violent Crime in Washington, DC: Results of the National Demonstration Project June–July 1993." *Social Indicators Research,* 47, 2, 153–201.

2. Sheldrake, R. 1995. *The Presence of the Past: Morphic Resonance and the Habits of Nature.* Rochester, Vt.: Park Street Press.

3. McTaggart, L. 2002. *The Field: The Quest for the Secret Force of the Universe.* New York: Harper Collins.

4. Dawkins, R. 1978. "The Selfish Gene." Oxford, U.K.: Oxford University Press.

5. Lipton, B. 1991. "Liquid Crystal Consciousness." Unpublished paper.

6. Dossey, L. 1997. *Healing Words.* New York: HarperOne.

7. Radin, D. 2008. Private communication.

Chapter 14

1. Sheila O. and Schroeder, L. 2007. Superlearning 2000. New York: Dell.

2. Moine, D. and Lloyd, K. 1990. *Unlimited Selling Power: How to Master Hypnotic Selling Skills.* New York: Prentice Hall Press.

3. Taylor, E. 1991. *Thinking Without Thinking.* Medical Lake, Wash.: R. K. Books.

4. Nelson, J. 1987. *The Perfect Machine: TV in the Nuclear Age.* Ontario, Canada: Dec Book Distribution.

5. Sacks, O. 1999. *Awakenings.* New York: Vintage Press.

Endnotes

Chapter 15

1. Bohm, D. & Peat, D. 1987. *Science Order and Creativity.* New York: Bantam.

2. Maltz, M. 1969. *Psycho-Cybernetics.* New York: Pocket Books.

3. Richardson, A. 1994. *Individual Differences in Imaging: Their Measurement, Origins, and Consequences (Imagery and Human Development).* Amityville, NY: Baywood Publishing Co.

4. Ibid.

5. Bandler, R. and Grinder, J. 1979. *Frogs Into Princes.* Boulder, Colo.: Real People Press.

6. Jung, C. 1968. *Man and his Symbols.* New York: Dell.

7. Diamond, J. 1989. *Your Body Doesn't Lie.* New York: Grand Central Publishing.

8. Penfield, W. 1955."The Role of the Temporal Cortex in Certain Psychical Phenomena." *Journal of Mental Science,* 1955 101:451–65.

9. LaBerge, S. 1991. *Exploring The World of Lucid Dreaming.* New York: Ballantine Books.

10. Taylor, E. 1991. *Thinking Without Thinking.* Medical Lake, Wash.: R. K. Books.

11. Hay, L. 1984. *You Can Heal Your Life.* Hay House. Carlsbad, CA.

12. Tolle, E. 2008. *A New Earth.* New York: Penguin Books.

13. Helmstetter, S. 1990. *What to Say When You Talk to Yourself.* New York: Pocket Books.

14. Hawkins, R. 2002. *Power vs. Force.* Carlsbad, Calif.: Hay House.

15. McCuksker, C. 2000. *Cranial Electrotherapy Stimulation.* **http://home. comcast.net/~charlesmccusker/website.htm.**

16. Taylor, E. 1988. *Subliminal Learning: An Eclectic Approach.* Medical Lake, Wash.: R. K. Books.

Chapter 17

1. Mandino, O. 1986. *The Choice.* New York: Bantam.

Chapter 18

1. King, M. L. 2000. *A Knock at Midnight: Inspiration from the Great Sermons of Reverend Martin Luther King, Jr.* New York: Grand Central Publishing.

Chapter 19

1. May, E.; Utts, J. M.; and Spottiswoode, S. J. P. 1995. "Decision Augmentation Theory: Toward a Model of Anomalous Phenomena." *Journal of Parapsychology.* 59, 195–220.

2. McTaggart, L. 2002. *The Field: The Quest for the Secret Force of the Universe.* New York: Harper Collins.

Chapter 20

1. Joyce, S. J. 2007. *Teaching an Anthill to Fetch.* Calgary, Canada: Mighty Small Books Publishing.

Epilogue

1. Buzan, T. 2002. *How to Mind Map.* New York: Thorsons.

2. Sheldrake, R. 1995. *The Presence of the Past: Morphic Resonance and the Habits*

of Nature. Rochester, Vt.: Park Street Press.

Appendix 1

1. Hess, J. 1981. "Subliminal suggestion during anesthesia to control postoperative complications." (Letter). *AANA Journal,* 49 (2), 209–210.

Appendix 5

1. Henley, S. H. 1975. "Cross modal effects of subliminal verbal stimuli." *Scandinavian Journal of Psychology,* 16 (1), 30–36.

2. Kostandov, E.; Arzumanov, J.; Vazhnova, T.; Reshchikova, T. & Shostakovich, G. 1980. "Conditional mechanisms of decision making." *Pavlovs Journal of Biological Science,* 15 (4), 142–150.

3. Miller, J. M. 1974. "The effects of aggressive stimulation upon young adults who have experienced the death of a parent during childhood or adolescence." *Dissertation Abstracts International,* 35 (2-B), 1055–1056.

4. Rutstein, E. H. & Goldberger, L. 1973. "The effects of aggressive stimulation on suicidal patients. An experimental study of the psychoanalytic theory of suicide." *Psychoanalysis and Contemporary Science,* 2, 157–174.

5. De Martino, C. R. 1969. "The effects of subliminal stimulation as a function of stimulus content, drive arousal and priming and defense against drive." *Dissertation Abstracts,* 29 (12-B), 4843.

6. Silverman, L. H. & Candell, P. 1970. "On the relationship between aggressive activation, symbiotic merging, intactness of body boundaries, and manifest pathology in schizophrenics." *Journal for Nervous Mental Disorders,* 150 (5), 387–399.

7. Lee, I.; Tyrer, P. & Horn, S. 1983. "A comparison of subliminal, supraliminal and faded phobic cine-films in the treatment of agoraphobia." *British Journal of Psychiatry,* 143, 356–361.

8. Galbraith, P. and Barton, B. 1990. "Subliminal Relaxation: Myth or Method." Weber State University, Utah.

9. Leclerc, C. & Freibergs, V. 1971. "The influence of perceptual and symbolic subliminal stimuli on concept formation." *Canadian Journal of Psychology,* 25 (4), 292–301.

10. Henley, S. H. 1975. "Cross modal effects of subliminal verbal stimuli." *Scandinavian Journal of Psychology,* 16 (1), 30–36.

■　■■　■■■■

ABOUT THE AUTHOR

Eldon Taylor has made a lifelong study of the human mind and has earned doctoral degrees in psychology and metaphysics. He's a fellow with the American Psychotherapy Association (APA) and a non-denominational minister.

A practicing criminalist for more than ten years while completing his education, Eldon supervised and conducted investigations and testing to detect deception. His earliest work with changing inner beliefs was conducted from this setting, including a double-blind study at the Utah State Prison from 1986 to 1987.

Eldon is president and director of Progressive Awareness Research, Inc. For more than 20 years, his books, audio programs, lectures, and radio and television appearances have approached personal empowerment from the cornerstone perspective of forgiveness, gratitude, self-responsibility, and respect for all life.

He lives in the countryside of Washington State with his wife and their two sons. Apart from his family and work, his true passion is horses.

If you've enjoyed this book and would like to learn more about tools to help you become the person you were meant to be, visit Eldon's Website at **www.eldontaylor.com**.

■　■■■━■

INNERTALK DISTRIBUTION

USA
Progressive Awareness Research, Inc.
PO Box 1139
Medical Lake, WA 99022
1-800-964-3551
1-509-244-6362
www.innertalk.com

UK
Vitalia Health
The Marina, Harleyford Estate
Henley Road, Marlow, Bucks S17 2DX
UK
011 44 1628 898 366
www.innertalk.co.uk

Germany
Axent Verlag
Steinerne Furt 78
86167 Augsburg
Germany
011 49 821 70 5011
www.axent-verlag.de

Mexico
Dialogo Interno
Calle Retorno Cerro De Acazulco No. 6
Col. Oxtopulco Universidad Del. Coyoacan
Mexico D.F. C.P.04318
Mexico
011 52 555 339 5742
www.dialogointerno.com.mx

**Malaysia/Singapore/Brunei/Australia/
New Zealand/Papua New Guinea**
InnerTalk Sdn Bhd
2–2 Jalan Pju 8/5E, Perdana Bus. Cntr.
Bandar Damansara Perdana,
47820 Petaling Jaya
Selangor, Malaysia
011 60 37 729 4745
www.innertalk-au.com
www.innertalk.co.nz
www.innertalk.com.my

Taiwan and China
Easy MindOpen
3F, No. 257, Ho-Ping East Rd. Sec. 2
Taipei, Taiwan, R.O.C
011 886 (227) 010–468(1)
www.iamone.com.tw

India
VAS InnerPotentia Solutions Marketing Pvt. Ltd.
T.C. 39/1730 (3), Pournami,
Manacaud P.O.
Trivandrum 695009
Kerala State, India
011 0471-2459444
www.innertalk.co.in

Distribution Inquiries

For information about distributing InnerTalk programs, please contact:

Progressive Awareness Research, Inc.
PO Box 1139
Medical Lake, WA 99022
1-800-964-3551
1-509-244-6362
www.innertalk.com

Hay House Titles of Related Interest

YOU CAN HEAL YOUR LIFE, the movie, starring Louise L. Hay & Friends
(available as a 1-DVD program and an expanded 2-DVD set)
Watch the trailer at: **www.LouiseHayMovie.com**

THE SHIFT: the movie,
starring Dr. Wayne W. Dyer
(available as a 1-DVD program and an expanded 2-DVD set)
Watch the trailer at: **www.DyerMovie.com**

■ ■

The Divine Matrix: Bridging Time, Space, Miracles, and Belief, by Gregg Braden

I Can Do It®: How to Use Affirmations to Change Your Life,
by Louise L. Hay (book-with-CD)

Everything You Need to Know to Feel Go(o)d, by Candace B. Pert, Ph.D.

The Force, by Stuart Wilde

The Law of Attraction: The Basics of the Teachings of Abraham®,
by Esther and Jerry Hicks

The Power of Intention: Learning to Co-create Your World Your Way,
by Dr. Wayne W. Dyer

Power vs. Force: The Hidden Determinants of Human Behavior,
by David R. Hawkins, M.D., Ph.D.

Virus of the Mind: The New Science of the Meme, by Richard Brodie

■ ■

All of the above are available at your local bookstore,
or may be ordered by contacting Hay House (see last page).